Accessible American History:

Connecting the Past to the Present

by Paul Swendson

Cypress Books
Cypress CA

Accessible American History: Connecting the Past to the Present. Copyright © 2012 by Paul Swendson. Cover was designed by Matt Key, with the photos accessed from Wikimedia Commons. All rights reserved. Printed in the United States of America. No part of this book may be used or reproduced in any matter – either printed or electronic - without written permission from the publisher. For information address the following:

Cypress Books
P.O. Box 54
Garden Grove, CA 92846

ISBN: 978-0-9850002-0-2

Special thanks to my wife and kids for their patience and support through all of the hours invested in this endeavor. Also, thanks to the many people who have given me so much feedback and encouragement by reading and commenting on my blog posts and articles online.

Table of Contents

Introduction: How and Why History Can Matter

I am not a historian. A historian, as I understand the term, is a person who studies primary source materials and uses this data to produce original historical information. Instead of becoming a scholar, I have chosen to be a community college instructor, a job that requires a different skill set. For while it is important for a teacher to develop and continually enhance his or her academic knowledge and skills, a good teacher, more than anything else, is a combination of a performer, organizer, coach, sage, critic, and enthusiast. A great scholar is not necessarily an effective teacher, and vice versa.

As a community college history professor, I have devoted my career to organizing and attempting to explain information produced by historians. I see myself as a "middleman" relaying this information to students who, by and large, are unlikely to spend much time reading in-depth historical scholarship. Let's face it. Much of what is called historical research is produced almost exclusively for historians and hard-core history buffs. If historical information is to have any impact beyond this small community of history lovers, then we need effective teachers who can make this stuff interesting and relevant for the general public. This is where I fit in.

In the community college survey courses that I have taught for the past eleven years, I try to help students learn the basics about all of the major events and trends in American history. There is therefore not enough class time to study any one topic in nitpicky detail. In fact, if students are overloaded with information, they tend to learn less than if you cover a smaller amount. Unfortunately, many people associate history with the memorization of a mass of random, disconnected facts. Because of experiences in past history courses where the material was not broken down in a manageable and meaningful way, many people have been cursed to forever hate history.

1

Being overwhelmed by random data, however, is only part of the problem. Even if the material is presented in an understandable way, many students will still see the study of history as pointless. Why do they have to hear stories and memorize facts about a bunch of dead people from the past? This is where the history teacher faces the most challenging and important task. We must help students to make some sort of a personal connection to the material, to try and imagine themselves in the situations faced by past human beings and recognize that in some ways, we all face similar experiences and challenges today. History never repeats itself completely, and we can never quite see the world through the eyes of people from other times and cultures, but there are general themes and patterns that seem to keep popping up. Also, there are certain fundamental traits that make up our human nature that remain consistent over time. People in the past, like today, enjoyed sex, tried to accumulate wealth, cared about their families, made stupid mistakes, and often feared change. By learning about the experiences of other individuals and societies trying to make their way in the world, we can learn lessons that will maybe make us a little wiser and more empathetic. In the end, history is the study of humankind's collective memory. All of our knowledge, whether personal or collective, is based on past experience. As individuals, we know that red lights mean stop, jumping off of a cliff can be painful, and politicians occasionally lie because of things we have been told or have personally experienced in the past. So if we lose our memories, then it is difficult to function.

Now some would say that the analogy between individual memory loss and historical ignorance works better in theory than in practice. Obviously, if you forget how to swim and fall into the water, then things will not end well. But does not knowing about some famous date, person, or event from hundreds of years ago have any impact on your life? I do agree, believe it or not, that many historical facts in themselves are irrelevant. Good historians and history teachers, however, are not primarily interested in compiling, memorizing, and presenting trivia. The goal is to draw more general, applicable meanings from all of the facts. And if history is done correctly, then you should gain a better understanding of how the world used to be and of how it became what it is today. The only way, after all, to make sense of the present is to turn to the past.

Studying history can also have another practical benefit. To be an informed citizen, a certain amount of historical literacy is required. When reading newspapers, magazines, books, or web pages that seek to be informative, references to famous people and events of the past will inevitably be made. In most cases, the writer will not bother to define or describe well-known historical references. If the Cold War is mentioned in some kind of a publication that is directed to a reasonably informed audience, the writer will not say, "This, by the way, was an indirect and undeclared war between the Soviet Union and the United States." The writer assumes that you know. Can you imagine a writer today bothering to stop and describe for readers the 9/11 attacks, Tiger Woods, Michael Jackson, or Hurricane Katrina? If an American has not spent several years in a coma, then he or she will probably know at least the basics about these events and people.

So a person without a certain amount of historical literacy will have a hard time getting the full meaning out of writings about history, politics, economics, current events, or many other subjects. History is unavoidably integrated into the study of virtually any subject, so historical illiteracy can contribute to a more general academic and cultural illiteracy. And if the ultimate success of our democracy rests with an informed voting public, historical and cultural illiteracy can be disastrous. So much of the battle over hearts and minds that we see in our country and world is a competition over which interpretations of the past will predominate. Whoever wins this competition will then have the greatest influence on our views of the present. In the course of this battle, history will often be twisted and misused to suit the needs of various powerful interests.

After almost 18 years of teaching history, I am more convinced today than ever of its relevance. People with basic historical literacy will not be so easily talked into questionable ideas. In a nutshell, studying history can make a person wiser. Too often, education is seen merely as a means of getting job skills. In recent years, as our country has faced some tough times, it is clear that our main problem is not a shortage of job skills. Instead, it is a shortage of wisdom. God help us if a college education degenerates into nothing more than a job-training program creating workers who have little interest in or understanding of the circumstances that have shaped our world.

So if you are interested in reading historical essays compiled by someone who has been out there in the community college trenches seeking to make American history manageable, meaningful, and relevant for the average 21st-century American, then you have come to the right place. Essentially, my essays on various history topics are lesson plans converted into written form. And in all my lesson plans, I make a continuing effort to show how the events of the past relate to the modern world. For if history teachers – and historians for that matter - make no effort to draw lessons from the data and to bring the facts to life, then we are merely engaged in a trivia exercise, helping students memorize enough to get their three units, forget the stuff immediately after the final, and move on to subjects that they see as actually relevant. Like journal articles and books rotting away in an old library, the hard work will not amount to much of anything.

Part One: The Colonial Period

1. Happy Columbus Day?

Columbus Day is officially recognized every October in the United States. Most Americans, I imagine, hardly notice. Few people, after all, get the day off from either work or school. Some would argue that this is for the best. Columbus the man, along with the "discovery" for which he is famous, is not worth celebrating anyway. Of course, there will always be people, myself included, who will take any day off that any employer is willing to offer. Any moral or historical objections, no matter how valid, will fail to interfere with my ability to find rest and relaxation.

Christopher Columbus, one of the biggest names in American history, also happens to be one of the most controversial. Some of this controversy relates to Columbus as a human being. Was he a brave visionary who accidentally introduced Europe to a "new world," or was he a bloodthirsty, greedy conquistador who initiated a Spanish policy of plunder and genocide? While there is little doubt that terrible things were done under Columbus' watch during those early days of Spanish colonization, I do not personally view Columbus as an unusually evil man. Instead, he was largely a reflection of the European society of his time, a society that by modern standards was disgusting in some ways: arrogant, closed-minded, and racist. And if someone else had governed that first Caribbean colony, things would have turned out the same. When you throw together cultures that have incompatible worldviews and lifestyles, and give one side all of the advantages – steel, "old world" diseases, guns, and horses – there is only one possible result. So is it fair to judge Columbus by modern standards? This question makes one wonder how future generations might judge the society of our time.

The debate about Columbus has little to do with him anyway. Those who view him in negative terms are mostly angry about the series of events initiated by his accidental discovery. For Native Americans, the arrival of Europeans would bring what was perhaps the worst population disaster in human history. Some died as a result of violence. Some could not survive because their habitat was overrun and destroyed. Most, however, died from diseases for which they had no immunity. So even if Europeans had made a legitimate attempt to coexist with Native Americans, it still would have been a disaster.

Most people living in the Western Hemisphere, of course, are not "full-blooded" Native Americans. Almost all of us are primarily descended from people who have immigrated here in the last few centuries. And if a person living in the Americas enjoys his or her life here, then he or she is forced to admit that Columbus' discovery was, on some level, a positive thing. In addition, it is important to recognize that Columbus' discovery did more than impact people's lives in Europe and the Americas. On many levels, for better or worse, his discovery transformed the entire planet. New world agricultural commodities – tomatoes, potatoes, manioc, chocolate, and many others – quickly became staples in countries throughout the world. "New world" silver was used to buy commodities from the east, stimulating inflation and increasing trade connections throughout the global economy. The African slave trade, which would have been a small-scale operation without the discovery of America, had an enormous impact on the future histories of Africa and the Americas, bringing enormous wealth for some and horrific suffering for many others. On so many levels, the world of today is impossible to imagine without the countless interconnections between the "old" and "new" worlds.

We are all the products of history, and like the world of today, the world of the past could be a nasty place. Societies rise and fall, and a piece of land is only yours until someone else takes it away. The history of the Americas is filled with tragedies, and those tragedies, whether we want to face them or not, are an integral part of who we are. I am living on conquered soil, and without that conquest, I would not exist. So how do you acknowledge that some of the very events that brought you into existence also happened to be horrific tragedies? Questions like this help me to understand why societies tend to mythologize their past or talk about it as little as possible. It is much easier to just let Columbus Day pass by, complain that you do not get the day off, or see if any department stores have been inspired to have a three-day sale.

2. The Blessing of Bad Geography

At its highpoint, the Spanish empire in the Americas was enormous, stretching from the southern tip of South America to much of what is today the southern United States. The heart of the empire, however, was in northern South America, Central America, and the Caribbean islands. Columbus first hit land in the Caribbean, and it was in Central and northern South America that the Spanish found great civilizations to conquer and significant populations of Native Americans to exploit as laborers. Many of the Native Americas who managed to survive exposure to old world diseases worked in horrific conditions in the lucrative silver mines found in these mainland regions.

But it was Portugal, the only other significant player in the Americas during the 16th century, that established the basic model for the other big money maker in the Spanish new world: cash crops. It was Portugal, in fact, that had gotten the ball rolling for European exploration in the first place. Beginning in the early 15th century, Prince Henry "The Navigator" began sending naval expeditions south around the coast of Africa. In addition to satisfying Renaissance curiosity, seeking to expand the "kingdom of God," and hoping to generate wealth in some way from Africa, the ultimate goal was an eastern sea route to Asia. By the end of the 15th century, the Portuguese had managed to send an expedition around the southern tip of Africa and to the coast of India. In the 16th century, the Portuguese would generate tremendous amounts of wealth from its growing control of the Indian Ocean trade routes.

While much of Portugal's focus was to the east, it also established one significant colony in South America: Brazil. And in this colony, they found an ideal environment for growing sugar, a crop that was rapidly growing in popularity at the time. The only problem was finding a labor force to plant, tend, and harvest the crop. Brazil did not have the types of population centers found in

Mexico or Peru, and the Native Americans who did live there made for a poor class of laborers due to their tendency to die from exposure to old world diseases. Fortunately for Brazil - and unfortunately for many of the people living on the West African coast - their travels around Africa solved their labor shortage problem. People, along with gold, became the most valuable commodities that the Portuguese acquired through trade with Africa. And Africans, due to centuries of exposure to old world diseases, withstood the terrible conditions in the fields better than Native Americans. Over the next few hundred years, approximately one-third of all of the slaves transported to the Americas came to Brazil alone. The Spanish, who also controlled ideal sugar-growing lands in Central America and the Caribbean, would replicate the Portuguese model of plantation agriculture.

Meanwhile, as the Portuguese and especially the Spanish generated tremendous wealth from the Americas, no other European nations had much of anything happening in the new world. Both the French and the English had sent expeditions into North America in the late 15th and the early 16th centuries, but these did not translate into settlements. The main goals of these navigators were to find lucrative fishing waters or to discover a northwest passage to Asia. And for good reason, they were not particularly impressed with the lands that they found. Unlike the Spaniards in Latin America, they did not see any signs of large empires to plunder or ideal climates for producing cash crops. And the Spanish, who sent explorers into the southern regions of North America, came to similar conclusions. Their North American lands remained thinly settled border regions for centuries, far away from the more lucrative lands of the south.

By the late 16th century, however, the English had resolved some of their internal conflicts and reached a point at which they could invest into overseas exploration. At first, their primary means of gaining wealth from the Americas was stealing it from Spanish ships. But by the early 17th century, they were able to begin establishing a string of colonial settlements along the North American East Coast. As latecomers to American colonial settlement, they were forced to settle for these "leftovers." Fortunately for the English, they were also able to gain control of some islands in the Caribbean, and by copying the Portuguese model of sugar production, these lands generated more wealth than the thirteen colonies. In the Southern colonies of the East Coast, however, they were able to grow some valuable cash crops – tobacco, rice, indigo, sugar, and eventually cotton – that generated significant amounts of wealth. And after a few decades of relying on European indentured servants for labor, they would eventually turn to the same African slaves used throughout the Americas.

In the colonies north of Maryland, however, the climate and soil were not well suited for plantation agriculture. Geographically, these Northern colonies seemed to have limited economic potential. But in a way, these geographic limitations may have proved to be a blessing for the North. Because they could not simply enrich themselves by exploiting land and manual labor to crank out the cash crops, Northerners were forced to become more economically innovative. Fortunately for them, the early settlers of New England, who were largely hard working, self-disciplined, educated Puritans, were inclined toward business activity anyway. So over the course of several decades, the North became the business and industrial center of the English colonies and, eventually, of the early United States. The South, on the other hand, would remain mostly content with cash crop production, cranking out the cotton for Northern textile factories. And when these regions came into conflict in the United States' only civil war, the industrialized north would prevail, establishing the dominance of its system over the nation as a whole.

If you were living in 1600, you would assume that Spain would be the dominant power in Europe and the Americas for decades to come. And even when the English and French began to build their colonial empires in North America, you would assume that the economic and political centers of the Americas would be found in the south. These were the areas, after all, that were blessed the most with ideal climates and natural resources. But instead, the English would eventually develop into the dominant economic and political power in Europe. And the English colonies on the East Coast of North America, which would ultimately develop into the United States, became the power center of the Americas and eventually of the entire world.

So how was it that the English, stuck with the colonial leftovers, created the dominant American society? And how was it that the Northern colonies and eventually states, which seemed to inhabit the inferior geographic regions of the country, would come to dominate this North American nation? Some of this may have resulted from cultural differences between England and Spain. The Spanish, for instance, more strongly maintained the medieval notion that landholding and military service were more noble pursuits than business activity. The colonial model in New Spain was essentially conquest, with wealth generated through the exploitation of land, labor, and natural resources. They extracted wealth. They did not produce it through economic innovation. The English, on the other hand, developed over time a more favorable attitude toward business activity. They also created a political system in the Americas similar to that found in England. For while Spain was an absolute monarchy, and the provinces of New Spain were governed by political appointees ruling in the name of the king, England developed a parliamentary system in which some of its citizens had a say in political matters. This outlet for political participation and the potential ability to shape policies more beneficial to the general public may have further encouraged the climate of innovation that is the key to long-term economic success. Englishmen and their colonial descendants, after all, were not expected always to give unquestioning obedience to the state.

In itself, however, cultural and political differences cannot completely explain the different circumstances in England and Spain or between the United States and Latin America. When English colonists had the opportunity, such as in the Caribbean or the Southern colonies, they were content to follow the traditional model of cranking out the cash crops. But in the Northern colonies, where plantation agriculture was not an option, a wider variety of economic activities would evolve. And over time, this society based more on towns, industry, and trade would become the dominant power in the new world.

Today, there are prosperous nations throughout the world that have benefited from the blessings of their geography. They may have a climate ideally suited for certain activities, plentiful natural resources, or a beneficial strategic location. Geographic blessings, however, do not guarantee long-term economic success. There are many resource rich countries with tremendous economic potential, after all, that are political and economic basket cases. In the end, cultural values may be more important in creating a prosperous society than the blessings and/or curses of geography. And since "necessity is the mother of invention," it is often the societies facing the greatest geographic obstacles that become the most resourceful and innovative. Hopefully, the United States will retain into the future those qualities that have helped it be so successful. For if Americans rest on their laurels and assume that they are somehow entitled to live in a prosperous and stable society, we may find someday that our nation, like the Spanish before us, will look back longingly at its former glory days.

3. Thanksgiving: Our Founders Day?

Thanksgiving has evolved into one of the central events on the American calendar, and like all holidays, it means different things to different people. For some, it is an opportunity to gorge oneself on traditional food items such as turkey, mashed potatoes, stuffing, and pumpkin pie. Only Super Bowl Sunday rivals Thanksgiving for total caloric intake. For others, it is a chance to watch football on a Thursday, see some balloons fly around in New York City, or initiate the Christmas shopping season. I am sure that many Americans, however, remember the deeper meaning built in to the holiday's name. It is, after all, supposed to be a day to give thanks for our many blessings, whether this gratitude is given to God or just good fortune.

I mostly associate the holiday with specific people and a place. For years, my side of the family has gathered at my parents' cabin in the mountains, so the holiday for me conjures up the sights, sounds, and smells of a place that has been my second home from birth. As my parents get older, I can't help wondering how much longer these family gatherings will last. It won't be the same without mom and dad, so I plan to make the most of the Thanksgivings that we have left.

As a History teacher, I also often think about the historical roots of this holiday. Only the Fourth of July rivals Thanksgiving as a holiday specifically rooted in an American historical event. Beginning in the early 20th century, this holiday, officially established during the Civil War, began to be linked to a harvest festival celebrated by a group most commonly known as the Pilgrims, who established the Plymouth Colony in modern day Massachusetts in 1620. According to this story that most Americans learn in childhood, the Pilgrims risked their lives to come to America in hopes of escaping religious persecution back in England. Then, after approximately half of those who came on the Mayflower survived that first difficult winter, they gave thanks by sharing a meal with local Native Americans. So within this story, we see the key ideals on which we like to believe our country was founded: seeking religious freedom, escaping political strife, and different cultures coming together as one.

As a kid hearing this story while growing up, I had little reason to question its basic outline. I was also under the impression that Thanksgiving was an American Founders Day. Because the Pilgrims received so much attention, I assumed that Plymouth was the first English settlement in North America. But as I grew up and started digging more into history, I realized that I was mistaken on both counts. The Pilgrims, it turns out, were not the great promoters of religious freedom that I once believed them to be. They were seeking a place where they could practice their faith without potential interference or harassment from the government sponsored and funded Church of England, an institution that they decided to separate from because they thought that it was too Catholic. This does not mean, however, that they wanted those with different religious beliefs to come to their colony seeking religious freedom. Before coming to North America, a group of Pilgrims – called "Separatists" at the time – moved to the Netherlands, the one place in Europe with true religious tolerance. After living there for a few years, they decided to leave and try their luck in North America, largely because they were afraid of the potential influence of this tolerant society on their children. Would they be able to maintain their identity and belief system in such a diverse environment?

The true, complete story of Plymouth is also not a great example of different cultures coming together. After a short period of decent relations between Pilgrims and Native Americans, things would gradually deteriorate. Once Pilgrims became more secure and established, particularly when they were followed in larger numbers by a much more significant group – the Puritans – they did not need Native American aid as much anymore. So within a few years, Pilgrims and Puritans were praising God for helping them to kill Native Americans, not for getting the chance to eat with them.

So the Pilgrims were not quite everything they were cracked up to be, but at least their goals were somewhat noble. The same cannot be said, however, for the first British settlement to survive in North America: the Jamestown Colony. This settlement, founded in 1607 in the colony eventually called Virginia, was primarily about money. They were hoping, like the Spanish before them, to find precious metals in order to enrich both the colonists and the investors who put up the money for the venture. Unfortunately for them, the colony was a disaster from the start. There was no gold in Virginia, but many early settlers wasted precious time and energy searching for it. Many of the leaders of the expedition were the sons of nobles, men who were not accustomed to any kind of hard labor, and the lower class men who came had little experience with farming. The site of their settlement was a marshy area ideal as a breeding ground for disease. Initially, Native Americans were willing to give some food aid to the Jamestown colonists, largely because they thought that these settlers could be politically useful. But the Jamestown settlers, as a result of both desperation and typically racist attitudes toward Indians, would raid settlements and try to force the native inhabitants to give even more. War inevitably resulted. So during those first 15 years, roughly 80% of those who came to Jamestown died of either disease, starvation, or from conflict with Native Americans. Without continuous reinforcements from England, the colony would have died out completely.

Eventually, however, the Jamestown colony found a way to turn a profit. It turned out that tobacco, a crop that had been growing in popularity over the previous few decades, grew very well in Virginia. The only catch was that they needed a large labor force to tend and harvest the crop. So they began to import indentured servants from England and throughout Europe. These servants, in return for free passage to America, agreed to work for a certain number of years. Then, when their term was up, they were free to start a new life in North America. Unfortunately for them, the horrible working and living conditions that they faced caused many to die before their term was up. Still, there were enough desperate people in Europe to maintain a steady supply of new workers. Virginia was still a death house, but for the landowners, there was finally a way to turn a profit.

When I first learned about Jamestown, I was surprised that it was founded 13 years before the Pilgrims landed at Plymouth. Jamestown, apparently, was our true Founders Day, and yet it gets nowhere near the fanfare of Plymouth. But when you look at Jamestown's history, you see little to celebrate. Who wants to be reminded that England's first surviving colony was founded for money, barely hung on in spite of the colonists' stupidity, and ultimately became profitable because of tobacco, a crop that has been killing people now for centuries? The Pilgrim story, particularly when you edit out some of the less attractive parts, is more worthy of celebration. The settlers of Jamestown, however, are as much a part of our heritage as the Pilgrims – and, more importantly, Puritans – who helped establish what would become Massachusetts. But like the people of all nations, we prefer to remember the more noble aspects of our history. After all, if we were settled by noble souls seeking freedom and embracing diversity, then maybe we are still a nation rooted in these principles. Thank God that we are not a nation founded by people willing to do anything to turn a profit. What would that say about us today?

4. Lessons from the Salem Witch Trials

The Puritans often get a bit of a bad rap. They are typically depicted as a bunch of hard-ass people walking around in plain black clothes who did their best to ensure that no one in their Massachusetts theocracy thought too independently or had any fun. They were just so damn puritanical.

One of the most famous American stories involving Puritans is "The Scarlet Letter" by Nathaniel Hawthorne. In this classic novel, a woman named Hester Prynne is condemned to wear a large "A" on her chest indicating that she is an adulteress. The fact that she became pregnant out of wedlock was a dead giveaway. But while the Puritans were known for public forms of punishment in order to deter negative behavior, there is no record of any women wearing scarlet letters. And while Puritan society frowned heavily on extramarital sex – especially for women who could not so easily get away with it – Puritans were not necessarily anti-sex in general. Letters written by Puritan spouses to one another could actually be very emotional, romantic, and a bit spicy.

The most famous true story related to Puritans would probably be the Salem Witch Trials. It has been the subject of several films, plays, and countless books over the years, and the town of Salem milks its notorious history year after year by attracting large amounts of tourist dollars. Because the story is told so often, it is easy to get the impression that Puritans were executing witches all of the time. But outside of the twenty who died in this one episode, only about twenty others (at the most) were killed as suspected witches in the first eighty years of colonial New England's history. Now for me, that is forty people too many. But compared to certain periods in European history when people were executed in large numbers as supposed heretics and witches, the Puritans were far less violent when it came to witch-hunting.

It is the relative rarity of New England witch executions, however, that makes the Salem case so fascinating. If these were not people who were normally in the business of killing suspected witches, then what caused this town to seemingly go witch-crazy over roughly a one-year period from 1692-1693? Historians agree on a few basic facts. The trouble apparently started when the town of Salem hired a new minister named Samuel Parris. He came to Salem to try his luck as a minister after failing economically in the Caribbean, and he brought a female slave with him named Tituba. Some young girls in the village, including Parris' own daughter, asked Tituba to teach them some black magic, an activity that would not go over well with their Puritan parents. Suddenly, Parris' daughter started to have horrible nightmares, and she became so traumatized that she could no longer even speak. Reverend Parris, of course, wanted to know what the hell was happening; so now it was time for the young girls to shift into damage control mode. Apparently, in order to distract attention away from their sins, they claimed to all be victims of witchcraft. From these innocent little games played by adolescent girls, things would ultimately snowball out of control.

It is difficult to determine what was going on in the heads of these young girls. Parris' daughter seems to have been truly traumatized. With the other girls, however, it is difficult to say. Maybe some of them truly believed that toying with black magic had caused them to be cursed, and their psychological guilt manifested itself as strange delusions and hallucinations. Maybe they had some mental health issues that could not possibly be diagnosed and understood at the time. Maybe they were initially trying to get out of trouble, but when the accusations began, a certain momentum built up that became impossible to stop. Once the first person was convicted and hung, it became difficult for any of them to admit that they were just making things up. Then, to ease their guilt, they may have unconsciously convinced themselves that they were actually telling the truth. Or it is also possible that these immature individuals did not have the capacity to understand the seriousness of what they were doing. In modern times, kids have been known to make some false accusations or commit some nasty crimes. The human mind can be a funny thing.

For me, however, the young girls' psychological makeup is not the most interesting part of the story. The real mystery is why anyone took them seriously. The evidence that they presented was, to say the least, pretty weak. In the court room during trials and at other times, the girls would start behaving in a crazy fashion: screaming, convulsing, claiming to have visions, crying out in pain, etc. They also claimed to have visions of a supposed witch's sprit or specter that would attack them late at night. Now it does not take a genius to see some issues with this "evidence." Anyone, after all, can start convulsing or claiming to have visions of another person attacking him or her. By definition, this "evidence" can neither be proven nor refuted. So why was this strange behavior the trigger event for the beginning of these witch trials? And why, after a while, did some adults get involved with further bits of "evidence" demonstrating that the accused must be "witches" because they either behaved in an unorthodox fashion or could perform feats that a normal person could not do?

The historical debate rages to this day. Some historians focus on political and economic factors. The 1690's were a time of economic stress, with land becoming increasingly scarce. People were worried about the prospects of their children becoming landholders. In addition, Salem was becoming increasingly divided between the townspeople who relied on business activity and those on the outskirts who were the more traditional villagers. Most of the accusers, it turns out, were more the traditional village types who lived in the western part of town, while the supposed witches were mostly eastern, more urbanized folk. Once the kids of one faction began having strange visions, their parents were happy to step in and encourage their children to accuse adults from the other faction. If people from a certain part of town were eliminated, it could both free up some land and reduce the number of those money-grubbing business types.

Early 1690's political strife came in various forms. From 1689-1697, the British and French were fighting one of their periodic wars, with some of this conflict raging on the western frontier, and most Indians sided with the French. In 1684, the British government revoked its charter to Massachusetts, establishing it as a royal colony in 1691. After years in political limbo, Puritans in Massachusetts did not know what this new, uncertain, political future would bring. There were already signs that Massachusetts was drifting into moral decay, so what would happen now that the Puritans had lost political control of the colony? Finally, the new Reverend Samuel Parris who I mentioned earlier was a controversial figure from the start. Many in the town opposed hiring him for the job, and as you may have figured, these anti-Parris individuals were often the ones who were accused of witchcraft. The anti-Parris people also tended to be the eastern, urban folk mentioned earlier.

Other historians focus more on social factors. People accused of witchcraft were often a bit unorthodox in their thinking and behavior, a fact that made them socially vulnerable. Single women, in particular, were common among the accused, a fact that should not be surprising in a male dominated, family oriented society. The only problem with this argument is that there were some prominent figures who were accused as well. (Even the wife of the governor was eventually accused, and as you might expect, the trials ended shortly thereafter.)

Still other historians focus more on psychological factors. I recently read an essay arguing that an outbreak of encephalitis occurred at the time and might explain the strange behavior of the girls. Given the limited medical knowledge at the time, witchcraft may have seemed to be a likely explanation. And even if one rejects the disease hypothesis, there may have been other psychological disorders that could arise in a 17th century society that tried so hard to regulate human behavior. A Freudian, after all, could have a field day with the Puritans.

From what I can gather, Salem in 1692 may have been a classic example of a "perfect storm." War, factionalism, economic insecurity, and unsettling political changes were all taking place at the same time. When under this type of intense stress, people may do and believe things that they would not consider in normal times. Arthur Miller, when he wrote "The Crucible," was drawing a clear parallel between events in 17th century Salem and the communist "witch hunts" of the late 1940's and 1950's, another time when hysteria gripped many Americans. Innocent until proven guilty, a concept Americans claim to hold dear, was somewhat thrown out the window during the Red Scare, and a man named Joseph McCarthy became a powerful figure by exploiting people's fears. The imprisonment of over 100,000 Japanese-Americans during World War II was an even more glaring example of the United States government tossing aside political principles in the name of security. Do Americans actually believe in the Bill of Rights, or do we only uphold our principles when we feel safe? It is hard to imagine literal witch trials happening again in the United States, but I can imagine many scenarios in which Americans might behave strangely when facing extreme stress. If, for instance, another major terrorist attack happens in the United States, I expect things to get ugly.

Still, you cannot take these historical parallels too far. It is impossible to understand the Salem Witch Trials without looking at the specific belief system of the Puritans. These were people who believed that an all-powerful God controlled all events past, present, and future, and that Satan and his legions were real beings trying to wreak havoc in the world. Without the widely held beliefs that witchcraft was a real possibility, and that meaning could be deciphered in all events, there could have been no Salem Witch Trials. In the mind of a common Puritan, the disastrous series of events in the 1680's and 1690's must have a cause. In this worldview, there is no such thing as a string of bad luck. So when young girls start to behave strangely, witchcraft can seem like a plausible explanation. There were just so many signs that Satan and his legions were running amok and that increasingly sinful citizens might be in league with the devil.

Today, it is easy to just laugh these people off. No one, after all, could ever be this stupid today. The problem with this reaction is that a large percentage of Americans today still believe in demonic spirits, and some may even believe in the reality of witchcraft. I have heard that some people do not want their children to read the *Harry Potter* series because of the "occult" practices depicted in the books. It is also common to hear people offer spiritual explanations for disastrous events such as 9/11, Hurricane Katrina, or the BP oil spill, claiming that these are signs of God's judgment. Now as far as I am concerned, people have every right to believe whatever they want. Religious beliefs that cannot be proven, however, must be kept out of any court of law. The Salem Witch Trials, along with an enormous list of other events, prove the necessity of separating church and state. When the weight of the government is thrown behind purely religious beliefs, then you can get in some serious trouble. A long time ago, it was decided that our legal system should judge guilt on the basis of measurable evidence. Physical evidence and eyewitness testimony may be imperfect, but it's a hell of a lot better than gyrating teenagers and other nonsense.

So most Americans, whether they believe in witchcraft or not, have no desire to bring back any witch trials. What concern me more are other fringe beliefs and movements that are generally written off as being ridiculous. Neo-nazis, extremist anti-government groups, conspiracy theorists, and many others are either reviled or laughed off by the majority. Few expect them to ever become particularly prominent. But as the Salem Witch Trials demonstrate, during times of stress, ideas that are usually out on the fringe may come into the limelight, and the general population may consider some things that they would normally write off without a thought. When the Nazis first emerged in Germany, I doubt that too many people believed that they could ever take over the country. But in a nation facing severe economic strife that was angry and bitter about the results of World War I, the Nazi message appealed to enough people to bring Hitler to power. This is why crazy ideas need to be taken seriously, and rational people must do their best to keep them on the fringes. Never underestimate the potential of the human race to believe just about anything, especially in times of stress.

5. Can Democracy and Extreme Inequality Coexist?

Throughout the history of civilization, political dictatorship and extreme economic inequality have been the norm. The two go hand-in-hand. Until the advent of modern machinery and industrialization, the only way for a small minority to achieve fantastic wealth was to exploit the majority as laborers. Human muscle - rather than electricity, petroleum, or natural gas - was the primary energy source. To maintain this system in which a small minority held most of the wealth through the labor of others, the majority had to be controlled by brute force. If some form of democratic reform were implemented, then the poor majority might produce and/or vote for leaders that implemented economic policies more beneficial to the masses. If protest was tolerated, then the system could come crashing down under the weight of these masses.

In 2011, political protest and revolution spread like wildfire throughout the Middle East and Northern Africa, and these movements were caused by more than just a desire for democracy. The unrest was also the result of high unemployment, widespread poverty, and extreme economic inequality. People were tired of systems in which a tiny class of elites ran the state as if it was its private source of cash. At the time of this writing, it was not clear how this "Arab Spring" would ultimately turn out. In some nations – Libya, Syria, Bahrain – governments resorted primarily to violent crackdowns. In others, such as Tunisia and Egypt, long-ruling dictators were swept aside under the weight of non-violent protest. But even in areas where governments have already been toppled, it may be years before we know if the dictatorships have been replaced with something fundamentally different and better.

Almost four hundred years ago, the elites of the Southern English colonies in North America – an area that would later become a significant part of the United States – were in a situation somewhat similar to what was recently faced by North African and Middle Eastern dictators. Jamestown, the colony that would eventually evolve into Virginia, was a complete disaster in its early years. Eventually, however, they found a crop that would make the place profitable: tobacco. The only problem was that a large labor force was needed to plant, tend, and harvest the crop. To fill this need, a simple strategy was developed. Since England was filled with desperately poor people, it would not be too difficult to find individuals desperate enough to try their luck in America. To get free passage to the colonies, a person simply had to agree to work for someone else for a given period of time - about seven years or so on average – and then he would be free to start a new life in America. For the first few decades of English colonial history, these indentured servants would be the primary labor force in the South.

Because conditions were still awful in the early years of Virginia and later Maryland, a large percentage of indentured servants did not live out the years of their contracts. For the owners of large plantations, however, this was fine. There were still plenty of people back in England who could be cheaply induced to try their luck in America. Also, with a limited number of people surviving to go free, the economy was able to absorb these survivors, so there was enough to go around to keep these people appeased. Eventually, however, a "problem" arose. Over time, an increasing percentage of indentured servants managed to live out their servitude and go free. Once freed, they now needed jobs or land in order to start their new lives. But with much of the land owned by a relatively small class of plantation owners who utilized indentured servants, it became increasingly difficult to find enough jobs and land to go around. So the options were pretty clear. The political and economic elites could implement a land reform program extensive enough to appease the masses. They could also, either in conjunction with land reform or not, improve the pay and work conditions for agricultural laborers so that people would more willingly take and keep these jobs. The problem, of course, with both of these options was that they would cut into the potential wealth of the elites. So if the powers that be wanted to maintain their extensive wealth, they could turn to a crackdown approach, turning poor European laborers into something closer to

25

slaves. Enslaving Englishmen accustomed by the 17th century to at least some basic rights, however, might not go over very well.

Fortunately for them, the Carolinas, along with the colonial model established in Latin America, provided another alternative. The African slave trade was in full swing by the late 17th century, with Britain taking increasing control over this lucrative business. The southern part of the Carolinas, with its profitable rice plantations, was the first British colony in North America to rely primarily on slave labor. Slaves were much more expensive to acquire than indentured servants, but owners were never required to set them free. Slaves would therefore never become the potential landless, jobless, troublemaking ex-indentured servants that threatened to cause political chaos, and landowners, by exploiting slave labor, could maintain their wealth. Also, by keeping the population of white people somewhat in check, there could be enough resources left over to keep these people satisfied and maintain stability. Because slaves lived in an absolute dictatorship, average white people could at least have some basic rights and relative economic prosperity. Ironically enough, enslavement of Africans made a certain amount of freedom, democracy, and prosperity possible for white men during both colonial times and in the early days of the United States. And even if a white person had a tough time in America, at least he knew that he was better off than a slave, and the fear of a slave revolt kept him from seriously questioning the system. White people, after all, had to stick together. Racism was both an effective tool for justifying slavery and for keeping the poor divided, making a widespread revolt less likely.

Slavery would continue to exist in the United States until 1865, and if the Southern United States had never chosen to secede from the Union, there is no telling how much longer slavery might have been maintained. Long before the Civil War, however, the Northern states had decided that slavery made no economic sense. It was more efficient to employ wage laborers, and the Northern economy had never relied so much on agricultural workers anyway. And as the industrial economy advanced and developed, it eventually became possible in the Northern states to sustain a large enough middle class to keep enough people content. Machines and mass production, rather than slaves and large tracts of land, became the basis for the fabulous wealth of the elite class. Workers were still exploited, and labor strife could often cause instability, but eventually the government gave in to limited demands for reform, establishing work regulations that would keep the masses appeased. The expansion of voting rights and development of a limited welfare state over time also served to maintain order. And even during tough economic times, many middle class people held poor people responsible for being poor, and politicians who called for more radical economic reforms were written off as socialists.

The large businesses and elite classes often protested the expansion of government's role, but as the economy continued to become more productive, they were often able to thrive in spite of the new rules and taxes. In recent decades, they have had some success in lobbying for lower taxes and deregulation. Even in the face of the closely related problems of large budget deficits and a near collapse of the financial system, the ideology of tax cuts and deregulation remains strong in the United States. Businesses have also been able to maintain profits by moving operations to countries where workers are cheaper and regulations less strict. And if the governments of these foreign nations maintained dictatorships in order to keep the laboring masses in control, American businesses and political officials either actively supported these dictators or looked the other way.

We still live in a world filled with political dictatorship and economic inequality. This is partly the responsibility of political leaders in underdeveloped nations who are more concerned with amassing fortunes than with meeting the needs of their people. It is also the result, however, of economic reality. If a nation is unable to produce enough wealth to both enrich its elites and appease an adequate number of its citizens, then dictatorship will be the norm. And if the economic and political elites of advanced nations are more interested in seeking out cheap labor or resources around the world than in promoting real economic development, dictators will be necessary to control the disenchanted masses.

You cannot separate politics from economics. Real democracy cannot exist without a certain level of economic development. Unfortunately, promoting democratic institutions and economic development is not easy. Decades of hard work and struggle may be necessary to get there, and numerous obstacles, both human and otherwise, stand in the way. At our current stage of technological development, the human race may not be able to produce enough wealth to sustain a decent standard of living for all of the world's citizens. So in an ideal setting, nation building is very difficult. In a world of flawed, self-centered, shortsighted human beings, it can seem downright impossible.

Still, I hope that people will not give up if the recent uprisings in North Africa and the Middle East fail to achieve significant improvements. As the history of the United States and other nations shows, change can be very slow, and at times, reforms can either stall or be rolled back. But if the more advanced and democratic parts of the world were able to make at least some improvements over time, maybe there is some hope for people today who are fighting the same battles that Americans fought in the past. And as science and technology continue to progress, we may someday be able to sustain throughout the world an average standard of living that is higher than currently seems possible. If people four hundred years ago were transported to our era in a time machine, they would likely be surprised by how far the human race has come. Unfortunately, however, there will also be some things that seem very familiar to them.

6. What Does it Mean to be American?

When the Fourth of July rolls around, you tend to hear a little more talk than usual about the founding of the United States. Unfortunately, there if often little depth to this conversation. We just hear the same old generic story about the evil British taxing and abusing our ancestors in various ways and those freedom-loving Americans rising up to fight for independence. We then go back to focusing on more important matters such as Fourth of July sales, blowing stuff up, and having nice block parties or barbeques.

But in this generic story that is a ritualistic part of the Fourth of July patriotic orgy, a simple question is not answered. Why, after 170 years of being generally happy with British rule, did these American revolutionaries decide to break away from their mother country? Did Great Britain turn evil all of a sudden? Did Americans just wake up one day and decide that they did not want Britain around any more? Committing treason, after all, and taking up arms against the most powerful nation on earth, were not decisions to be taken lightly.

When you ask why history transpired as it did, there are no definitive answers. We can state with some certainty the date of the battle of Lexington and Concord or the day when the Continental Congress voted to declare independence – July 2nd, by the way - but explaining why these events took place is much trickier. In my American History classes, I go over multiple factors that apparently played some part in leading up to the American Revolution. Most of these are not specific, measurable events that occurred at some single point in time. Instead, they are mostly long-term trends that developed over the course of decades. Long before Americans even thought about revolution, a potentially revolutionary environment formed in the thirteen colonies. And while historians debate about which factors were the most important, I think that most would agree that everything in my following list played some role in causing the American Revolution. They would also agree that this was a more complex story than some freedom-loving Americans getting fed up with horrible, abusive Great Britain.

You could make a good case that the most important factor in creating the revolution was not British tyranny. Instead, it was decades of British neglect. Because the thirteen colonies were three thousand miles from Great Britain, and circumstances both within Britain and in other parts of the world – mainland Europe, India, the Caribbean – were considered much more significant than those in North America, American colonists were largely free to govern themselves. When each colony was founded, the British government granted a charter to an individual, a small group of people, or a corporation to govern and develop their colonies as each saw fit. Over time, most colonies eventually became royal colonies with a governor appointed by the crown. But these men did not generally do a lot of governing. Important decisions regarding the day-to-day operations of government were usually made by town councils and colonial legislatures, with governors by and large rubber stamping these actions. Over the decades, colonists grew accustomed to running their own affairs. And so long as Britain was able to generate a certain amount of wealth from its thirteen colonies, it was willing to tolerate American colonial autonomy and to not enforce very strictly the trade regulations that it passed in order to profit from colonial trade. American colonists grew accustomed to defying the British Navigation Acts, and Britain was unwilling to invest a great deal to enforce them. Most trade, after all, flowed to and from Great Britain anyway.

Also, as people well aware of the British parliamentary tradition, colonists felt that they possessed the same "Rights of Englishmen" as those citizens back in Great Britain. Americans, as much as we hate to admit it, did not invent the concepts of individual rights and representative government. These concepts were largely brought here from Great Britain. And these were not the only ideas emerging in Europe that affected the American colonies. The 18th century is often referred to as the Enlightenment, or the Age of Reason. During this time, intellectuals argued that ideas should only be accepted as truth if they could be backed by logic and/or scientific experimentation. Traditional ideas in the areas of science, religion, philosophy, and politics were called into question, and people influenced by the Enlightenment were not going to accept ideas and institutions simply because they represented the way things had always been. By nature, the Enlightenment could be a spur to revolution, and many of our nation's Founding Fathers were steeped in Enlightenment philosophy.

In themselves, however, our British heritage of self-government and the influence of the Enlightenment were not enough to start a revolution. As long as Great Britain failed to govern the colonies very closely, Americans would be content with their situation. Sure, there were plenty of problems within the colonies. Colonists from the western frontier regions often resented the power, wealth, status, and lifestyle of those in the east. The wide variety of religious and ethnic backgrounds of colonists could cause tension and conflict at times. Large disparities of wealth, as in all societies, could lead to various social problems and class conflict between rich and poor. And a large colonial middle class, people who had a taste of the good life, often wanted a bit more, but they felt excluded by more traditional elites. Ultimately, most of the problems in colonial America involved conflict between colonists, not policies imposed by Great Britain. But if Britain were to ever change its ways, assert more control over the colonies, and implement unpopular policies, these lingering forms of colonial tension and resentment might be directed toward the mother country.

Eventually, Britain did change its ways. From 1754-1763, the British were engaged in the fourth of a series of wars with France in a struggle largely over global territory and trade. In the United States, we refer to it as the French and Indian War, largely because most Native Americans sided with the French. When the British finally won, the French lost all of their considerable territory in North America, and the British had added significantly more land into which its colonial empire could expand. After investing so much into this victory, the British government decided to govern its new, larger, North American empire more closely, and they decided that American colonists should help pay some of the debts from this war and the costs of this increased government presence. This was the beginning of the British actions that get all of the publicity in our American Revolution stories: new taxes, restrictions on where Americans could settle, tougher enforcement of trade regulations, soldiers quartered into people's homes, etc. In America today, these are depicted as the actions of a terrible, dictatorial government. But if you look back more objectively, it becomes clear that these actions were not that big of a deal. Americans today are taxed more, subject to more regulations, and live with a much larger military presence under the United States government than the colonists under Great Britain. But after years of being left alone and liking it, any increased involvement by the British crown was going to be perceived as onerous. And when coupled with factors mentioned earlier – the belief in the "Rights of Englishmen," the Enlightenment, and lingering tensions between colonists – these changes in policy proved to be the spark that ignited a long developing fuse.

When years of American protest finally led to war in April of 1775, the goals of American rebels were not quite clear. Were they trying to convince Britain to go back to the days before the French and Indian War, or would this inevitably become a fight for independence? Was the goal to be British subjects with all of the rights that this implied, or were we now Americans attempting to create a new nation? It was not until July of 1776 that this question was finally settled. But even before the conflict with Britain began, Americans had a sense that something new was being created in these thirteen colonies. Rather than simply being an extension of the nation of Britain, a distinct, and some would say superior, American culture was being formed.

From the beginning, American colonists did not represent a cross-section of the British population. People willing to cross an ocean to a new world tended to be a bit more adventurous, ambitious, brave, and/or desperate than your average person. The colonies often attracted people who were, for lack of a better term, oddballs. But this weirdness went beyond personality. People who were religious minorities in their homeland, such as the Puritans, could become the dominant group in an American colony. Also, many of the people who settled in British colonies were not British not all, with significant numbers of Germans, Dutch, French, Swedish, and Irish people settling here. With the development of slavery, you also had a much larger African influence in the colonies than anywhere in Europe. In general, the people who developed many of the colonies were more interested in getting wealth-producing bodies than in maintaining any degree of cultural homogeneity. So from the beginning, the thirteen colonies represented an interesting hodgepodge of people from various backgrounds.

Geography also played a major factor in causing colonial American society to diverge from Great Britain. Most notably, there was just so much open space in North America. Prospects for an average person to become a landowner were so much greater than Britain, a place where you often had to be lucky enough to inherit the limited amount of land available. Particularly during those early days, the colonies truly represented a "land of opportunity." Also, the climate and terrain in certain colonial regions bore little resemblance to that in England. It should be no surprise therefore that the economy and culture of a place like South Carolina would bear decreasing resemblance to that of Great Britain.

So over the course of many decades, these peculiar, not-so-English Englishmen lived thousands of miles from a mother country that often bore little geographic resemblance to the places they now called home. Technically, the thirteen colonies were a political extension of Great Britain. But over time, they developed cultures distinct to this new world. So what were the particular qualities of this new American culture? These societies were so young, and from the start they were so diverse, that it may have seemed premature to declare at the time that there was any such thing as a new culture here. Still, there was a growing sense that something new was being born, so when the British government decided to govern these colonies more closely, Americans were more inclined to resist. The colonists, after all, had already sensed for some time that they were different from those British overlords anyway. And in the minds of those patriots, this new society upheld principles such as representative government and individual human rights much more than those British people who claimed to believe in them.

As I write this in the year 2011, the United States is 235 years old. But even now, it is difficult to define exactly the cultural traits of this society that we have built. As it was in the beginning, modern American society is characterized by diversity, and some would question the notion that there is any such thing as a single American culture. Still, if you were to ask non-Americans about our culture, I suspect that specific thoughts might come to their minds. Some associate America with the products of our popular and consumer culture: McDonald's, Wal-Mart, Coca-Cola, Hollywood, etc. Others around the world might judge us by our leaders and powerful institutions. Hopefully, there are still some around the world who associate our nation with freedom, democracy, and opportunity. In spite of our many flaws, after all, many throughout the world still flock here for the same reasons our colonial ancestors came hundreds of years ago.

While I recognize that any attempt to define American culture will lead to gross overgeneralization, I think that there are some cultural traits that make us distinctly American. For better or for worse, we are still a very individualistic society. We tend to think that people should take care of themselves, and that people should have the opportunity to get rich if they play their cards right. So closely related to this individualism is a materialistic streak, with many Americans judging others by the amount of money that they have. But while we respect the rich, we don't show them the same deference as some more traditional societies, and we tend to celebrate wealth that is earned, not inherited. Partly in the quest to get rich, a strong entrepreneurial sprit has existed since colonial times, and the United States remains arguably the most innovative society on earth. After decades of astounding success, a certain American arrogance also permeates our culture. Many still believe in American exceptionalism, this notion that our country is somehow different than others and can achieve what other societies cannot. This individualism, materialism, and arrogance can get us into trouble, but is has played a major role in our success stories as well.

The United States began as an experiment, and it remains the same today. 235 years sounds like a long time, but as societies and nations go, we are still relatively young. And in recent decades, we have become more ethnically and culturally diverse than ever. Some are apparently worried, although they don't directly express it, that this growing diversity will make the United

States lose some of what made it great. Personally, I think that diversity has always been one of our nation's greatest strengths. Sure, other peoples and cultures will change the United States. But the principles that this nation was founded upon, and the culture that has evolved through our unique history, also have the power to shape those who come. And in more cases than not, people who come here for many of the same reasons as our ancestors will be happy to cast their lot with the rest of us oddballs.

Part Two: The American Revolution and the Constitution

7. The Meaning of the Fourth of July

On July 2, 1776, representatives of thirteen British colonies in North America voted to break free from British rule and form a new nation. Two days later, a document was officially drafted that attempted to explain the reasons for this action. The date written on this "Declaration of Independence" would ultimately become the officially celebrated birthday of the United States of America, a day that Americans generally (and "creatively") refer to as the Fourth of July. The most quoted parts of the Declaration of Independence come from its opening two paragraphs, and they have become a significant part of our national creed:

> "We hold these truths to be self-evident, that all men are created equal; that they are endowed by their Creator with certain unalienable rights; that among these are life, liberty and the pursuit of happiness. That to secure these rights, governments are instituted among men, deriving their just powers from the consent of the governed; that, whenever any form of government becomes destructive of these ends, it is the right of the people to alter or to abolish it, and to institute a new government, laying its foundation on such principles and organizing its powers in such form, as to them shall seem most likely to effect their safety and happiness."

It sounds simple enough. Governments exist to protect individual rights – a radical idea at the time – and if a government fails to perform this function, then the people have a right to get rid of it. You can make a strong case, however, that the people of the United States have spent the last 235 years struggling to determine the exact meaning of these noble words. To some Americans today, the Fourth of July is a time to celebrate the greatness of the United States, a nation that is history's ultimate embodiment of a land where all people are guaranteed their basic rights. To others, the words in the Declaration would be the first of many examples of blatant American hypocrisy.

"All men are created equal." At least the Founding Fathers were somewhat honest in only referring to men. Women in early American history, after all, had the legal and political rights of children. Still, the founders could have been more honest by saying, "all property-holding, white men are created equal." Black slaves had no rights, Native Americans were viewed as obstacles to settlement that needed to be displaced, and in many states, people without property could not vote. This was hardly the embodiment of a democratic, freedom loving society where all were created equal.

Of course, concepts like "equality" and "rights" are vague and tricky to define. If you ask Americans today of various political persuasions how they define these words, you are likely to get a variety of answers. Does "equality" refer to the distribution of goods, or is it limited to equality of opportunity? Do all humans have a right to basic needs like a college education, health care coverage, and housing, or are these reserved to those who can afford them? I wonder how the Founding Fathers would have answered these questions? Given the fact that Thomas Jefferson, the primary author of the Declaration of Independence, was both a slaveholder and plantation owner, it is clear that his views on equality and human rights were not particularly radical. It is difficult to generalize, however. The founders, after all, were a collection of opinionated individuals, not a single entity with one point of view.

In a sense, the American Revolution did not end when the British decided to stop fighting. Instead, the revolution has been an ongoing process. Displacing the British was only part one. When the British were gone, the truly difficult questions had to be answered. What system of government would this new nation have? What policies would it follow? Who would rule this new nation? On the surface, the answers seemed easy. We would have a government free from Britain that protected individual rights, and Americans would rule themselves. Americans, however, both then and now, have never agreed with one another on everything. We have always been a society divided by ethnicity, race, gender, age, social class, religion, and political ideology. These divisions that existed in colonial times did not magically disappear once the British were gone. Even during the Revolutionary War, Americans who fought for the patriot cause had various motivations for doing so, and they had different visions for this new nation's future. The revolutionary concepts of freedom, liberty, and equality were defined in a wide variety of ways.

Too often, particularly on the Fourth of July, we Americans mythologize those first patriots who founded our nation. In comparison to those glorious people of the past, our country today can seem pretty lousy. But when you take a closer look at the past, you will see that they were not all that different from us. If anything, their society was much worse. Over the course of the last 235 years, our country has expanded voting rights, abolished slavery, established better work conditions, and improved its attitudes toward and treatment of ethnic minorities, women, children, homosexuals, and the disabled. There is obviously still a long way to go, but progress has clearly been made. Many people and events, of course, have played a role in these social changes, but the principles laid out in the Declaration of Independence have been a significant, consistent, revolutionary force.

The United States does not live up to its noble ideals. No nation ever does. So Americans should not simply rest on their laurels every Fourth of July and celebrate how great we are. Ideals must not be confused with reality. This does not mean, however, that we should all become cynical and depressed because our country falls so woefully short. The United States, in spite of all of its weaknesses and problems, has taken steps over the course of its history toward more closely realizing its creed. A recognition that revolutions never really end, and that progress is possible, should inspire all Americans to push our nation closer to those ideals that we claim to believe.

8. The Battle Against Childish History

A couple of years ago, we tried a home schooling experiment with our younger daughter. Since I was the resident history professor, "Social Studies" was my responsibility, and I immediately ran into a problem. History, like the present, is not always a pretty picture. And just as most responsible parents, I assume, try to shelter their kids from some of the ugly aspects of the modern world, I was tempted to edit out certain aspects of the past. Right away, of course, I reached a point in our "class" where we talked about what happened when Europeans came into contact with Native Americans. Try as I might, I could not think of a way of making this a happy story. Native Americans, after all, were largely wiped out through warfare, disease, and habitat destruction. It would be ridiculous, of course, to call this an insignificant detail and leave it out of the story. So I decided to keep things simple. We talked about a few reasons why these two groups might fight, and then we discussed a few factors that would help Europeans win that fight. We then moved on, and I managed to avoid going into any gory details.

As a parent, I have become more sympathetic toward the idea of feeding kids fantasies. Santa Claus, the Easter Bunny, the Tooth Fairy – some would even put religion in this category – were invented in part to give kids a positive impression of the world. These magical figures are out there, after all, handing out gifts to children out of the goodness of their hearts. All parents know that some day kids will figure out that these characters are not real and that there are people and forces out there that might do them harm. But when should that moment of facing up to reality come? Ultimately, this question will be answered at some point for us parents whether we like it or not.

When it comes to history, I suspect that many people never face up to reality completely. In some ways, it is not their fault. Grammar schools, in addition to sheltering kids from some of the ugly aspects of history, are filled with teachers with little historical training. Kids are therefore given a simplistic history, and in some cases, an inaccurate one. The media reinforces these trends by altering history in order to make it more entertaining and inspiring for kids, just as many movies and TV shows continue to do for adults. Theoretically, this is fine if people are exposed to more sophisticated historical information as they grow up, and I know from personal experience as a student and teacher that there are people at the high school and college levels who are trying to do just that. People who teach these older students, however, are fighting a difficult battle. First of all, many people, to say the least, do not particularly enjoy studying history. They will often do the minimum amount of work necessary to memorize enough stuff to pass the class. Then, when the tests are over, most of that information quickly exits their brains.

Teachers can only hope, therefore, that students will remember some of the major events that were discussed and that they will, more generally, gain a more accurate view of the world. The problem, however, is that the basic worldview of all human beings is largely developed when they are children. In other words, the stuff we learn as a child sticks with us more than the things that we learn as adults. So if details tend to fade away and we are only left with the major ideas, these will mostly be big ideas absorbed while we were kids. Then, when you combine this fact with the power of visual media like TV and movies, one thing becomes very clear: Hollywood (especially *Disney*), parents, and grammar school teachers often have a much greater impact on beliefs about history than college teachers like me. My colleagues and I are competing with some very powerful forces.

Many people of my generation, and even some younger people, remember *Schoolhouse Rock*. These were a series of little cartoon music videos that would be shown in between Saturday morning cartoons beginning back in the 1970's and would teach basic lessons about grammar, math, science, and, of course, American History. Obviously, you cannot expect a three-minute song designed for little kids to provide detailed historical information. You can expect them, however, to at least be somewhat accurate. In my American History classes, I show one of these little videos called "No More Kings" to introduce the unit on the causes of the American Revolution. Before showing the video, I tell my students two things. First, I ask them a simple question: "If someone asked you why the American Revolution happened, would this video basically be your answer?" Then, I tell them that if they ever use this *Schoolhouse Rock* summary as an answer to any future test questions, then their grade will not be particularly high. There are several problems with this video. First, the king of England did not resemble the strange mutant creature portrayed in the video. (Although European royal family inbreeding may have sometimes had some nasty effects.) Second, the king did not start taxing Americans to simply show them that he was in charge, and he did not take away practically everything that they owned. Libertarians and Republicans today would love to go back to the kind of tax rates faced by American colonists. The video also gives the impression that all Americans banded together to fight and defeat the evil British. The truth is that many Americans either tried to stay out of the conflict or actively supported the British. The American Revolution was as much of a civil war as it was a war for independence.

The facts just listed, however, would not make a particularly inspiring children's video. It is not a story that adults particularly want to hear on the 4th of July either. The purpose of *Schoolhouse Rock*, of course, is not merely to educate; these videos are primarily designed to entertain, to inspire kids to do great things, and to teach kids to love the United States. In other words, the primary purpose is propaganda. Now I can understand why a society would want to teach this kind of "history" to kids. All societies throughout history have created myths and legends to instill cultural values into their children (and adults). The problem is that many Americans do not recognize these as legends. So even after I spend an entire class covering the American Revolution in detail, and I specifically tell them not to give me the *Schoolhouse Rock* answer on a test, a few people still recite the cartoon video on exams. When students fail to study, they fall back on what they learned as kids.

So is this such a bad thing? As a history teacher, I am professionally obligated to say yes. Yet even if I look at things from the perspective of a non-history professor, I see some major problems with a society that never moves beyond a childish view of history. First of all, a childish version of history is not particularly interesting. The good guys are too good, and the bad guys are too bad, to be interesting characters. Events are also described in a superficial and simplistic way. When history is presented in this way, it does not seem real. Personally, I did not acquire much of an interest in history until college; at this level, I finally had professors who described in rich detail the realities of the past with its flawed characters and sometimes stupid, ugly, and pointless circumstances. The stories were not always pretty, which was exactly why they were so interesting. Unfortunately, there are a larger number of students out there who were probably turned off to history at an early age. Since they have always found it boring, they are no longer able to consider the possibility that there could be something interesting and relevant in a history course.

A childish history, however, does more than distort the past. It also creates an inaccurate, often pessimistic view of the present. If the past was filled with glorious characters and events, then the present by comparison seems really crappy. How can modern politicians ever live up to the legends of George Washington, Abraham Lincoln, and John F. Kennedy? How can average citizens today ever match the bravery of the men who fought the American Revolution or World War II? How can a country that has deteriorated so much hope to solve any of its problems? But if you study history with all of its complexities, you realize that the people of the past were at least as messed up as we are. So if they could have occasional moments of wisdom and glory, then maybe we are not completely hopeless.

I have heard it reported many times that a significant percentage of Americans believe that we are living in the "end times." There may be many causes for the prevalence of this belief, but I think that one source is this inaccurate view of history. As I said before, if the past is romanticized, then the present by comparison can seem really bad. Then, an ideology that describes a hopelessly sinful world in a state of constant deterioration seems pretty convincing. I have also heard it reported many times, however, that by most of the measures that we use to determine happiness and prosperity, the world today is better than it has ever been. This is not to say that the world is without problems. I am merely recognizing the fact that the world has always been a mess. If people, through the study of history, could gain this same insight, they might become more engaged in attempts to solve problems, and they may be less likely to hope for a divine being to show up one day to bail them out.

Paradoxically, a romanticized history could also in some cases make people overly optimistic. If people are taught that the United States throughout its history has been primarily a force for good in the world, then they might be inclined to believe that it is mostly doing good today. So, for example, if a political figure argued that the United States, through military force, could bring democracy to a foreign nation with no history of democratic government, historically illiterate Americans might be inclined to agree with him. Who else but Americans raised with a romanticized history would buy that idea?

9. The More Powerful Country Does Not Always Win.

When Great Britain decided to put down the revolt in its thirteen colonies, there were plenty of reasons to think that it would succeed. It was stronger than those troublemaking American colonists in every way. The British had a well-trained and fortified army. The rebels were trying to piece together an army from its various semi-trained militia groups. An island nation, the British had always placed great emphasis on their navy, which was without a doubt the most powerful on earth. The Americans, on the other hand, initially had a "navy" consisting of whatever boats they could dredge up. In those early days, the American military was essentially a bunch of guys with guns and a few boats. They had military potential, but it would take time for this potential to be realized.

To help fund its effort, Great Britain also had the backing of the most sophisticated economy on earth, including access to resources from a global trading network. The Americans had great economic potential, but much of the colonial economy was based on exports to Great Britain. With access to this market cut off, they would have to go through a difficult adjustment period. The British also had a well-established government that backed a stable currency, could easily borrow money, and would continue to exist regardless of the outcome of this war. Meanwhile, the Americans were trying to form a single nation from what had traditionally been separately governed colonies. It was not until near the end of the war, in fact, that they settled on an official system of government. And the abilities of this "government" to create a stable, accepted currency and to borrow money to fund the war were restricted by the lack of any guarantee of its continued existence. Loaning money to this new nation or even accepting its paper currency carried with it a certain amount of risk.

So outside of having a weaker military, economy, and government, things were looking pretty good for the Americans. But the colonies' problems did not end there. A significant percentage of American colonists did not actively support the cause, and many others remained strongly loyal to the British. For American colonists, this was as much of a civil war as it was a war for independence. Even under ideal circumstances, with an overwhelming majority behind the cause, this was going to be a difficult fight for the Americans. This lack of unity, however, stacked the odds even more in the favor of the British.

So how did those American revolutionaries manage to win? People who believe in divine providence, the "God bless America" crowd, might see this miraculous victory as evidence of the reality of supernatural intervention. While there is no way to disprove this hypothesis, it is not necessary to resort to the supernatural in trying to explain this amazing victory. In spite of seeming weaker in every tangible way when the war started, the Americans also had some important things going for them. For one, the colonists were fighting on their home soil, which had some definite practical benefits such as knowledge of the terrain and proximity to supplies. But this also had some important intangible benefits. People fighting on their home turf might fight a bit harder and longer than a soldier far from home. Also, the American civilian population, with its significant number of people who did not take sides when the war began, would tend to become more sympathetic toward their fellow colonials as the conflict dragged on. If nothing else, the patriots were fighting for their homeland. British soldiers, on the other hand, were either military professionals following orders or mercenaries fighting for money. For many of them, the thirteen colonies were God-forsaken places where they really did not want to be. These men were outsiders, and when neutral civilians are caught in the crossfire, they tend to vent their frustrations against the foreigner.

By nature, outside invaders, which British soldiers essentially were, have a difficult task. They have to win battles, capture important pieces of territory, and then hold on to what they have captured as they seek to gain even more territory. They also have to transport men and materials over significant distances, securing ports and protecting supply lines. Given the technology of the late 18th century, the thirteen colonies represented a large piece of territory for the British to try and control. This task was made even more difficult by the loose political organization of the colonies. People in these areas were accustomed to being governed locally, and there was no single place whose capture by the British would guarantee victory. Also, in the late 18th century, the Atlantic Ocean was a significant barrier, and shipping men and materials was only part of the problem. Orders also moved very slowly across this ocean before the existence of the telegraph, telephones, or internet connections. And back in Great Britain, the tremendous distance separating civilians from the colonies had an important psychological effect. Since the thirteen colonies were so far away, and American colonists posed no direct threat to Great Britain, British civilians were likely over time to start wondering if the fight was really worth it.

Victory in war often has as much to do with motivation as strategy, weaponry, and money. In the end, the winner is often the one willing to tolerate the highest level of sacrifice. When the Revolutionary War began, George Washington wanted to build an army that could take on the British in battle and win conventional military victories. But because of British advantages mentioned earlier, his army spent more time retreating in the early days of the war than winning glorious battles. Fortunately for him and his new nation, British generals, either because of indecisiveness or overconfidence, generally did not push hard enough to finish Washington off when they had the chance. When the winter kicked in, the British figured that they could just finish the job in the spring. There were also moments during these early years when Washington barely escaped due to luck or because he was wise enough to know where and when to run. Over time, Washington realized a simple truth. He and his nation's armies and part-time militiamen did not necessarily have to win this war. They just had to not lose. So long as armies were in the field, and American soldiers and militiamen were able to harass the British on occasion, the dream of American independence was still alive. And the longer that this war lasted, the more likely it was that the British would realize that it just was not worth it any more. Washington's biggest contributions, therefore, were not the occasional victories that he won. It was his ability to somehow keep an army in the field. And for the sake of survival, he was man enough to declare a retreat.

These early Americans, however, do not deserve all of the credit for this victory. It turns out that they had some help. About halfway through the war, France, still stinging from its defeat at the hands of the British fifteen years earlier, decided to enter the war officially on the side of the American revolutionaries. (They had started to send aid secretly two years earlier.) This was not done, of course, out of the goodness of their hearts. In addition to payback, declaring war against Britain while that nation was distracted might create opportunities for France to make gains throughout the world at its enemy's expense. Suddenly, Britain had to worry about more valuable colonial possessions in the Caribbean and in Asia. They also had to consider the possibility of cutting their losses in the thirteen colonies. So upon France's entry into the war, the British began focusing their efforts on the Southern colonies. Because of the cash crops cranked out by their plantation economies, the Southern colonies were considered much more valuable than those in the North, and there were more colonists loyal to Britain in the South as well. So as Washington sat largely idle outside of New York City, most of the action had shifted to the South. Finally, in 1781, the opportunity arose in Yorktown, Virginia for Washington, with major support from French army and naval forces, to trap and capture the main British army in the South. With the American victory at Yorktown, the British finally came to the conclusion that the costs of this war had become too high. After two years of negotiations, Britain, seven years after colonists had declared independence, recognized the sovereignty of the United States.

Today, it's hard to believe that the United States started off as a nation of underdogs. For the last seventy years, the United States has been a military superpower. And today, no nation comes close to the United States in terms of military spending and sophistication. We should have learned from the beginning, however, that power does not guarantee victory in war. With the right combination of intangibles – and maybe some outside help – the underdog can sometimes outlast the superpower. Nearly two hundred years after the American Revolution, the United States relearned this lesson in Vietnam. For many of the same reasons that my forefathers succeeded – knowledge of terrain, a greater motivation to fight, a decentralized country, distance from its enemy, outside aid – Vietnamese communists outlasted the United States and ultimately created a single Vietnam.

With its more recent invasions of Afghanistan and Iraq, many fear that the United States may ultimately learn the same lesson again. In a conventional sense, the United States military seemed to achieve quick victories in both of those countries. But Iraqis, Afghans, and foreign fighters who oppose American goals in these countries are not going anywhere. And they know that as time passes, Americans will lose patience with military intervention in places so far from home. Will these insurgents, by harassing and inflicting damage on American troops, domestic security forces, and the civilian population, prove once again that the highly motivated underdog can outlast the superpower? Recent events indicate once again that patience is not one of America's strengths, and many see the costs as just too high. In my mind, the only hope is that political leaders and security forces within Iraq and Afghanistan develop the competence and legitimacy to maintain some semblance of order. For as history has made clear, brute strength exercised by an outside power is often not enough.

10. Why was the Articles of Confederation Replaced by the Constitution?

A movement within the Republican Party calling itself the "Tea Party" became an important political force in 2009 and remains so to this day. But why have the "members" of the Tea Party movement chosen that particular name? From what I can gather, Tea Partiers are trying to connect their movement to our nation's historical roots. Just as those first patriots (dumping tea into Boston's harbor) rebelled against a powerful central government that tried to tax, regulate, and control them too much, believers in this modern movement are fighting to restore our nation's original ideals of freedom and limited government, ideals embodied in our nation's Constitution. In their minds, the federal government has grown too large, taxes and spends too much, and has gotten involved with issues over which it has no Constitutional jurisdiction.

There is no doubt that those first American revolutionaries were generally afraid of a powerful central government. Given their experiences with Great Britain, these fears were understandable. So shortly before the Revolutionary War ended, the thirteen states agreed to a political system called the Articles of Confederation. In this system, the national government had the bare minimum of powers: forming a military, negotiating with foreign powers, establishing a postal service, and creating currency. Essentially, it dealt only with matters that concerned the nation as a whole, namely national defense and interstate trade. Most significant, however, were the powers it did not have. For one thing, the national government could not tax. It could merely request money from the states to fund its various activities. There was also no national court system. Instead, state and local courts handled all judicial matters. If interstate disputes arose, the national government was supposed to be the arbitrator. The system for doing this, however, was extremely complex and cumbersome, and there was no powerful executive to enforce much of anything anyway. You could make a good argument, in fact, that the European Union today is a more united body than the United States was under the Articles of Confederation. The United States was essentially a military and loose economic alliance of thirteen nation-states.

To people who believe in a limited federal government and states' rights, this original political system must sound great. Because most of the power was at the state and local level, government was more responsive to people's needs. Your vote carried more weight in this system because each individual citizen constituted a larger percentage of the population in the important state and town elections than they did in the mostly irrelevant national elections. A mayor of a town, after all, is more willing and able to meet with an individual constituent than the president of an entire nation. Also, because the size of the state and city bureaucracies would be smaller than with a powerful national government, there was less possibility of corruption and waste.

The only problem with the Articles of Confederation was that it did not work. States did not provide adequate funding when the federal government requested it, making it impossible to get much of anything done. Debts to foreign nations and to Revolutionary War soldiers remained unpaid. States sometimes created their own currencies and established tariffs on goods coming from other states, making it difficult for merchants to conduct any kind of interstate trade. Businessmen, in fact, were some of the biggest advocates for changing the system. Finally, the federal government under the Articles was unable to perform the most basic functions of government: defending the state and maintaining order. Spain and Great Britain encroached on American territory with no consequences, and in 1787, a man named Daniel Shays led a rebellion of indebted farmers that had to be put down by the Massachusetts state militia.

So in 1787, 55 men from 12 states got together with the official purpose of amending the Articles of Confederation. Very quickly, however, they agreed to go much further than that. The result was a system in which the federal government would be much stronger than before. It could now collect taxes to fund itself.

A national court system was created that could override the decisions of state and local courts. Only the federal government could create currency, and tariff barriers between states were forbidden. A separate executive branch was set up, headed by a president, which would carry out the laws passed by a Congress, consisting of a House and a Senate. Interstate disputes could now be resolved by this new federal government that clearly had the final say.

Some historians, like many Americans in the late 1780's, view the Constitution as a counterrevolutionary document. The Articles, based on the principles of democracy, personal freedom, and states' rights, embodied the original revolutionary spirit. But the elites of society, in this thesis, felt threatened by the Articles. Shays Rebellion seemed like an indication of things to come, with poor people grabbing their guns and taking the law into their own hands. More future events like this were bound to happen in a society with too much democracy and a weak federal government. The next thing you knew, the poor would be pushing for the passage of laws or taking violent actions that would confiscate the property of the wealthy. Businessmen also saw limited potential for profit in a system that had no consistent rules regarding currency, trade, and contracts.

So with the Constitution, these 55 men, who mostly represented the elite classes, created something that would protect their interests. This new government would be strong enough to maintain order, and it would not be overly democratic. In fact, the only officials in the Constitution as it was originally written that were directly elected by voters were the members of the House of Representatives. Senators were selected by state legislators. The president was chosen using a strange Electoral College system (that we are still stuck with), and Supreme Court justices were nominated by the (non-democratically elected) president and approved by the (non-democratically elected) Senate.

So was this a conspiracy of elites, or were the framers of the Constitution merely creating a system that would compensate for the weaknesses of the Articles? There is no doubt, after all, that these so-called self-centered elites had their own suspicions about excessive government power. This was why power was divided into three branches, with each branch having the ability to check and balance the primary powers of the other two. Even the limits on democracy do not necessarily constitute a conspiracy. At the time, choosing leaders through elections was not exactly the norm around the world, so relative to other nations at the time, the Constitution allowed voters to participate a great deal.

Ratification of this new government was by no means a done deal. In the end, concessions had to be made in order to get majority support in the required nine of thirteen ratifying conventions. It was agreed that a Bill of Rights would be added to set limits on this new national government. So amendments one through ten were added two years after the Constitution went into effect, and to many Americans, some of the principles found in the Bill of Rights represent the crowning achievements of the Founding Fathers. The conspiracy theorists mentioned earlier, however, can point out that the Bill of Rights was not part of the original plan. They were only added in order to get the Constitution ratified, indicating that the original framers saw them as unnecessary and possibly even a threat to their plans. All of those individual protections, after all, could make it more difficult to keep order.

Whatever your point of view on the framers of the Constitution, it is fascinating that the Tea Party, a movement primarily focused on limiting federal government spending and power, views itself as being rooted in Constitutional principles. They are celebrating, after all, and on some level mythologizing, a document that greatly increased the power of the national government. It makes you wonder if Tea Party people would have been among those Americans 220 years ago who were trying to block ratification of the Constitution. Still, when they argue that the federal government is doing things today that go beyond the limits set in the Constitution, they definitely have a point. But even the most ardent libertarians within the movement must recognize a simple truth demonstrated by those early years when the nation was under the Articles of Confederation: a federal government that is too weak cannot carry out the two duties that Tea Party people and conservatives in general care about the most: defending the nation and encouraging business activity. Believe it or not, a powerful federal government is not necessarily bad for business.

11. Alexander Hamilton: Liberal or Conservative?

If Alexander Hamilton were alive today, would he be a Democrat or a Republican, a conservative or a liberal? It's an impossible question to answer. Some of the major issues of our day, after all, are very different from his time. Still, there are some basic political questions that are eternal, so it may be possible to make an educated guess. The problem, however, is that Hamilton seemed to be a Democrat/Republican hybrid. He had two fundamental goals – the creation of a strong national government and the promotion of business activity – that many Americans today believe are in conflict. How could anyone, after all, think that a powerful central government could be good for business?

The nation's first Secretary of the Treasury, Alexander Hamilton had been a delegate to the Constitutional Convention where a plan was formulated to get rid of the weak national government of the Articles of Confederation and replace it with the more powerful federal government that we have today. He also wrote about half of the essays that make up the "Federalist Papers," which were published to convince people that this new Constitution should be ratified. Many Americans, after all, were understandably nervous about the idea of a powerful central authority. The negative experiences with Great Britain that had triggered the American Revolution were still a recent memory. Hamilton, however, even as he argued for ratification, had a different concern. He felt that the Constitution had not gone far enough in creating a powerful national government. Great Britain, rather than being a source of fear, was in his mind a political and economic role model.

So which political party today is more supportive of a powerful national government? The answer depends on which aspect of the government you are talking about. Republicans, after all, are happy to give the national government the power that is necessary to maintain our security. They often promote heavy defense spending, and they want to give our intelligence services the tools that they need to keep Americans safe. This does not mean, of course, that Democrats are anti-security. They are more likely, however, to call for needed cuts to the military and to express concern about the protection of individual rights. Democrats are happy, however, to give the national government the power to provide social services and to regulate business, activities that Republicans believe, if taken too far, can be wasteful and harmful to business.

So what kind of big government did Hamilton want? To a certain degree, you could make the case that he wanted both security and business regulation. (In the late 18th century, social services were not seen as the responsibility of the government, especially at the federal level.) Hamilton, like many of the men who wrote the Constitution, was horrified by the lack of security and potential for anarchy that existed under the Articles of Confederation. Under the Constitution, the federal government would have the assets necessary to protect the nation from foreign invasion, and more importantly, it could prevent the masses from threatening the security and wealth of society's elites. Unlike Jefferson, who tended to glorify the independent farmer majority, Hamilton did not trust the "common man." He felt that you needed a strong political authority to keep the masses in line, and during the Constitutional Convention, he had even proposed a system in which an indirectly elected president and senators would serve for life and check the power of a democratically elected House. Clearly, his proposal was based on the British system with a monarch and House of Lords to check the power of the House of Commons. Of course, we ended up with a Constitution that was more democratic than Hamilton's proposal, but Hamilton could at least take comfort in the fact that the Constitution gave voters less of a direct say in political affairs than under the Articles of Confederation.

Outside of security concerns, the other big problem under the Articles of Confederation was the lack of a coherent, functional economic system. States often produced their own currencies, states issued tariffs on goods imported from other states, and contracts agreed upon in one state might not be honored in another. The federal government, which had no power to tax, was unable to pay back the debts it had accrued during the Revolution, and would therefore struggle to find lenders in the future. In this situation, the United States could never become the commercial, manufacturing power that Hamilton envisioned. When there are no set rules or standards that everyone can agree upon, trade cannot function. So under this new Constitution, economic standards were established. There was now only one American currency. Interstate tariffs were forbidden. The Congress was given the power to establish uniform standards regarding bankruptcy laws, copyright rules, contracts, and "Weights and Measures."

When the Constitution was ratified, and Hamilton was sworn in as Secretary of the Treasury, he laid out policies that would utilize this newfound national government power. Tariffs were established on European imports in order to encourage American manufacturing, and a controversial excise tax was placed on whiskey in order to raise needed revenue. A significant amount of the money raised on these taxes would be used to begin paying off the nation's debts, with the federal government taking full responsibility for all money previously borrowed by the national government and the individual states. And to help the national government to conduct its operations, and to inject investment into the nation's economy, the Bank of the United States was established. In this case, many argued that Hamilton had proposed something that was unconstitutional. There is nothing in the Constitution, after all, about establishing banks. But Hamilton, convinced that the Constitution made the national government too weak, argued that a national bank would be "necessary and proper for carrying into execution" powers that were listed in the Constitution, specifically those related to economic regulation. For the first four decades of American history, this national bank would remain a controversial issue. Looking back, however, there is no doubt that Hamilton's programs put the nation on a much firmer financial footing than before.

Clearly, one of the main motives for creating the Constitution was to provide economic regulations. In Hamilton's time, it was about establishing the basics: stable currency, fulfilling debt obligations, consistent business laws, etc. But what would Hamilton have to say about regulations regarding work conditions, environmental standards, or consumer product safety? Many people today argue that these types of rules tend to strangle private industry and make it more difficult for American companies to compete with foreign businesses. It seems that Hamilton, that great promoter of business activity, would recognize the dangers of excessive regulation. If nothing else, the "anti-business" attitudes of liberals would make him a conservative today, right?

While conservatives who want to claim Hamilton can make a legitimate argument, I suspect that Hamilton would also recognize the dangers of excessive deregulation. He knew from firsthand experience, after all, what happens when you lack consistent rules. We learned this recurring American history lesson once again in 2008. In the years preceding the crisis, exotic financial instruments such as Mortgage Backed Securities and Credit Default Swaps were being bought and sold without any government oversight. Essentially, a "shadow economy" worth trillions of dollars existed without most Americans even realizing it. Then, when the real estate bubble popped and financial institutions started going under, fear and panic caused the financial system to freeze up. Since few people understood these "toxic assets" that multiple, interconnected institutions were stuck with, there was no way to determine how bad off a company might be. In this crumbling, shadow economy that operated without rules, it became impossible to do business. Then, of course, the national government and Federal Reserve had to step in and inject trillions of dollars in order to save the system.

Alexander Hamilton, a man with a generally negative view of human nature who believed that most people were not too bright, understood that you need a government watchdog powerful enough to enforce some basic financial rules. At the same time, however, he also dreamed of America becoming a prosperous economy where private industry thrived. So in the end, Hamilton today might be numbered among the moderates. He supported raising taxes, paying off the national debt, promoting private industry, enforcing consistent business regulations, maintaining order, and protectionism. Both political parties today may be able to stake a legitimate claim on him.

12. Is the Federal Budget Constitutional?

When people express alarm about federal government spending, they can take two basic approaches. Some focus on the numbers, referencing statistics that demonstrate the foolishness of the federal government. By throwing around these big fat dollar amounts, they are hoping to show that current spending is unsustainable, wasteful, and/or ineffective. Another line of attack, however, is more theoretical. In this line of reasoning, excessive spending is more than just stupid; it is often unconstitutional. Today's bloated federal government, many argue, is engaged in tasks that are not authorized by the Constitution.

So I decided to pull these two lines of attack together in this little essay. First, I will look at the Constitution to try and determine what the federal government is authorized to do. Then, I will look at how the federal government currently spends most of its money, comparing its apparent priorities with the guidelines set in the Constitution. It sounds simple enough. All that I have to do is read the Constitution, find a statistical breakdown of the federal government's budget, and see how they line up.

The powers that the Constitution gives to the federal government can be found in Article 1, Sections 8-10. Section 8 is a list of things that "The Congress shall have Power To" do. It consists of seventeen paragraphs of one sentence each, with most of these statements related either to national defense (7) or economic regulation (6). Sections 9-10, on the other hand, are lists of things forbidden by the Constitution. About half of these are restrictions placed on individual states, reflecting the efforts being made to fix the Articles of Confederation, a system that gave almost all power to state governments. The rest are laws or actions that the federal government cannot pass nor take.

Reading the Constitution proved to be the easy part. The modern federal budget is a much larger animal. There are plenty of web sites out there that publish charts and tables chronicling the amount of money spent by specific government departments and programs. The problem is that they don't always match up. Dollar amounts for different types of spending can differ slightly, and web sites vary in how they categorize various programs. Yet even with these various discrepancies, it does not take long to form a general picture of where most of the money goes. The overwhelming majority of the dollars, no matter what statistics you consult, go to two general areas: national defense and social services. National defense, as I am defining it, includes military spending, the various agencies within the Department of Homeland Security, the State Department, and benefits paid to veterans. Social services, representing the largest chunk of cash, include retirement pensions, medical services, education funding, housing programs, unemployment benefits, and direct aid to the poor through either cash payments or food stamps. The rest of the money, a comparatively small amount, goes to various forms of what might generally be termed economic regulation and/or stimulus, activities carried out by Departments such as Labor, Transportation, Commerce, Agriculture, Treasury, and Energy.

So how well do these spending priorities line up with the guidelines set in the Constitution? While one can easily question the wisdom of spending almost as much on national defense as the rest of the world combined, it is difficult to argue that defense spending is unconstitutional. A large chunk of Article 1, Section 8, after all, is devoted to issues related to national defense. More effectively providing for the "common Defence" was one of the main reasons the Constitution came into being in the first place. The only strong constitutional issue one can raise has to do with the secrecy that exists within the Defense Department and the various intelligence agencies:

> "No money shall be drawn from the Treasury, but in consequence of Appropriations made by Law; and a regular Statement and Account of the Receipts and Expenditures of all public Money shall be published from time to time." (Article 1, Section 9)

Are the military and our various security agencies only spending money in congressionally authorized ways? Is the public still made aware of how all national security money is being spent? I am not enough "in the know" to answer either of these questions with any certainty, but let's just say that I have my suspicions.

The other parts of the federal government that are clearly constitutional are those related to certain types of economic regulation. Section 8 clearly states that the federal government can borrow money, regulate commerce, establish bankruptcy laws, coin money (and regulate its value), establish post offices, build roads, and create copyright laws. These are activities today that are carried out by the Departments of Commerce, Treasury, and Transportation. Of these departments, however, only Treasury spends a significant amount of money, and much of that is the interest on the public debt. The crucial duty of regulating the money supply is handled by the Federal Reserve, which can create billions of dollars out of thin air in some serious "off-budget" spending. (You could have a long discussion, in fact, on just the constitutionality of the Federal Reserve.)

The Departments of Labor and Energy, along with the Environmental Protection Agency, regulate the economy in ways that are not directly authorized by the Constitution. Of course, when the Constitution was written, slavery still existed; the only sources of energy were human, muscle, and water power; and our impact on the environment was minimal compared to today, so mention of these types of regulations could hardly be expected in the late 18th century.

Spending on social services is also on a weak constitutional footing. Article 1, Section 8 does not directly authorize the federal government to perform any of the services that it spends so much money on today. There is no mention of retirement pensions, unemployment benefits, medical insurance, or anything else. Supporters of social service spending, however, do have two statements to base the constitutionality of "welfare" programs. The first sentence of section 8 says, "The Congress shall have the power to... provide for the common Defence and general Welfare of the United States." Social service spending, according to some, fits under the category of "general Welfare." Many would also argue that programs designed to stimulate the economy, which are also not directly authorized by the Constitution, fit under this category. When you consider that hundreds of billions of dollars of government aid are flowing every year, it is clear that the overwhelming majority of Americans has accepted this interpretation. Only the hard-core libertarians argue that providing for the general welfare does not include various forms of government aid, an argument strengthened by the fact that federal welfare as we currently define it did not appear until the 20th century.

But even if some people reject the general Welfare argument, advocates of social service and stimulus spending have this final statement from Article 1, Section 8 to support their case:

> " (Congress shall have power) to make all laws which shall be necessary and proper for carrying into Execution the foregoing Powers, and all other Powers vested by this Constitution in the Government of the United States, or in any Department or Officer thereof."

This is the famous elastic clause, which authorizes the federal government to do things that are not expressly mentioned in Article I, Section 8. Ever since the days when Alexander Hamilton was trying to support policies not expressly supported in the Constitution, this "necessary and proper" clause has been used to justify all sorts of federal policies. All that you need to do is make a connection between a policy that you support and something that appears in the Section 8 list. Obviously, the Constitution could not list every single thing, in painstaking detail, that the federal government could ever do. Instead, it lists some general powers, and then it throws in this last clause in order to make clear that the list was not intended to cover everything in detail.

There is a problem, however, with such a broad reading of the 'necessary and proper" clause. Namely, it seems to contradict the Tenth Amendment, which says the following:

> "The powers not delegated to the United States by the Constitution, nor prohibited by it to the States, are reserved to the States respectively, or to the people."

So if the Constitution does not clearly grant the federal government a certain power, then only an individual state can exercise that power. So what wins out, the Tenth Amendment or the elastic clause? That argument has been going on ever since followers of Alexander Hamilton, the advocate for a strong national government, competed with the faction agreeing with Thomas Jefferson, who wanted to keep as much power as possible within the states. And like the early days of our republic, the debate about the proper role of the federal government rages on.

The Constitution was designed as a general framework for running a government, and like anything created by human beings, it has its imperfections. It cannot answer all of our modern, complex political and legal questions. And because lawyers on both sides of the political spectrum can make a good case to support their points of view, I am left with some of the same simple questions that the Founding Fathers had when they wrote the Constitution: What works? What must the federal government do for us? What should the federal government never do? We can argue until we are blue in the face about who is more constitutional, and to a certain degree, these are important conversations to have. In the end, however, we are forced to be practical. So Americans need to move beyond political rhetoric, look at the numbers, do the math, and make some tough decisions. The Founding Fathers are not around to do all of the governing for us.

13. If the Ten Commandments Were a Legal Code

Every now and then, a controversy comes up regarding the erection of religious-oriented monuments on government land. Sometimes, this involves the display of the Ten Commandments in some sort of a court building. Supporters of these displays argue that they are merely acknowledging these rules as a major foundation for our legal system. In my view, these people are seriously misled. The Ten Commandments, rather than being a foundation for our legal code, contradict the Constitution in some cases. In addition, certain commandments could never be practically enforced as legal ordinances. The Ten Commandments are primarily religious and moral codes, not legal ordinances, a fact that I will briefly demonstrate by taking a quick look at each commandment.

1) "You shall have no other gods before me." The opening statements of the First Amendment guarantee the freedom of religion. So the Constitution guarantees our right to commit the ultimate Biblical sin of worshipping other Gods. So unless you think that the United States should be a theocracy, it is hard to justify placing a code in a legal building with an opening command that flies in the face of such an important Constitutional principle.

2)"You shall not make for yourself an image in the form of anything in heaven above or on the earth beneath or in the waters below." See my response to commandment one. In my view, if religious monuments are to be placed in public places, then we should give equal treatment to all religions. So right next to the Ten Commandments, crosses, or anything else, we should erect some "brazen images" and "idols" from other religious traditions. Since the state is constitutionally forbidden from "respecting an establishment of religion," we should acknowledge all religious traditions in public places or none at all. Plus, if the term "image" was interpreted very broadly, and this second commandment became the basis for any laws, then a lot of artists could get in some serious trouble.

3) "You shall not misuse the name of the LORD your God." I have heard this explained in different ways. Some would say that this forbids blasphemy or the use of God's Hebrew name, but I have heard this also interpreted as a command against more general profanity: "God damn it!", "Jesus Christ!", etc. Either way, it seems to contradict freedom of expression. Of course, some could counter that there are restrictions on freedom of speech and the press such as rules regarding obscenity. And there was a time when the censors were much tighter regarding the mainstream media. So assuming that these rules do not in principle contradict the First Amendment, maybe this commandment could be seen as a foundation for "obscenity laws." Hopefully, however, no one wants to go back to stoning people for "blasphemy." That could get ugly fast.

4) "Remember the Sabbath day by keeping it holy." To make this a legal code, you would first have to determine which Sabbath to keep holy. Should it be the original Sabbath of Friday evening until Saturday evening, or should we go with the more recent Christian tradition of observing it on Sunday? Plus, legal scholars would have to spend a lot of time defining what is meant by work. It's hard to imagine this ever being strictly enforced. Many Americans (and shopping malls) would freak out without weekend shopping. Also, it would eliminate Americans' true national religion of watching sports on the weekend. You would need a very large Sabbath police to keep the masses in line.

Laws are supposed to be created in order to promote the public good: to maintain order, defend the state, and protect individual rights. They are designed to stop people from engaging in behaviors that harm others. Try as I might, I can't see how the breaking of commandments one through four infringes on the rights of others. Worshipping idols, working on the Sabbath, and misuse of God's name have no measurable, negative impact on anyone else. Obedience of these commands does not in itself promote ethical behavior or civic responsibility. Instead, these commandments attempt to shape the theological beliefs of people and promote obedience to God for its own sake. Personally, I do not want to live under a legal code that seeks to promote a certain mode of thought and forces me to follow a purely religious tradition. An orthodox system of belief is impossible to enforce anyway. People may give the appearance of faith, but there is no way to determine if it is legitimate.

5)"Honor your father and your mother." Because I cannot read Hebrew, I'm not quite sure what was meant by honor. As we all know, there are some parents out there who are not worthy of honor or obedience. In some cases, the honoring of parents can lead someone into behavior that is downright evil, behavior that contradicts other commandments. Still, respect of elders is a nice ideal to strive for. It cannot really be enforced, however, as part of a legal code. If people were punished every time that they dishonored their parents, there would be a whole lot of fines being paid or prison sentences being served. You would need an enormous police force just to deal with the damn teenagers.

6)"You shall not murder." This is one commandment that has to be a part of any rational legal code. It's basically a no-brainer. Killing another person clearly infringes on that person's rights. There may be some debate, however, regarding what murder actually means. Most people with a Judeo-Christian belief system, after all, believe that killing is justified in certain situations: self-defense, policing, military action, etc. Extreme pacifists, however, might see all killing as murder. But given the fact that Old Testament law mandated the death penalty as punishment for just about anything, along with the fact that the Biblical God frequently kills people or instructs his followers to do so, it is difficult to both accept scripture as truth and be an extreme pacifist.

7) "You shall not commit adultery." If I am not mistaken, adultery is defined as sex outside of marriage, not merely cheating on one's spouse. Either way, it is hard to imagine this instituted as law. For lawmakers, after all, this would hit too close to home. If adultery were punished, however, it would at least force "Family Values" conservatives to go after one of the behaviors – along with divorce - that actually threatens marriage. It could also go a long way toward either reducing budget deficits through the collection

of fines or increasing the already swelling prison population. It would also create the opportunity to produce a reality show called "Sex Cops," although this would have to be on cable due to graphic content.

8) "You shall not steal." This is another legally enforceable commandment that is a no-brainer as part of a legal code. Protecting property is one of the essential functions of government. The term "steal," however, can be a bit tricky. If a government taxes its people beyond what is reasonable or necessary, is this stealing? If a worker is exploited to the point that he or she cannot reasonably survive, would it be wrong for this worker to steal food? In a world filled with massive social inequality and injustice, a world in which governments often exist to serve the leaders rather than the general population, is it okay to disobey unjust laws instituted by lousy lawmakers? The Bible does not seem to provide any clear answers to these obvious questions.

9) "You shall not give false testimony against your neighbor." In certain circumstances, you can be punished for lying: perjury, slander, fraud, etc. It can be difficult to determine, however, when a "little white lie" crosses over into illegal territory. If people were punished for every lie, that would definitely take care of all the people not already paying the price for breaking the Sabbath, committing adultery, or dishonoring their parents. And the politicians and lawyers charged with making, interpreting, and helping to enforce laws would have trouble winning elections and cases without the ability to stretch the truth.

10) "You shall not covet your neighbor's house. You shall not covet your neighbor's wife, or his male or female servant, his ox or donkey, or anything that belongs to your neighbor." I think that I could probably avoid coveting my neighbor's farm animals or servants. But I hate to admit that envy may occasionally creep in when it comes to the other items in commandment 10. I probably have no need to worry. This one would really be a bitch to enforce. In theory, however, it may be possible someday to detect coveting with technology. A certain part of the brain may trigger when we feel envy, so maybe a covet detector could be created that will go off at the appropriate time. A message could then quickly be sent to law enforcement so that they could instantly withdraw funds from my bank account. Man, talk about taking a cut out of budget

deficits. But without this kind of technology, I guess that we would have to go with the covet police or with citizen's arrests in which people are quickly cited when they get that covetous look in their eyes.

The principles of amendments five through ten can at least be viewed as the moral foundation for many laws. Instead of dealing with religious beliefs, they deal with how people interact with one another. The enforceable ones, however, are pretty obvious and vague, and they do not represent a major legal or moral insight by the people who compiled the code. Others represent noble ideals to strive for but not rules that could be reasonably enforced. So arguing that these somewhat vague, unoriginal, and often unenforceable commandments played a major role in the development of our legal system is a bit of a stretch.

Of course, Jewish law was much more detailed than the Ten Commandments. Few Americans, however, would ever want to go back to that legal system. The rules are often too outdated or silly, the punishments are too harsh, and way too many animals had to be dismembered every day to offer sacrifices of atonement in order to make up for our constant disobedience. If you don't believe me, try a simple experiment. First, try to find someone who knows little about the Bible. In the United States, that is just as easy as finding someone who knows almost nothing about the Constitution. Then, pick and choose some random Biblical laws and the punishments for breaking them. When you are done, ask them what they think of this legal system. Whether the person is Jewish, Christian, agnostic, or atheist, I think that you can predict what his or her response will be.

Part Three: 19th Century Economic and Social Change

Part Three: 19th Century Economic and Social Change

14. Benjamin Franklin in the 21st Century

Imagine that Benjamin Franklin in 1785 was given access to a time machine. Then, for some unknown reason, he was transported into one of my classrooms in the year 2011. What would first draw his attention? What would most blow his mind about this classroom of the future? He might be surprised by the ethnic diversity in the classroom and wonder what country he might be visiting. If the room had mounted, wall-to-wall carpet, he might wonder how it was ever cleaned. The clothing worn by the students, I imagine, would also seem rather strange. (And from what I know about Mr. Franklin, he might find the clothing of the women in the classroom particularly stimulating.)

I doubt, however, that the students and décor would stand out the most for him. It is more likely that he would look up at the lights and wonder where the candles were. Then if I, or preferably a scientifically competent student, were able to explain the concepts of electric power and light bulbs, he would feel gratified because of his own contribution to the development of this modern wonder. Still, as amazing as modern lighting may be, it is likely that the screen displaying my *Power Point* presentation would catch his eye first. He might touch the screen and look behind it to see where the words were coming from. When he was told or he noticed for himself that the information came from a projector mounted on the ceiling, he would have a host of questions trying to understand how information could be transmitted through the use of this light source.

I would then be forced to dismiss my freaked out class so that I could show him the personal computer that was the source of the information. After getting over the shock of what this device could actually do, he would then have a field day using this modern wonder called the internet to see what had become of both his country and world. He would learn rather quickly that virtually anything you want to know could be accessed in this way. He would also conclude very rapidly that this country and world of the future were even stranger than he first imagined. Modern people transport themselves in things called automobiles that can move at speeds in excess of one hundred miles per hour. When they want to travel even faster, they can get on flying devices called airplanes that travel several hundred miles per hour at a height of approximately 30,000 feet. Hardly anyone in this society works the land as farmers or in small workshops as craftsmen any more. In fact, few people make anything for themselves. Machines do much of the hard labor, which frees many of the people up to perform less labor intensive highly specialized tasks, earn money, and buy virtually everything at places called supermarkets and department stores. There are apparently more people in the entertainment industry than in food production, and people have several different mediums they can use to receive this entertainment: television, radio, movie theaters, and, increasingly, this amazing internet. They can communicate instantly with others using various types of computers and phones, can cool and heat their homes just by pushing buttons on devices called thermostats, and are taxed somewhat heavily by a huge federal government that provides a wide array of services. (Although, as in Franklin's time, there was still a great deal of waste and corruption.) And this short list, of course, only scratches the surface of the many differences between Franklin's time and ours.

Now imagine that you were able to drag Mr. Franklin away from the computer and put him back in the time machine. You decided for the heck of it to send him back approximately 3,300 years to hang out with Moses. Amazingly, after he arrived and spent some time there, it would become clear that the world of Moses was more familiar to Franklin than our world of today. After all, things have changed more in the last two hundred years than in the preceding thousands of years. You would then be forced to put Franklin back in the time machine and use its built in memory-erasing device. After all, he needed to go back to 1785 so that he could participate in the writing of the Constitution and fill in the last entry of one of the greatest resumes in American history.

Because we were born into this industrialized, technology dependent society, we generally fail to realize just how weird our world is. Prior to the mid-19th century, most people would die in a world that differed little from the one into which they were born. Today, we expect change. In fact, we demand it. Whenever the latest smart phone, computer, or video game system comes out, we are bored after a little while and wonder when the next big thing is coming. And the pace of change only accelerates. Both computer speed and the accumulated knowledge of the human race double every two years or so. So where will we be in 20, 50, or 100 years? Will we be on our way toward *Star Trek*, living in some sort of a technological utopia?

With this rapid pace of change, some speculate that the industrial age is already ending. We are now at the dawn of a new era, an Information Age, that promises to transform society in the next 50 years as much as the Industrial Age did in 200. Due to future advancements in automation, certain types of industrial workers, service sector employees, and office workers will become obsolete, just like early 19th century farmers and craftsmen in the earlier transformation. And just as early industrial entrepreneurs capitalized on the possibilities created by railroads, telephones, and mass production, future information age visionaries will capitalize on developing methods of information sharing that will create economic opportunities that most others fail to foresee. Through their efforts, overall standards of living will rise, just as they eventually did during the Industrial Age. This growth in income, however, promises to be exponentially higher. And because information technology is more readily accessible to all – not just those with large amounts of capital - we may once again gravitate back toward an economy less dominated by large corporations.

Some, however, would argue that we are not headed toward *Star Trek*. Instead, the future is more likely to be *The Terminator, The Matrix,* or *Wall-E*. Either the computers are going to take over, or this planet will someday become uninhabitable. We face some serious problems that our fancy technology has played a big part in creating. We have seven billion people (and counting) on this planet, all of whom would like to enjoy the benefits of the modern world. Can a system based on the burning of fossil fuels provide a quality standard of living to this large of a population? Fossil fuels are finite resources, and everyone – even the doubters of global warming – agrees that they do environmental harm. And while

71

Information Age technology is fantastic, we are still biological creatures who need to consume physical commodities. Will we be able to produce enough food, fresh water, housing, clothing, and the countless other wants and needs of this enormous, expanding population? Because every day we are in completely uncharted territory, there is no way to answer these questions. Modern society as we know it has not been around for very long, so it is much too early to tell if it can last.

Unless you are a person waiting for some sort of an apocalyptic, religious event which will bring a new world order, then there is only one hope: technology, which got is into this mess, is going to have to get us out. It's too late to turn back now. The problems are daunting, but the human race, particularly in recent years, has demonstrated a remarkable capacity to innovate. To Ben Franklin, the world of today would seem as unlikely as *Star Trek* seems to us. Maybe we should hop back into that time machine and bring him back. Benjamin Franklin, one of the most innovative minds in our history, might be able to help us out.

15. The Changing Value and Definition of Work

One of my favorite topics in American history is economic change in the early nineteenth century. Now I may be going out on a limb here, but I doubt that this subject gets you particularly excited. This is because many people associate economics with boring, complicated stuff like supply/demand curves, interest rates, and Dow Jones Industrial Averages. But when you strip economics down to fundamentals – particularly when you focus on microeconomics - it all comes down to a simple question: how do individuals meet their basic needs?

I start off this topic by painting a general picture of how the American economy operated in 1790. At this point in history, the overwhelming majority of Americans, as in much of the world, were farmers. Somewhere between 80-90% of people worked the land, with the majority of these living on relatively small, family farms. To a large degree, people on family farms took care of themselves. In addition to making their own food, they also may have built their house and furniture, sewed their own clothes, and made their own candles and soap. They also produced their own heat by chopping wood and gathered water from a river or well. If they were cut off from the rest of the world, they could survive for some time. They also knew that if they did their work, and Mother Nature more or less cooperated, they would eat that year. In the modern world, many of us do not have that same sense of security.

These farmers were not entirely self-sufficient, however. There were certain goods and services that they could not provide. Occasionally, they would have to take a wagon ride to town to get certain types of manufactured goods – metal products, shoes, glassware, etc. – acquire certain types of food products such as tea and salt, and find skilled individuals to perform services for them: doctors, printers, lawyers, etc. In town, therefore, you would find people who were similar to most modern Americans: specialists. Towns and cities were filled with people either working in the manufacturing industry, the professions, government service, or some type of business activity. Like almost all of us, they focused on one particular occupation and bought everything else that they needed. Unlike farmers (and like most of us), they were almost entirely dependent on other people to receive the goods and services needed to survive, which is why they lived in towns. Also, unlike farmers, they did not have the security that came from having a piece of land that, at the least, could provide them with enough food.

After giving students this general overview of the economy in 1790, I give them an activity to demonstrate how our economy works today. I ask them to name a breakfast cereal that is particularly bad for you. (As you will see, this assignment works better for food items that have all kinds of chemicals and crap pumped into them.) Then, I tell them to describe in painstaking detail every step in the process of producing a box of this type of cereal. This list should include all of the ingredients, packaging, and workers necessary to get the job done from the farm (or chemistry lab) to the grocery store shelf. After looking at me strangely as they wonder why I am trying to make them experts on *Lucky Charms*, students then proceed and generally have a good time with this assignment. (I let them do it in groups to make it even more fun.)

So other than killing a few minutes and giving both myself and the class a break from listening to me talk, what is the point of this sugary cereal study? What I want them to see is how incredibly complex our modern economy really is. Just to get a simple box of cereal made, you are required to have a huge variety of raw materials from all over the country and world, a large number of workers with various occupational skills, and a complex communication and transportation network. In addition, a highly mechanized process must be created at the cereal plant to produce the tens of thousands of boxes of cereal that are needed every day in order to fill store shelves all over our country and world. (The leprechauns can't quite handle it.) Unbelievably, when this complex process is complete, the *Lucky Charms* are pretty darn cheap. (Plain wrap is even cheaper.)

On the family farm more than two hundred years ago, food production was simpler. First, you grow wheat. Second, you grind the wheat. Third, mix the flour with eggs and milk. Last but not least, you bake the bread. Food production was now complete. And when the farmer ate the bread, he or she was able to taste something very tangible that he or she was personally responsible for creating. A craftsman at this time could also see in a very tangible way the finished product that was the result of his individual labor. And if these self-employed farmers and craftsman were able to sell some or all of their finished products, they received all of the money generated from the sale. Whether consuming the product themselves or exchanging it for money, the workers knew very specifically the value of the commodity that was produced by their labor.

As our country began to industrialize and evolve into the country of today, many people would lose the ability to measure the value of their work. There are few farmers or craftsman in the United States today. Only 1-2 % of Americans work the land. The rest of us work in manufacturing, professions, business activities, and government service. Far fewer Americans today are self-employed than in the past. Many of us work in large businesses, corporations, and government organizations. And for the many Americans who work in large organizations, it is very difficult to see or measure in a tangible way the fruits of their labor. They sell labor, not a commodity. Factory workers do not make things from start to finish. They perform one step in a complex process. (No one can ever say, "I made that box of *Lucky Charms*.") Workers in office buildings play no part in producing something tangible. Instead, they play one part in a complex process of promoting products and/or keeping track of information. People in professions such as teaching, medicine, and law, who perform services for a living, can also have a hard time tangibly measuring the value of their work, particularly if they work in a large organization.

In a modern, industrial society, work for many Americans is a place. The word work is often used more as a noun than a verb. And for many, the location where they go for their job is not a happy place. It is a place where they go through an ordeal that is necessary for survival. Now I am not going to argue here that people in 1790 were necessarily overjoyed with work either. The work of a farmer or craftsman required a lot of time and hard, manual labor. They had two things, however, that many employees of large organizations lack: a sense of accomplishment and a tangible way to measure the value of their labor. A craftsman could say, " I made that." He could also reap all of the rewards of his labor. Do workers in an office or factory know what their labor is worth? Is there any tangible way to measure how much wealth their job is producing for the corporation? I can tell you one thing for sure. If an employee works for a profitable enterprise, then this person is not getting paid what he or she is worth. Profit, by definition, is the revenue left over after costs are deducted. So if a company is making more money than it is spending, with its workforce being one of many costs, then workers are not being paid in proportion to the wealth that they generate. And the big money, of course, often goes to upper management and the stockholders, not the workers on the ground level. This is a major development in economic history: the separation of labor from ownership and management.

There is a natural tendency to focus on the benefits of technology and industrial development. All things considered, if I was given the choice of living in the twenty-first century United States or time traveling to any other point in its past, I would stay here. Still, I can understand why many Americans in the nineteenth century were sorry to see the old ways go. I can also understand why many Americans today are dissatisfied with their jobs, looking to change careers, or striving to become self-employed. Many want to get more out of work than just a paycheck

16. The Second Great Awakening, Social Reform, and Personal Responsibility

In the early 19th century, the Second Great Awakening swept through the United States. People attending evangelical, Christian revival meetings converted in large numbers through what was often a powerful emotional experience of the spirit of God coming upon them. This "born again" conversion experience would sometimes manifest itself through people speaking in tongues, twitching uncontrollably, prophesying, passing out, or being miraculously healed. And it was on the western frontier that these tent meetings and the message of salvation often attracted the largest numbers of spectators and converts. In a region of the country where circumstances were particularly tough and people were often living on the edge, the promise of eternal salvation, along with the alternative prospect of perpetual damnation, were very powerful messages.

In the early days of this revivalist movement, the emphasis was on saving souls. But as the years passed, and as the country began to go through the sometimes painful shift from an agrarian to an industrial society, Christians began to interpret their mission on earth in various ways. New social problems began to appear or become more severe, particularly in the growing urban areas: homelessness, poor sanitation, crime, lousy work conditions, and overcrowding. So when confronted with the human suffering associated with these problems, many Christians concluded that they needed to do more than simply preach the message of eternal salvation. They also needed to find ways to heal the sick, feed the hungry, and help the orphan. Preaching a sermon or handing out a Bible tract was simply not enough to fulfill the duty of living out the gospel of Christ.

Anyone who accepts the Christian worldview is forced to confront the same basic issue as those reformers of the early 19th century. When you see a homeless person starving on the street, what is it that this person really needs? Obviously, the immediate need is a roof over his or her head and a meal. But providing a temporary solution at some sort of a homeless shelter or food bank is not going to solve the long-term problem. Something must be done about the individual behavior or circumstances that were the underlying causes of this individual's homelessness. But even if this were somehow accomplished, a Christian believes that there is still a more fundamental issue. Since this life is temporary, resolving the physical problems of any individual does nothing about that person's ultimate need. Whether rich or poor, all people are sinners, and unless they repent and accept Jesus into their lives, they will experience an eternity of suffering far worse than anything on earth. So if the ultimate need is spiritual, should the primary focus be on preaching? Or, by helping to alleviate a person's immediate physical needs, do Christians communicate a more powerful message of God's love than they would through the preaching of a sermon?

Christians then, like Christians today, answered these questions differently. Some churches continued to focus on preaching the gospel. Other religious organizations tried to integrate preaching with efforts to solve social problems. Still others became so focused on solving social problems that over time, they ceased to preach the Christian gospel at all. But in spite of their differences, these churches and organizations that struggled for social reform and could often trace their roots to a common, evangelical ancestry continued to share one core idea: for people to improve their individual circumstances, they needed to become better people. And for America to become a better place, individual Americans needed to make more ethical, responsible choices. So even when reform organizations stopped being evangelical Christian in a conventional sense, they still generally stressed the importance of the "born again" experience.

This reform impulse was primarily carried out through the creation and reform of social institutions. And while these orphanages, prisons, schools, hospitals, and "insane asylums" were focused on alleviating specific social problems, they also tried to deal with the same, basic "spiritual" need. Orphanages provided housing for children, but they were also designed to teach these kids the values necessary for ensuring that they did not grow up to give birth to future orphans. Prisons punished criminals and kept dangerous people off of the streets, but they also strove to reform inmates so that they could turn their lives around and become productive members of society. Schools tried to teach basic academic skills, but they also sought to instill in children the values necessary to become successful members of the work force. So in all of these institutions, they combined the effort to meet an immediate, physical need with an attempt to instill in people the values necessary to turn away – to "repent" if you will – from the behaviors that were the underlying causes of social problems.

But in their attempts to teach "proper" values, were these reformers truly motivated by a desire to create a better world? Or were they mostly concerned about their personal safety and security? The world is less scary, after all, when the people who surround you are not too "different." This may help to explain some of the "nativist" streak that developed in these reform movements. As the first major wave of European immigrants began arriving in the 1840's, efforts were made to Americanize these foreigners as quickly as possible. For if these efforts failed, people feared that the white, middle-class, protestant values that made America great would be threatened, and those foreigners would drag the United States down. With movements rooted in the underlying principle that teaching proper values is the key to solving problems, their followers unavoidably developed an arrogant, closed-minded streak that permeated whatever they did. Since reformers knew that the solution was for everyone to live like the reformers, they may have often had a limited capacity to listen, adapt, and evolve. There is little incentive to learn and to change when you already have all of the answers.

But this arrogant drive to alter the values of others may not have been the biggest weakness with their approach. There is also a fundamental flaw with their belief in personal responsibility. We all know, after all, that people are often impacted by circumstances that are completely out of their control. And the biggest factor in influencing the future prospects of any individual is the circumstance of that person's birth. On average, people who become prisoners, alcoholics, or homeless had a tougher upbringing than those who wind up being successful. We are not entirely victims of circumstance, but our condition in life is not purely the result of our personal choices either. Encouraging people to make wiser choices is important, but it is also necessary to confront systemic, societal problems that get in the way of individual success. Over time, many Americans interested in social reform came to realize that efforts to change the values of individuals were not enough. By the late 19th-early 20th centuries, there was an increased focus on creating government regulations that were designed to alleviate systemic social problems. But even as these Progressives focused more of their efforts on political policies that would reshape society as a whole, they retained the belief that so-called traditional American values were superior to those held by the waves of immigrants pouring into the country. And in addition to reforming and regulating corporations, living conditions, and government itself, they also tried to snuff out "immorality" through political action.

So if you see or hear about people who are suffering from poverty or homelessness, what is your initial reaction? Some might wonder what a homeless man did to put himself into that situation. Others might feel sympathy for this person who is clearly the victim of an unjust world. You can learn a lot about a person's political ideology from his or her answer to this simple question. Conservatives would tend to see the person as a screw up. Few, however, would argue that all homeless people, regardless of circumstances, should be left to rot on the streets. They generally support the idea of charity, but they tend to think that private charitable organizations do a better job of helping the poor than government. Still, only the hard-core libertarians argue that all government social services should be eradicated. Liberals, on the other hand, would be more likely to see the person as a victim. In their minds, government is obligated to help the homeless fulfill their basic human rights, and steps must be taken to deal with the systemic problems that create homelessness in the first place. Few, however, would argue that government should give lavish benefits to all poor people, even those who are perennially lazy. Individuals, after all, must have some incentive to be productive citizens.

People who still allow themselves to think deeply about these complicated issues realize that it is neither practical nor desirable to drift too far toward extremes. We all know that our circumstances result partly from our own efforts and partly from luck. Too often, however, discussions about controversial issues get bogged down with rhetoric and abstractions. Conservatives might dream of an ideal world in which all people are rewarded (or punished) for their individual efforts. Liberals might dream of a world in which no one is a victim of injustice and all people have their basic needs met. Since we do not live in an ideal world, there is little point in spending too much time arguing about which side has the superior ideals. Because when you get down to the tough work of formulating political policies or establishing charitable organizations, you realize that extreme positions are not satisfying. You can't simply blame individuals for every mistake and misfortune, and you cannot turn everyone into a victim. Instead, you must recognize that we live in a messy, complex world filled with individuals who, at different times in their lives, have been screw-ups, winners, victims, and lucky bastards. So if every thinking person is some form of a moderate, then why do discussions about politics and social reform often degenerate into shouting matches in which people mock and even demonize those that drift toward the other end of the spectrum? I suspect that this is because it is easier to stick with rhetoric and abstractions. Dealing with practical details, after all, takes so much time and effort, and there are never any simple answers. Unfortunately, telling people to just stop being so immoral and stupid is probably not enough.

17. Why are the Smart Kids Unpopular?

I am not sure when it happened, but at some point in my life, I stopped caring so much about what other people think about me. By virtue of being human, I will always experience a certain amount of self-consciousness. But these neurotic tendencies are nowhere near the level that they were in high school, or even college. This change may be part of the natural process of becoming an adult. Over the years, I have noticed that my older students are far less inhibited than the younger ones. These older students are so uninhibited, in fact, that it is sometimes hard to get them to shut up. I think that my personal reduction in self-consciousness, however, is also the result of spending about eighteen years in the teaching profession. Because in this job, you cannot be very effective if you care too much about what others think of you.

Excessive self-consciousness is one of the strongest impediments to education in American culture. It can sometimes be a problem for teachers, although I suspect that teachers who are always seeking approval from students do not last very long. The main concern is its impact on students, a phenomenon commonly known as "peer pressure." In American culture, peer pressure may be the most common explanation for an assortment of behaviors, particularly with young people experiencing "adolescence."

One of the ultimate examples of the impact of peer pressure, of course, is the attitude of many adolescents toward school. Because for "teenagers," school is one of the ultimate evils of the universe, most likely in a close tie with parents (and old people in general). The last thing a young person wants, after all, is to receive one of the many negative labels that our culture has produced for people who do well in school, terms such as "nerd," "geek," "brown nose," or whatever the current terminology may be. On the other hand, many students take pride in academic failure, bragging about their poor study habits and lousy grades.

Now in college teaching, you would think that this is no longer a problem. College students, after all, are supposed to be in school by choice. In some cases, however, I still have students who have not broken out of this "adolescent" way of thinking. These students are still trying very hard to present the image of a person who does not care, and they often pay the price when they play this role too well. Of course, this explanation for student failure fails to answer a simple question: why does peer pressure often push young people in a negative direction? Why is there often so much hostility toward school?

Now I would never claim to be a psychologist, but I am somewhat familiar with common psychological explanations for adolescent behavior. There is of course the "raging hormone" argument, which has been used, with some accuracy, to explain all sorts of irrational behaviors. Hormones, for example, may cause adolescents to think a bit more about the opposite sex (and sex in general) than academic pursuits. They may also lead to emotional outbursts that interfere with human reason. Another of these "biological arguments" focuses on the particular qualities of the adolescent brain. I have heard more than one expert over the years arguing that the teenage brain is not fully developed, with the "common sense" part of the brain not reaching full maturity until a person is in his or her mid-twenties (and sometimes never). Some would also argue that adolescent behavior is a natural part of the transition to adulthood. An attempt to assert one's independence should be expected of people in this age group, and this is not necessarily a negative thing.

In my view, all of these psychological explanations have a certain amount of validity. As a history teacher, however, I am inclined to look for historical explanations for behavior. Could modern adolescent behavior also be a product of historical forces and not just a result of teenage biology? In my American History classes, there are two units in which I directly address the issue of adolescent hostility toward academics. One unit where this topic comes up is the 1920's, a time period in which a distinct American "youth culture" was starting to form. This term "youth culture" refers to the development of a distinct way of life among so-called "teenagers" involving certain types of dress, speech, music, and other behaviors. Today, it is taken for granted that young people in

America want to develop a way of life that is different from their parents and from old people in general. The quickest way for something to become "uncool," after all, is for a teenager's parent to start liking it.

So why did this particular way of life begin to appear in the 1920's as opposed to some other period? It seems that the appearance of this youth culture coincided with the development of public high schools and the increasing perception that a high school degree was crucial for success. The only way, after all, for adolescents to develop a distinct way of life was for them to have the opportunity to spend large amounts of time exclusively with other adolescents. (In addition, the growing prevalence of automobiles at this time created opportunities outside of school.) In the past, people in this age bracket never had the chance to hang out so often with exclusively teenage friends. In the nineteenth century and earlier, fifteen-year-olds may have been working on the farm, learning skills as an apprentice, or working as a manual laborer. In other words, they had somewhat made the transition to being an adult, and they were spending time in the adult world.

Now let us return to the raging hormones. Biologically, adolescents are becoming adults in their teenage years. In modern American society, however, they are not recognized as such. Instead, they are bottled up in high school, unable to make much of a contribution to society until they get that high school degree. Today, in an age where the college degree is seen as increasingly mandatory, young people are bottled up in school even longer. It can be very difficult to make a decent living on your own in America until you are in your mid-20's, and in many fields – medicine, law, college teaching – the wait is even longer.

The biological definition of an adult, therefore, no longer matches the cultural definition. And because of this disconnect, we have a society that is populated by a large number of frustrated "wanna-be" adults who are stuck in school. It is only natural, then, that high school and sometimes even college students will lash out against educational institutions. Of course, "teenage rebellion" is directed against more than just school. If you look at a list of the behaviors that many – not all, of course – adolescents think are "cool," you will see a list of some of the dumbest behaviors that a human being can engage in: drinking oneself into oblivion, driving

84

like a maniac, having unprotected sex, and doing extremely dangerous things for no apparent reason other than showing off your "coolness." To a certain degree, I think that teenage frustration is directed against authority in general. Authority figures, after all, are older people seemingly impeding the entrance of young people into the adult world.

To understand this anti-school phenomenon, however, you must look beyond a discussion of adolescence and recognize a broader aspect of our American cultural heritage. So it is here that I bring up the second American history topic that relates to anti-school hostility: the Jacksonian era. When historians speak of the Jacksonian era, they are referring to American political history of the 1820's and 1830's, a period in which Andrew Jackson was the most influential political figure. It was also a period in which the United States became a somewhat more democratic nation, a phenomenon Jackson would take advantage of in his rise to power.

When our country was founded, only a small percentage of Americans had the right to vote. The majority of Americans were disqualified for a variety of reasons. Women and slaves were ineligible throughout the United States, and in many states even free black men were disqualified. Many other states, as had been common in colonial times, required that an individual owned a certain amount of property to be able to vote. The typical voter, therefore, was a white, male, and free property holder.

In the early nineteenth century this situation gradually changed as a movement grew in support of "universal white male suffrage." In other words, people pushed for the elimination of the property requirement mentioned previously. (Other barriers to voting, of course, still generally applied.) Most of the new western states that were rapidly being created established themselves without these property requirements. Over time, many states in the east were pressured to do the same. And as an increasing number of "average guys" gained the right to vote, politicians began to adapt their campaigns to appeal to this new kind of voter.

This movement toward democracy, however, involved more than simply changes in voting rules. It was also an ideological movement in which people came to believe that average, everyday Americans should have more of a say in the political system. When our country was founded, many Americans felt that citizens should defer to higher status people whose success and educational backgrounds qualified them to rule. Our Founding Fathers – George Washington, Thomas Jefferson, James Madison – generally came from this class of people. By the 1820's, however, many voters, particularly these new non-property holding voters, came to see elite status as more of a negative. A person with a large amount of wealth and education, after all, would be out of touch with the needs of the "common man."

It was in this environment that Andrew Jackson rapidly rose to prominence in the 1820's. While he was hardly a common man, he effectively presented an image that common men found appealing. Jackson was a farmer, a Westerner, and a war hero. He was a self-made man, not a person born into wealth and status. He was also a man that even his supporters would never describe as a great intellectual. Some would describe the rise of Andrew Jackson as the beginning of "mass politics." Campaigns from that point forward utilized techniques that appealed to the masses: rallies, parades, picnics, catchy slogans, and the careful cultivation of a candidate's image. Jackson then rewarded his supporters by hiring them to political positions, signifying even further the entrance of the average guy into politics.

So what does this nineteenth century history lesson have to do with modern education? This historical discussion began as an attempt to figure out why many young people are hostile toward education. I then proceeded to explain how early twentieth century adolescents began to create their own distinct subculture. Now while I still hold to my teenage subculture thesis, I also believe that the adult dominated, broader American culture still manages to impact adolescents. And as much as older Americans preach the importance of education, there is to this day an anti-intellectual, anti-elite bias in American culture that can be traced back to the days of Andrew Jackson.

To see this, just look at recent political campaigns. George W. Bush, in my mind, was an excellent example of a Jacksonian politician. Like Jackson, he was hardly a common man. Most people were not born into the wealth that his family possessed. Most did not have a father who was recently president. And yet he did a very effective job of appealing to the average American voter. More than once I heard voters say that George Bush seemed like a guy you could have a beer with. His famous grammatical and pronunciation "issues," rather than being detrimental, may have helped him cultivate this image of the average guy. On the other hand, Al Gore and John Kerry were caricatured by the Republican Party as stiff, snobby, liberal elites. (Their lack of anything resembling charisma only served to strengthen the caricatures.) Even Barrack Obama, an African-American man raised by his single mother and grandparents, was described by Republicans during the 2008 campaign as a member of the liberal elite. His Harvard degree, a degree I assume he earned through intelligence and hard work, was seen by many as evidence of his elitist attitude. Then, in this same campaign, Republicans turned to Sarah Palin, the ultimate example of the candidate designed to appeal to the "average" voter. She, after all, was a "soccer mom" just like millions of Americans. She also talked the language of the average voter, and she did not have all of those fancy degrees or elite political credentials.

Now you may be wondering why I have suddenly degenerated into a stereotypical liberal professor promoting the Democratic Party. Believe it or not, this is not my point. I am merely trying to demonstrate that "elite" status, something often associated with intellectual achievement, is often viewed negatively in American culture. And in a culture that often describes educated people as arrogant, out-of-touch nerds, it should not be surprising that young people pick up on some of this anti-intellectual hostility. Personally, I find this general hostility toward "smart" people disturbing. I want highly educated, intelligent people running for high office. I do not particularly want average guys (like myself) running for congress and the presidency. Most of us "average guys" are not remotely qualified for these jobs. This does not mean, of course, that a fancy degree in itself qualifies a person for political office. It also does not mean that a person without impressive educational credentials should be instantly disqualified. There is much more to life experience, after all, then "book learning." But holding intellectual achievement against someone is simply ludicrous.

Having made these various arguments, a part of me wonders if I have made all of this too complicated. It is possible, after all, that people simply dislike school because it is so difficult and monotonous. Once you have stopped being a student for a while, it can be easy to forget how hard it was to get through school. This can be particularly true for teachers, who after many years can forget what it was like to be the test taker. It is important, therefore, for teachers to try and maintain a certain amount of empathy for students. The majority of my students, after all, are still growing up in a culture where it is hard to become an adult. They are also trying to become educated in a society that often does a poor job of helping them, either because of poor teachers or because a quality education can seem increasingly unavailable or expensive. In addition, they listen to preaching from adults about the importance of education in a society that continually uses negative terms to describe intellectuals. In short, it is not easy being a student, especially when you are young (and those damn hormones keep raging).

18. The Immigrants are Coming (Again)!

Too often, the discussion of complex issues degenerates into emotionally driven shouting matches between two sides arguing about how the world should be. One of the classic examples of this tendency is the issue of illegal immigration. Some people emphasize that the United States should be a place that is welcoming to potential immigrants and treats all people, "illegal" or otherwise, with dignity and respect. Others put the priority on carefully regulating our nation's borders, arguing that only a carefully controlled number of people who have followed a legal and orderly process should be allowed to enter and stay.

I wish that both of these ideals could be realized. Unfortunately, reality gets in the way of the ideals: a high demand in this country for cheap labor; Latin American nations with much higher poverty and unemployment rates than the wealthier United States; and a large, difficult to regulate border to the south. In this situation, it is easy to predict what will happen. Desperate workers who are not far from the United States will come seeking economic opportunity, and if employers can get away with it, they will gladly pay wages that are as low as possible. The question, therefore, is how to respond to a less than ideal reality. Due to our nation's reliance on low wage immigrant labor from Latin America, deporting all of the "illegals" may not be feasible. Our nation, however, cannot absorb all of the people who might come if the borders were wide open. As always, the best path is a compromise, with a system set up in which larger numbers of people from Latin America are legally admitted than from other parts of the world. If more of the inevitable immigrants are able to achieve legal status, then they will be able to "come out of the shadows," reducing the prospects for labor exploitation and potential security problems. People who hope to immigrate into the United States from other parts of the world may see this as unfair, but I do not think that "fair" is a practical option. Whether people like it or not, our nation must face up to geographic and economic reality.

In many ways, the current situation regarding immigration is nothing new. For generations, immigrants have come to this nation either escaping hardship or seeking opportunity. And like today, the "native" population has expressed the same old concerns. The first large wave of immigrants to the United States arrived in the 1840's and 1850's, and these were mostly people from northern and western Europe: Ireland, Germany, France, Great Britain, Scandinavian countries – that's my dad's side of our family – the Netherlands, etc. The complaints from that era sound familiar: they are taking jobs away from Americans; they form gangs and corrupt political organizations; they are polluting American culture with their foreign ways. The Irish in particular bore the brunt of these complaints. More people came from this country than any other, and they were escaping horrible circumstances back at home. Their desperation fed perceptions that they were lesser breeds of humanity willing to live in horrific conditions. Their Catholic religion made them seem particularly foreign in a nation traditionally dominated by Protestants. Stories are told of signs hanging outside of stores that said, "Help Wanted. No Irish Need Apply" or "No Dogs and Irish allowed."

An even larger wave of immigrants came from 1870-1920, with the largest number coming in the early 1900's. Many continued to come from northern and western Europe, but there was also an increasing number of so-called "New Immigrants" from southern and eastern Europe: Italians, Greeks, Poles, Russians, Serbs, Croatians, Hungarians – those last two would be my mom's side of the family – etc. These New Immigrants seemed more "foreign" than even the Irish. Everything about their culture – language, religion, food, customs – seemed so radically different from previous immigrants. Many argued that a big push needed to be made in recently created institutions called public schools to Americanize these people as quickly as possible.

With all of the similarities between then and now, there are two significant differences. First, in the mid-19th to early 20th centuries, the concept of "illegal immigration" hardly existed. We basically had on open border policy (unless you were Chinese. See "Chinese Exclusion Act"). Immigration restrictions on Europeans were not put into place until the 1920's. So when people expressed their fears about immigrants, they could not use today's common argument: "We just want the government to enforce our immigration laws." Now to be fair, I am sure that there are many Americans who are fine with immigration so long as it is legal. I tend to think, however, that there are many others who share the same fears as past anti-immigrant, anti-foreign Americans but cannot in our political climate voice these concerns so openly. So they fall back on the more politically correct legal argument.

The second difference between then and now is even more significant. European immigrants, no matter their country of origin, shared one common trait: a white face. So if a family came to America and stayed here for a couple of generations, the cultural traits from the home country would mostly fade away. The grandkids of the original immigrants would essentially be white Americans, and they would have now earned the right to complain about immigrants. On the one hand, being labeled a "white" American is rather insulting. There is an assumption in that label that I do not have any ethnicity. When I fill out forms that ask for my ethnic identity, I typically get one box to check off: "White (non-Hispanic)." There is no box for "Norwegian-American," "Croatian-American," "Hungarian-American," or any other European-American. (I am basically a European "mutt" anyway.) According to every survey that I have ever seen, I am just a run-of-the-mill white boy. Of course, by having this generic non-ethnic identity, I am able to blend into the mainstream.

Now imagine if you were the descendant of a Chinese-American family that came to the United States during the gold rush of the 1850's. Culturally, you are no more Chinese than I am Norwegian. And yet, because of your physical appearance, you are still perceived as being ethnic. If a person does not have a white face, they are ultimately unable, according to some, to enter the mainstream. Many Americans would deny that they feel this way, and on a conscious level, they may be telling the truth. But there is no denying that our society for whatever reason defines non-white people as ethnic while essentially ignoring and stripping away the ethnic heritage of Europeans. By clearly defining whites as mainstream Americans, everyone else stays a foreigner.

Personally, immigration does not make me nervous. In fact, I see immigration as absolutely essential to our country's past and future success. When people are born into prosperity, they tend to take it for granted. We therefore need a fresh influx of highly motivated people who appreciate the opportunities that they have in this country. I joke with my students sometimes by saying that we need a large-scale citizen exchange program with other nations. We can then export certain Americans in exchange for talented, hard working immigrants. I say we start by exporting many of the people who have been guests on *The Jerry Springer Show* or plaintiffs/defendants on *The People's Court* and go from there.

Some might argue that our country will lose whatever it is that makes us distinctly American if too many immigrants come. I don't buy this argument. Current immigrants will most likely be integrated into American society in the same way as my ancestors, with American culture – whatever that is – being altered and enriched by their customs, ideas, and values. What make me nervous, however, are the potential future reactions of the white mainstream to its soon to be minority status. People from various Latin American and Asian nations are the fastest growing groups in America, and as long as many white Americans view these people as foreign due to their physical appearance, future tensions and backlashes are inevitable. Racism, which has cursed our nation for centuries, is not quite dead yet. The election of President Obama is definitely a sign of progress. Some (not all) of the criticism against him, however, particularly widespread conspiracy theories about his supposed Muslim faith or fake birth certificate, indicates that racist smear campaigns can still be effective. When these types of campaigns are no longer able to stir up traditional anti-foreign, racist fears, we will know that our nation has made some real progress.

19. Do Americans Have a Right to an Education?

Throughout our history, Americans have struggled with the question of what constitutes a human right. What do people deserve by virtue of being human, and what are merely privileges reserved to those who have earned (or can afford) them? This is a core question in some of the most difficult political issues of our time, issues such as health care, welfare reform, homelessness, and education.

One of the first attempts to clarify the rights of Americans was the adoption of the Bill of Rights. These first ten amendments were an attempt to set limits on the newly formed, much more powerful national government that was created by the Constitution. These are essentially political and legal rights, with some amendments guaranteeing the rights of individuals to voice political dissent and most of the others ensuring that the government cannot indiscriminately arrest and punish people. Freedom of religion and the right to bear arms were also implemented in order to make sure that the government did not impose a certain belief system, aided by a monopoly on gun ownership.

What you have with the Bill of Rights, then, is a list of things that the government is not allowed to do, and I, like most Americans I assume, am glad that they are there. What you do not see in the Bill of Rights, however, is a list of things that the government is obligated to do. So the Constitution guarantees a right to freedom of speech, the press, religion, a fair trial, and gun ownership. It does not guarantee, however, a right to have food, a house, adequate health care, and an education. So if you were to ask most Americans to make a list of their most basic needs, they would find that there is no legal guarantee of being able to meet them.

When our country was formed, most Americans did not expect or really want the government to do very much. Government basically existed to maintain order, defend the nation, and lay the basic groundwork for a functioning economy: transportation, stable currency, communication, etc. Today, government at all levels takes on responsibilities that people in early American history could hardly imagine. The federal government provides various forms of aid with Social Security, provides medical insurance to the poor and elderly, and distributes various forms of financial aid and other benefits to the poor. State governments, in addition to contributing to this newly emerged "welfare state," spend enormous amounts of money providing free and mandatory public education, something that was unheard of in early American history. In a sense, this paragraph has answered the question that I started with. Apparently, the people of the United States have come to the conclusion over time that Americans have a right to meet their basic human needs. Well, we have sort of come to this conclusion.

Compared to the majority of industrialized nations, the welfare state of the United States is still fairly limited. We are the only industrial nation that does not have a national health care system for all. The government will help you out if you are poor enough, old enough, a veteran, or disabled, but if you do not fit these categories, and you work in a job that does not provide insurance, good luck. Even when (or if) the 2010 health care bill goes into effect, millions will still be uninsured. Welfare benefits may be available, but they are generally more limited than those provided by other countries, and in recent years, welfare reform laws have set limits on how long a person can collect benefits. Our nation does provide public education, but only up to a point. When you get to the college level, the free ride (sort of) ends.

Until fairly recently in American history, college was a luxury largely enjoyed by a privileged elite. Today, some sort of higher education degree is increasingly mandatory for a person who wants to find a decent job. In a sense, this is nothing new. Public schooling originally developed in the 19th century in response to our country's gradual transition from an agrarian to an industrial society. Our country needed more white-collar workers – engineers, office workers, professionals – who needed to master at least some basic academic skills in order to do their jobs. When we were a country of farmers and manual laborers, there did not seem to be as much of a need for an educated work force. (Remarkably, however, American literacy rates were extremely high in spite of a lack of mandatory public education.) School was not made free and (eventually) mandatory to do citizens a favor; it was done to make sure that we did not have a bunch of useless people running around in this increasingly industrial society.

Initially, people were only required to go to grammar school. Then, as the accumulated knowledge of society grew and as parents increasingly found themselves working away from home, public high schools became increasingly common. (Schools are, after all, effective baby-sitting institutions.) This trend toward the average American spending increasing time in school has continued over the past century, and now many Americans see college as absolutely mandatory. Does this mean that government has taken on the responsibility of providing a college education to everyone who wants one?

To a certain degree, the government has taken on this responsibility. Public universities are common throughout the United States. And while these institutions are by no means free, in comparison to the costs of attending a private university, they are a pretty good deal. An even better deal is the ultimate example of the government funded college education: the community college. In California, community college fees were recently raised to $26 per unit, which is remarkably cheap. During this time of state budget deficits, however, there is increasing concern that in my state and throughout the nation governments may increasingly move away from the concept of a publicly subsidized college education. In California, not only have fees been going up, particularly in the Cal State and UC systems, but schools have also been admitting fewer students. This has led many students to turn to community colleges, where fewer classes are being offered. Demand for low-cost classes has outstripped supply, and there are no simple answers.

Some Americans who question the whole idea of a publicly funded college education would argue that this "crisis" is not really a problem. After all, why should some Americans pay taxes to subsidize the education of other Americans? Some make the same argument about public education at all levels. Why should parents whose kids either go to private school or are home-schooled pay taxes to support public schools? Essentially, this is the same argument used by Americans who complain about all aspects of the welfare state. The United States, after all, has a long tradition of believing that individuals must be personally responsible for meeting their basic needs. At the same time, however, there is the more recent tradition of government being held responsible for guaranteeing, to a certain degree, that Americans have these basic needs met. This American ambivalence toward government aid can be seen in many of the most intense political debates in America today, and it is not at all clear how this will be playing out in the next few years.

Public education advocates can use a variety of arguments in their attempts to maintain or increase government investment into education. They can compare the amount of money spent on education to other government programs, arguing that priorities may sometimes be out of whack. They can appeal to people's love for children, mixing this with good old-fashioned guilt through questions like, "Aren't our children worth it?" They can also use the human rights argument, claiming that a just society is obligated to meet this basic human need.

These education advocates should probably avoid these types of "bleeding heart," "liberal," emotional arguments. Any argument that does not recognize Americans' historical ambivalence toward the idea of government aid will not be particularly effective. Instead, they should focus on the practical benefits of public education. Investment in education not only leads to a more productive economy for everyone; it also reduces the number of unproductive, potentially dangerous people in our society. Americans have always been comfortable with the idea of a government that promotes economic development and provides security for its citizens, so why not emphasize these functions of government that almost everyone agrees are legitimate. In the long run, education may even save the government money. It is cheaper, after all, to educate someone then it is to house that person in jail for decades.

So is education a right? I must admit that I am somewhat ambivalent on this question, just as I am with all questions involving government aid. I don't know if certain members of society should be obligated to pay taxes in order to help meet the needs of others. In the end, however, I find this question regarding human rights somewhat irrelevant. When dealing with political questions, it is best to not get bogged down in discussions about general ideals and abstractions. I prefer to be practical. And when I look at this question in practical terms, I conclude that a society that provides the opportunity for people to become educated and successful is probably a nicer place to live than one that does not. So I am therefore willing to have some of my tax dollars go to this purpose. Is this an entirely fair and efficient way to do things? Probably not, but it is better than the apparent alternatives, and in politics, choosing the best of the flawed options is all that you can do.

Part Four: The Western Movement

20.   Tecumseh: Hero or Enemy (or Both)?

Imagine that an ethnic minority represented most of the population in a remote area that was considered by the white majority to be part of the United States. This ethnic minority was by no means united. Instead, they were broken up into a variety of tribal and cultural groups that often did not get along with one another. As the population of the white majority grew, many looked to these remote areas as places where they must expand and settle. Unfortunately, some of the ethnic minority groups that lived there viewed these white settlers as outside invaders who posed a grave threat to both the natural environment and to their traditional ways of life. One of these tribal leaders, a man particularly hostile toward white settlement, had a simple insight. He realized that the only hope for his people was to convince the various tribal groups to come together as one to violently resist the United States. If tribal groups continued to fight amongst themselves, or if some chose to accommodate the United States, then they would all be overrun.

If a man like this existed today, Americans would have many labels for him. He would be viewed by most as an enemy of the state, terrorist, extremist, murderer, and/or any number of various racist slurs. He would also be seen as an obstacle that stood in the way of our nation's continued progress. Of course, as you may already know, this man did exist about two hundred years ago. His name was Tecumseh, and for a while, he was able to strike fear in the hearts of American citizens and of the United States government. Unfortunately for Tecumseh, as he was traveling on a great journey to unite as many Native American tribes as possible, the central village of his movement was attacked and destroyed by the United States military. He would continue to resist the United States until his death in the War of 1812, but his dream of building a pan-Indian resistance movement had long since faded. Because Native American groups had no history of uniting on this scale, and Native Americans were so outnumbered by white Americans, his efforts were likely doomed from the start.

The first 115 years of American history plays like a broken record when it comes to the United States' dealings with Native Americans. Some Native Americans reacted violently to United States' efforts to settle the frontier, and "Indian Wars" were constantly in the backdrop of early American history. At other times, certain Native American tribes would do business with whites or give in to their requests to sign over land through treaties. At some point, however, most would come to realize that they could not coexist with these new settlers while maintaining their ways of life, and the United States government was either unable or unwilling to honor those treaties. So accommodation would often change into violent resistance, with all of these efforts ultimately suffering the same fate as those of Tecumseh.

As one would expect, Native Americans were portrayed in a very negative light by the United States media in the nineteenth century. Western "dime novels" of the late 19th- early 20th centuries depicted them as savages constantly in conflict with Western heroes. This continued in the thousands of 20th century Western films and television shows that were made from the dawn of the film industry until the 1960's. Since the late 1960's, however, Native Americans have generally been portrayed in a different light. Instead of being bloodthirsty savages constantly threatening white pioneers and soldiers, Native Americans over the last forty years have generally been portrayed as victims, overrun by the United States as it conquered the frontier.

So how should Americans judge a man like Tecumseh today? Should he be remembered as a bitter enemy of the United States, or was he, like all Native Americans, a valiant victim of an invasion? The tendency over the past four decades has been to view men like Tecumseh in a much more positive light than he was seen during his lifetime. There is a simple, unavoidable question, however, for anyone who sees him as a heroic victim. Would it have been a good thing if he were successful in repelling United States expansion or, at the very least, if he had helped Native Americans hold on to a larger percentage of their lands and traditional lifestyles? People who believe that Native Americans were victims of injustice are compelled to say yes. The problem with answering yes, however, is that the United States today would be a fundamentally different place if men like Tecumseh had been more successful. And since most of the people living in the United States today are descendants of recent immigrants to this land, a significant percentage of Americans who are currently enjoying their lives here would likely not even exist. Like all places on earth, the United States is conquered soil, and without the conquest, this nation would hardly be recognizable.

Also, when I think about Tecumseh, there is another simple question that I cannot avoid. For decades, Native Americans were viewed in almost a completely negative light. Today, they are not judged so harshly. In fact, Native Americans are typically portrayed in the media today as people who were more peaceful, wise, and in touch with nature than those conquerors from the United States. So are there people and groups living today who future generations will judge differently than we currently do? Are there people that most of us judge as enemies, terrorists, or other forms of evil who will be seen as freedom fighters or victims in the future? Being so ingrained into the thinking of my time, I am ultimately unable to answer this question with any certainty.

One thing I do know, however, is that the tough historical questions are the ones most worthy of being asked. History is so much more than memorizing facts and details. Instead, it is about trying to put oneself in the place of others and see things from multiple points of view. It may be very difficult to determine who was in the right during a certain historical period or to figure out how future generations will judge us, but facing the tough questions is what ultimately makes the whole enterprise worthwhile. It also makes it very difficult to place people like Tecumseh, or just about anyone else in the past or present, into the simplistic category of either "good guy" or "bad guy."

21. Could We Survive the Oregon Trail?

I doubt that I would even last a day on the Oregon Trail. For me, after all, a two-day camping trip is a bit of a grind, and I am usually on a campground with actual toilets and showers! It's actually hard for me to decide what would suck the most about taking this five-month, two- thousand mile hike to the West Coast. First of all, of course, there was the constant knowledge of all the various ways that one might die on the trail: disease, starvation, prairie fire, injury, Indian attack (which was rare, by the way), nasty weather, getting stuck in the snow, being eaten by a fellow traveler, etc. According to a film that I show to my Early American History students, one out of seventeen pioneers on the Oregon Trail died on the trip. How many middle-class Americans today would even consider taking a journey with that kind of a death rate? When we travel by plane, car, boat, or train, we begin with the assumption that we will reach our destination safely. How many of us take off for work or on a vacation crying with our loved ones out of fear that we may never see them again? We live in a world, after all, where people travel great distances for the fun of it. In the time of Columbus, people would have thought you were nuts if you sailed off into the open ocean on a pleasure cruise.

One of the great blessings of the modern world – and some would say curses – is that you never feel like you are isolated and alone. We always have our trusty cell phone at our side. The national weather service can warn travelers of impending trouble. GPS devices can help us to know at every moment our specific location, and if we end up stranded somewhere, all sorts of modern transportation and communication devices can be used to get to us. On the Oregon Trail, of course, travelers were cut off somewhat from civilized society. If you got injured, sick, or struggled to find food and water, there was no way to call for help and often no nearby store where you could shop for supplies. You could wait by the trail in hopes that someone might show up, but there was no way to know when or if this might happen. If bad weather lay ahead, there was no warning. And if you ran into some bad guys, you better be able to fight them off. Few people in a modern, industrial society have any concept of what it means to be isolated. For many, the phone is practically implanted to their ears or to their rapidly texting fingers so that they never have to feel anything resembling loneliness and isolation.

I have a feeling, however, that the constant fear of various forms of death would not be the hardest thing about life on the trail. The worst thing, in fact, might be plain old mind-numbing boredom. For a person like me who considers an eight-hour car ride or five-hour flight to be an almost unbearable ordeal, it is impossible to even comprehend what a five-month journey across the plains and through the Rocky Mountain passes would be like. Can you imagine hanging out with the same people, most likely your family members, every day for that length of time? And to make matters worse, you would not have an IPOD, radio, video game device, DVD player or anything else to keep you occupied (and distracted from the annoyances of your siblings.) You would be forced to talk to people, read books, and engage in other non-electronic, archaic activities. Hangman, twenty questions, and the "let's count the blades of grass game" could only be entertaining for so long.

So why were people of the past able to do this? How did they withstand the physical ordeal, the fears, and the mind-numbing boredom and drudgery of trail life? The simple fact, I would argue, was that trail life was not a huge deviation from their normal, day-to-day lives. In the America of the 1840's, death could always be around the corner. Before the advent of modern medicine, a significant percentage of the population died by the age of five. If a disease was contracted, doctors could do little to cure you, and some of their misguided practices could play a big part in finishing you off. Many people were still forced to adapt to and deeply respect the whims of nature since they did not have the modern technologies that lead us to believe that we can overcome weather, natural disasters, and time and space itself. Since death always stared them in the face, their fear of it was probably not as great as modern Americans who often do everything in their power to put their impending mortality out of their minds. It takes so little, after all, to freak us out. Almost every year, we hear the story of some disease that is apparently going to wipe out all of humankind: SARS, West Nile Virus, Mad Cow Disease, Swine Flu, etc. Now while I recognize that these diseases do some real damage, the death rates are microscopic in comparison to the epidemics, plagues, and day-to-day diseases of the past. Would one hundred people dying of West Nile Virus freak people out 160 years ago?

People of the past were also well acquainted with boredom and drudgery. Without modern labor saving devices, they were forced to perform many time consuming, physically demanding tasks that most modern Americans have never had to do. Doing laundry, chopping wood, gathering water, and producing food required both time and hard labor. For me, the ten or fifteen minutes that I must spend on laundry, the half hour at the grocery store, and the twenty minutes spent doing dishes feel like an overwhelming ordeal. I wonder how long I would last on a mid-nineteenth century farm? And when I managed to get some free time, would I know what to do with it? Before Facebook, cell phones, video games, ESPN, and DVD players, what the hell did people do with themselves?

In a sense, people 160 years ago were almost a different species than I. Because their lives were harder, they became tougher. Because they were well acquainted with drudgery, they tolerated boredom more effectively than many of us would, and a good book or conversation was often the ultimate form of entertainment. They were not conditioned to need continuous visual stimulation. And because they knew that death was a possibility no matter how risk-averse one might be, they may have been willing to take more risks. Still, I can't imagine that the journey on the Oregon Trail was remotely easy. So like the Polynesians who ventured throughout the Pacific, the people who first crossed the Sahara Desert, or the men who were crazy enough to set sail with Columbus, the pioneers on the Oregon Trail deserve the awe and respect of the wimps of modern society. I don't know if we will ever truly see the likes of them again.

22. Myths and Realities of the Old West

When we cover the late 19th century American west in my History classes, I have students start with a simple exercise. I have them brainstorm a list, either in pictures or in words (or both), of whatever comes to mind when they think of Western movies. Over the years, it has been amazing to see how consistent these lists are: cowboys & Indians, gunfights, gold prospectors, ghost towns, saloons, outlaws, desert landscapes, wagon trains, etc. Decades after the golden age of the American Western, these images are still embedded into our minds.

These powerful images of the West can be summed up with three basic ideas. First, there is the belief that this was the "Wild West," a crazy place filled with crime, duels, drunks, gamblers, bar fights, and dancing girls/prostitutes. As a place that was new and somewhat unsettled, law and order had not quite been established. Without a sheriff that was fast on the draw and a decent deputy or two, you would basically have anarchy. A second, subtler idea is the West as a land of independent pioneers. On the frontier, you were forced to take care of yourself. So if you were tough, devious, and/or smart, you could become a successful farmer, gold prospector, cattle rancher, or small town businessman. Finally, the West is often depicted as an unspoiled wilderness, a land of wide-open spaces untouched by the environmental effects of civilization. Because the western plains, Rocky Mountains, and southwestern deserts were tough places to survive, early 19th century pioneers often skipped these lands on a perilous journey to the West Coast. But by the late 19th century, these were the only frontiers left in the continental United States. So if you wanted to see the last of America's natural landscapes, and if you were tough enough to survive, it was time to "go west, young man."

But after taking a little time to look at the historical record, it becomes clear that the real west was a bit different from the typical depiction in Hollywood. Native Americans, rather than being the

105

savages blocking western settlement that were so often depicted in old Western movies, were generally victims of expansion rather than impediments to it. By the late 19th century, they were generally rounded up onto reservations, no longer able to live fully their traditional ways of life. The West could certainly get violent at times, but western towns were far less violent than in the movies. Gunfights were spontaneous acts of ugly violence rather than glorified duels in the middle of the street, and the "good guys," who were not always easy to identify, did not always win in the end. And when people were shot, they did not necessarily die instantly with a single bullet wound to the chest. Instead, they might die slowly, complete with blood, guts, excruciating pain, and dismembered body parts. Over time, the independent gold prospectors, "open range" cowboys, and family farmers became less common, replaced by mining companies, large cattle ranches enclosed by barbed wire, and big commercial farms. As in the rest of the country, corporations became increasingly common, and a growing number of Westerners found themselves employees rather than independent pioneers. And after years of trampling, farting, grass-eating cattle; large scale industrial mining; and primitive farming practices on land ill-suited for agriculture in the first place; the untamed wilderness began to lose its pristine quality.

These inconvenient realities, however, have not stopped the images of the "Old West" from staying very popular. It is not difficult to understand why. When Western dime novels began appearing in the late 19th century, Americans ate this stuff up for one basic reason: these Western stories seemed to be the polar opposite of their lives in the east. For this was a time when urban, corporate, industrial America began to truly take hold, with a growing number of Americans finding themselves living in crowded, unsanitary cities; working in horrific factory conditions; and watching most of the profits go to corporate tycoons. The idea that there was still a place with wide-open spaces where the independent pioneers could still thrive was very appealing. In the West, real men dominated, surviving on their toughness and their wits. I imagine that people would have paid good money to watch John Rockefeller in a gunfight against Wyatt Earp or Buffalo Bill Cody, just as people today would love to watch Bill Gates in the ring with the ultimate fighting champion. We would also love to see if one of those corporate geeks could make it as a farmer, gold prospector, saloon owner, or cowboy.

Western movies are not as common as they once were, although the genre still lives on. And in the general culture, you can still see the glorification of our Western past. The ultimate modern example of this would be the cowboy. Strangely, modern people who might identify themselves as cowboys are unlikely to work with cattle. Rather than being a job, the cowboy has become a person who follows a certain lifestyle: cowboy hat, leather, boots, a truck (complete with a gun rack), country music, rodeos, and NASCAR races. Now while I am stereotyping just a little, there is no doubt that the term cowboy has taken on a meaning very different from its original connection to cattle ranching. And what was formerly a pretty lousy occupation filled with potential injuries, nasty weather, loneliness, and rashes/ pain/ numbness in places that I will refrain from naming, has evolved into some sort of tough, manly, heroic figure holding on to so-called traditional values. The iconic figure of the American cowboy, more than anything else, demonstrates the degree to which the realities of the Old West evolved into myth and legend.

When I finish discussing the Old West, I leave students with one, final half-serious task. I tell them that someday, I want one of my students to become a great filmmaker who utilizes his or her skill in making the true American Western. Instead of heroic cowboys taking on bad guys and Indians out on the plains or in a one-street town, I want a movie filled with farting cows, industrial mining operations ran by corporations, cowboys with hemorrhoids, physical abuse of prostitutes, and spontaneous gunfights where someone gets shot in the back and dies slowly. This would undoubtedly be a blockbuster, earning dozens of dollars at the box office. And while it may be a commercial flop, at least this future great filmmaker can take solace in its historical accuracy. Or then again, maybe future filmmakers should stick with the John Wayne formula.

23. Wide Open Spaces

Our family typically goes on two types of vacations. First, there is the type where we travel to one location, stay there for several days, and mix rest and relaxation with some local attractions and activities. Then, there is the more ambitious road trip vacation where we travel to multiple places seeing some of the sights in this huge country. The following essay was originally written during a trip through part of the American Southwest, with the main attractions being Las Vegas, The Grand Canyon, and Bryce Canyon.

Driving around through parts of four states in six days can get a bit exhausting and monotonous, particularly when exposed to a steady dose of Hannah Montana and The Jonas Brothers. One cool thing about this kind of a trip, however, is that you get a better feel for the layout of this amazing country in which I live. The American Southwest so often conjures up images of nothing but deserts and barren landscapes. And while we have seen plenty of shrubs and cacti, we have also gone through forests; seen some amazing canyons, mountains and cliffs; and driven through green plains and meadows.

The most distinctive quality of the land, however, and something that I always notice while taking these kinds of trips, is emptiness. The overwhelming majority of the landscapes we have seen are basically devoid of people. It's amazing how quickly your idea of what constitutes a city can change when driving through mile after mile of nothingness. Suddenly, if you see a few houses and businesses, you feel like you have once again rejoined civilization. In Southern California, there is no way in hell that one of these little conglomerations of buildings would even register as being remotely urban. But when out on the open road, a town of 500 is a major population center. And if a town has a real supermarket, a Starbucks, or a Wal-Mart, then it is clearly a thriving metropolis.

Rural environments and general emptiness are still pretty common in the United States. Amazingly, even though our population has increased tremendously over the last one hundred years, there is almost as much empty space today as there was in the early twentieth century. This is because we Americans, like people in all industrialized societies, have a habit of packing into huge cities. As people have become increasingly dependent on commerce to survive, they have been compelled to live in cities. After all, if you rely on trade, then you are forced to live near other people with whom you need to trade.

When the United States was first developing in the nineteenth century, people saw the "empty" lands on the western frontier as a great blessing for our nation. If problems like overcrowding, unemployment, homelessness, or shortages of land and resources developed, then people could look to the West for new opportunities. This was why some Americans were nervous at the end of the 1800's when it seemed that the frontier was gone. Without this "safety valve" to ease tensions in the more settled, urbanized areas, our country would lose its uniqueness. We would no longer truly be the land of opportunity, and we would develop the kinds of problems seen in the more developed parts of Europe.

Clearly, these fears were largely unfounded. The idea that struggling Americans living in urban areas needed the frontier is clearly a myth. People are not leaving the cities to flock to the frontier. If anything, the opposite has been happening for decades. Southern California, in spite of all of its problems, continues to snowball in population. Meanwhile, states like Montana, South Dakota, North Dakota, Idaho, Wyoming and several others are filled with cheap land and wide-open spaces. Some of this can be attributed to geography. Southern California has access to the ocean and nice weather. Montana, of course, is landlocked and gets freaking cold. But this is also part of a general American and global trend in which most human beings are compelled to cluster into urban areas.

So in a sense, the American frontier never actually disappeared. It is still out there. I've seen quite a bit of it in my travels over the years. But most Americans, from what I can gather, are not itching to move there. Maybe the increasing importance of the internet will play some role in reversing this trend. If people can sell goods and services on-line rather than in person, then they can theoretically live anywhere. A certain

109

amount of human concentration, however, seems inevitable. Certain business transactions must still happen face-to-face, and goods and materials will continue to flow through urban centers that thrive due to their location. Plus, large cities are like a magnet, sucking people in to do business with those who are already there.

I always tell my students that they should get the heck out of California when they graduate from college and get some cheap land out in North Dakota. I then assure them that I will keep an eye on things for them out here in Orange County. The frontier is a nice place to visit from time to time, but I don't know if I could live there. I'm spoiled by Southern California weather, and a teaching job in a "town" of 150 might not pay very well. So I better get off to bed. For tomorrow, we will leave this iconic symbol of the American frontier – The Grand Canyon - and head back toward Southern California, iconic symbol of the modern age.

24. Why do Americans Stink at Geography?

For years, I have heard (and seen at times for myself) that Americans are terrible in geography. I decided to do a little quick research, and sure enough, when I googled "Americans Geography Knowledge," several links came up confirming how dismally Americans perform on geography tests. Some might see this as one of many symptoms of a generally lousy American educational system. Knowledge of global geography in the United States, however, seems to be uniquely bad. In one study, the United States scored 117th out of 193 countries on a test of global geographic knowledge. For the wealthiest nation on earth, a place that intervenes in the affairs of countries all over the planet, this is both disturbing and embarrassing.

It is easy to blame either the educational system for failing or the American people for choosing to be dumb. These, however, are simplistic explanations. Americans often display an amazing capacity to memorize information. The problem, many would say, is the information that they choose to memorize: sports stats, details about the lives of celebrities, movie/TV trivia, the intricacies of computer games, etc. So if the memory function of the American brain is clearly still intact, then why can't we find anything on a map? It's pretty simple. People memorize information that they care about. Clearly, Americans often don't care enough to bother learning very much about the outside world. So how can you explain this lack of interest? As a history teacher who took a lot of geography in college, I believe the answer can be found by looking at both our nation's geography and history.

For roughly our first one hundred years, both the American government and people did not pay much attention to the outside world. The global center of power, Europe, was across the Atlantic Ocean, a major barrier at this point in history. To the south and west were Spanish colonies that, in most cases, turned into new, relatively weak nations by the early 1800's. When we eventually expanded to the West Coast, the Pacific Ocean served as a massive barrier. To the north Canada, which was controlled by Britain throughout the 19th century, posed a threat in our early days. We fought a war with the British from 1812-1815, which would be the last time that a foreign army invaded the continental United States. Within a relatively short time after this war, however, relations with the British improved, and the prospects of Canadians invading us (wielding hockey sticks) subsided. We did not, therefore, face any serious threat from a foreign nation during the 19th century. The only war we fought against a foreign nation on the continent of North America was the Mexican War, a war that the United States provoked in order to gain control of Mexican territory.

As the Mexican War demonstrated, when Americans looked outward, the tendency was to look west. In addition to being blessed by geographic isolation, we were also blessed with seemingly unlimited, empty space (once Native Americans and Mexicans were knocked out of the way, of course). The United States from its inception was always in expansion mode. We just had plenty here in North America to keep us busy for a while. Of course, the frontier would eventually be tamed and somewhat settled. In addition, our economy by the late 19th century was becoming industrialized, creating the need to seek out new sources of raw materials and new markets where we could sell all of these mass produced goods. So once the frontier was settled, and the need to expand seemed stronger than ever, Americans gradually started looking beyond their borders. Latin America was the most natural place to turn first, but there were also efforts to acquire islands in the Pacific – sometimes violently, as in the Philippines - to gain access to the Asian market. Still, most American trade and manufacturing took place at home, so most Americans focused on events here. Europe was by far our biggest trading partner, but Americans, as always, took little interest in getting involved in European politics.

So what does this little history lesson have to do with bad geography tests? During our nation's formative years, Americans had little reason to care about the outside world. We had plenty here in the Western Hemisphere to keep us busy, and there was little reason to worry about external threats (except for those "pesky" Native Americans). Now I don't know if studies were done in the 19th century to measure American geographic literacy, but it would not surprise me if their knowledge of world geography and global events was pretty slim. Our country's geographic isolation and its enormous amount of physical space for expansion may have left a cultural imprint on us that has cursed our people to forever suck on geography tests.

You should see a problem with my argument, however. If you have some knowledge of the past one hundred years of American history, then you know that the United States became much more involved in the outside world over this past century. The United States in World War I was eventually dragged into its first European war. After it was over, disillusioned Americans decided to go back to the isolationist policy we had always tried to follow. It would therefore take an attack on Pearl Harbor to officially drag us into the Second World War. When that war ended, the United States asserted itself as a global superpower, a position that it is yet to relinquish. We then spent forty-five years on a global crusade against communism, and today we are engaged in a War on Terror. And throughout the last century, our global trade interests have consistently grown in scale. Some would argue, in fact, that our struggles against the evils of communism and terrorism have often been a cover for promoting economic interests. Where businesses go, the military must follow.

It seems logical, then, that as our country became more involved in the outside world, the American people would also show more interest in international affairs. Clearly, however, this has not happened. Why? While I cannot answer this question with certainty, I think that our continuing geographic ignorance is the result of another trend that corresponds with our emergence as a global superpower. After World War II, the United States quickly emerged as the most wealthy, technologically advanced nation in history. And as Americans became enraptured and distracted by new gadgets like televisions and their beautiful suburban "clone homes," it was easy to put out of their minds events around the world that were a bit scary and depressing anyway. After the Great Depression and World War II, Americans wanted escape to a place, both mentally and physically, where they could feel safe. And as scary as the Russians might be, they still seemed far away from suburban Orange County (and Disneyland). Geographic location used to be the main factor in helping Americans feel safe. To some degree, it still does. Today, however, and for the last sixty-five years, a massive military and, maybe more importantly, unprecedented material prosperity are the main factors in creating our little bubble of security out here in North America.

There have been times since World War II that global events captured our attention: Korea, the Cuban Missile Crisis, Vietnam, the Iranian Hostage Crisis, the fall of the Soviet Union, the first Gulf War. Still, it took a catastrophe on American soil on September 11, 2001, to truly burst our bubble of security. For the first time in 60 years, large numbers of Americans were killed by foreigners on American soil. Suddenly, international news really seemed to matter. And yet here we are, more than a decade into the War on Terror, and most Americans cannot find Iraq on a map. I bet a lot of them, however, can tell you the name of last year's NBA Most Valuable Player, some of the winners of the "American Idol" competition, or what the hottest computer or video game might currently be. Once again, material prosperity and entertainment can suck us in every time. The outside world, after all, seems so damn scary, depressing, and far away.

Part Five: Slavery, The Civil War, and Reconstruction

25. Nat Turner: Terrorist or Freedom Fighter?

In 1831, Nat Turner, a slave from Virginia, was convicted for leading the most famous and violent slave revolt in the history of the United States. Before the rebellion was eventually put down and he was captured, approximately fifty white people had been killed over the course of five days. This event would remain embedded in the consciousness of the South for decades, and in various ways, it would change somewhat both its attitude toward slaves and its techniques for controlling them.

In my Early American History classes, we read an excerpt from an interview that was given to Turner shortly before he was executed. Many historians believe that the interviewer may have jazzed up the story a bit in order to help it sell, and some doubt has even been expressed about Turner's actual guilt and supposed confession. But even if you assume that the writer added some grizzly details for dramatic effect, and that Turner's confession may have even been fabricated, there is no denying that this was a horrific event. Today, however, since I assume that most people believe that slavery is wrong, typical readers will find themselves feeling ambivalence toward the Turner described in this interview. At first, when you hear how Turner formulated his plans, you cannot help rooting for him. A part of you wants him to make those slaveholders pay, and you hope that he is able to perform a miracle and set thousands of his fellow slaves free. But over the course of the story, things get increasingly ugly. From the start, Turner and his followers had decided to kill every white person who came across their path, a plan that they generally upheld. At one point, they massacre an entire household and then begin moving on to the next place. Suddenly, one of Turner's people remembers that they forgot to kill a baby at the home. So one of them returns to stay true to the original plan and finish the job.

116

When that image of a baby being hacked to death by a machete enters your mind, you cannot help but ask yourself if Turner's people had gone too far. Their cause was noble, but does even the most noble of causes justify the strategy, "by any means necessary"?

As you might imagine, Southerners did not feel ambivalence toward Turner. In their minds, Turner was a violent fanatic, and their emotions were similar to Americans' feelings about Osama Bin Laden ten years ago. Some gunned down slaves in response to the Turner uprising out of fear and/or a desire for vengeance. Throughout the South, a crackdown was implemented, with restrictions placed on slaves' ability to become educated, gather together with other slaves, or carry any object that could be utilized as a weapon. If they implemented tougher security measures, and steps were taken to make sure that slaves did not think or question too much, then they believed that the Southern way of life could be maintained.

Most Northerners were also horrified when they heard what happened. Some, however, believed that a crackdown was not the most effective response. William Lloyd Garrison, an abolitionist who had begun publishing an anti-slavery newspaper shortly before the Turner uprising, basically said, "I told you so." In his mind, slave revolts were the inevitable result of an unjust system. If you treat people as non-human beasts, at some point, they are going to lash out against you. So the only way to stop future slave revolts was to stop slavery itself. Garrison, however, was not trying to justify what Turner had done. Even an abolitionist like himself felt that Turner had gone too far. Explaining why someone resorts to a certain type of behavior, after all, is not the same as justifying that behavior.

Before the Turner uprising, there were times when Southerners expressed reservations about the slave system. Shortly after this revolt, Virginia engaged in one of these periodic dialogues, with the state assembly actually holding a vote on a plan of gradual emancipation. In a close vote, this measure failed to pass. Unfortunately, this would be the last case of a Southern political institution holding this type of a discussion. In addition to implementing a crackdown against slaves, the South went into clampdown mode against anyone who questioned the "peculiar institution." After decades of relying on arguments that emphasized the economic and social necessity of maintaining slavery, there was an ideological shift in which Southerners argued that slavery was actually a positive thing. In general, the South was no longer apologetic. Slavery was good, and any Southerners who disagreed should keep their mouths shut. After all, if the South did not rally around its way of life, future Nat Turners might exploit their weakness and initiate more bloodshed. And the last thing that the South needed was an abolitionist like William Lloyd Garrison planting ideas into the heads of slaves. So as the South became increasingly defensive and protective of its way of life, prospects grew for future conflicts over any issue involving slavery, and any hope that Southern states might willingly abolish slavery on their own faded.

So in the minds of Southerners, Nat Turner was an exception. He was not the product of an unjust system. He was just a crazy fanatic – a terrorist, if you will – who rounded up a few evildoers to wreak havoc. Slave revolts were pretty rare, after all, and with adequate security measures, the threat of these occurring again could seemingly be minimized. In their minds, most slaves followed their masters and were basically content with their situation. Since slaves were believed to have the mental capacity of children, Southerners saw it as irresponsible to set them free. It would be like cutting loose a five-year-old to go and make it in the world. The fact that runaways were fairly common, and that overseers often had to use compulsion to force slaves to get stuff done, did not deter Southerners from their belief that slaves were basically content. If people want to believe something badly enough, they can talk themselves into anything. Engaging in this type of cognitive dissonance was easier for Southerners than taking an honest look at themselves and at the system that made their lifestyles possible. It was easier to label Nat Turner as evil and William Lloyd Garrison as a man who stirred up slaves with his dangerous, radical, anti-Southern rhetoric. To Southerners, anyone who expressed any sympathy with a man like Turner or made any attempt to understand his irrational behavior was essentially a terrorist sympathizer.

"One man's terrorist is another man's freedom fighter." There is no denying the truth in these often expressed words. We all have the tendency to support actions carried out by countrymen and allies that we condemn when taken by enemies. Still, I don't believe that morality is completely relative and that the righteousness of politically motivated violence is simply a matter of point of view. In my mind, a 19th century slave had more justification for turning to brutal violence against the American system than a 21st century Islamic jihadist. But like Southerners 200 years ago, Americans today have two general ways that they can respond to people who carry out violent actions against our people and interests. We can violently go after our enemies and impose stricter security measures to keep ourselves safe, or we can try to understand and minimize the forces which caused these enemies to turn against the United States in the first place. Force is sometimes necessary, but if you make no attempt to understand your enemy or to determine if your own mistakes or weaknesses may have contributed to the enemy's actions, then you make the battle much more difficult. Simply labeling enemies as evil and refusing to question the system that produced them can be a losing battle.

Someday, future generations may judge weaknesses in our society in the same way that most Americans look at the pre-Civil War south today. Fortunately, our nation eventually changed, and we no longer have to worry about slave revolts. There are plenty of other violent threats, however, both domestic and international, that stem at least partly from systemic problems. The easy "solution" is to "get tough on crime" or "go after" terrorists. Unfortunately, this limited approach, in itself, can be ineffective and expensive. Hopefully, unlike those early 19th century Southerners, we will demonstrate a willingness to look more closely at ourselves and our cherished way of life. If not, future historians may feel some sympathy for those who rose up to fight the system.

26. Was the Civil War Worth the Cost?

Approximately 620,000 Americans died in the United States' only Civil War, and another 400,000 were wounded. These numbers in themselves are difficult for Americans to wrap their minds around. But when you consider the fact that there were approximately 32 million people living in the United States when the war began, the casualties become even more unimaginable. After all, just the population of California today is significantly higher than 32 million. Can you imagine a war in which there were one million casualties in California alone?

So whose fault was it? If you can still find Americans who are aware that there was a Civil War, I imagine that the majority of these respondents would view the South as the "bad guy." After all, eleven Southern states "started it" by committing treason against the United States and attempting to form a separate country. Also, typical explanations for the causes of the war focus on slavery, and the South in this narrative becomes the evil region defending slavery against Northerners who were (supposedly) against it. Reality, however, is a bit more complicated. When I cover the Civil War with my history classes, the root cause I keep coming back to is Southern paranoia. Mistakenly, they believed that the North was filled with people who wanted to abolish slavery, and if the North was ever able to gain complete control of the federal government, then they might force the South to change its way of life. The attempt of a crazed, white, Northern abolitionist named John Brown to violently liberate slaves, and the election of a Republican named Abraham Lincoln who supported policies only advocated by the North, fed into these fears and pushed some Southern states over the edge. The facts that Lincoln clearly stated that he, like most Northerners, was not an abolitionist, and that the majority of Northerners condemned the actions of John Brown, were not enough to extinguish these fears that had been building for some time. Then, like now, political beliefs often had little to do with evidence and reason.

120

One could just as easily, however, blame the North for the war. The South, after all, wanted to leave the Union peacefully. In their minds, our country was first and foremost a collection of independent states, and these individual states had the right to withdraw from the Union at the time of their choosing. Southern states were simply asserting the same right as the British colonies when they formed the United States in the first place. The North, of course, did not see things this way, so the decision was made to invade the South and put down this rebellion. At that point, the war truly started.

But what if the North had made a different decision? They could have told the Southern states to just go ahead and leave. Think of all the benefits of this decision. Hundreds of thousands of people could have avoided death, maiming, and psychological damage. Families who lost loved ones could have kept their husbands, sons, and brothers. All of that money poured into military supplies could have been saved. (Mississippi and California would no longer have to share the same country.) President Lincoln must have spent a lot of sleepless nights wondering if he and Congress had made the correct decision. Given the fact that he was a man inclined toward intense mood swings, his job must have been agonizing.

Of course, if the North had made a different decision, it is hard to predict how American history would have played itself out over the past 146 years. Some would argue that conflict was going to happen eventually even if the Southern states were allowed to secede. Much of the tension that led to the war was caused by decades of competition over the western territories. Both regions wanted expansion. The problem was that they had different visions for what the West would someday look like. The South had visions of plantations, cotton fields, and slave labor; the North saw a future of family farms, businesses, towns, and wage labor. So if the country split in two, how would they divide the undeveloped lands in the southwest, Great Plains, and Rocky Mountains? Would the United States and Confederacy peacefully draw a line down the middle, or would they compete in a land grab that might ultimately lead to war?

Also, what would happen the next time that a state or group of states had a gripe about a federal policy? If Southern states were allowed to separate peacefully from the Union, then a legal precedent would be set. It is possible, therefore, that our currently large country with many regional differences would have ultimately been carved up into multiple smaller nations. A map of North America today might resemble that of Europe.

I wonder if California, for instance, would still be in the Union. If any state seems like a candidate for secession, it would be my home state. Much of the rest of the country thinks that we are nuts anyway. Plus, we have Disneyland, Hollywood, Silicon Valley, redwoods, wine country, central valley farms, a hell of a lot of beachfront property, one of the largest economies in the world, and not too long ago, we had the "Terminator" as governor. As an independent nation, California could also solve its fiscal problems like the federal government: by cranking our more currency and borrowing until the end of time. Come to think of it, I better stop this line of reasoning. People might think that I am some sort of a "Californiaist" revolutionary.

Last but not least, how long would slavery have continued if the South was allowed to secede? In order to win the war, save the Union, and prevent future conflicts, the North eventually took the drastic step of freeing the slaves. If the South had never seceded and triggered the Northern invasion, then slavery would have stayed intact indefinitely. And when you consider the fact that the post-Civil War system of segregation lasted until the early 1960's, you must conclude that if the South was left to itself, then slavery would have lingered for some time. Today, almost fifty years after the Civil Rights Movement, the lingering effects of our nation's legacy of racism are all around us. Imagine the conditions faced by African-Americans today if slavery was a much more recent phenomenon.

It's fun for historians to speculate about what might have been. But unless someone invents a time machine and goes back to mess with the past, we will never know how different decisions might have played out. So we are left with speculating about and ultimately shaping our future. And as I look to the future, I wonder what it would take for Americans to endure the kinds of sacrifices made by people of the Civil War era. What cause would we consider righteous enough to sacrifice hundreds of thousands of our fellow Americans in a war?

Clearly, the United States government does that think that Americans are willing to make significant sacrifices in the War on Terror. Apparently, they are worried that we do not see the cause as adequately vital to our survival and/or just. Taxes have been kept historically low, especially relative to past times of war. Few politicians would even consider the possibility of resorting to a draft. It has been politically easier to add another trillion or two to our national debt and to squeeze the volunteer soldiers (and their families) to the breaking point. Yet even as they try to shield most Americans from the cost, some of our citizens have long been fed up with the conflicts in Iraq and Afghanistan. Apparently, about $100 billion per year (out of a budget of three and a half trillion) and approximately 6,000 American deaths (out of a population of over 300 million) are too high of a cost for many. Many others seem apathetic and perfectly content with living their lives as if our nation was not at war. So those who want Americans to awake from their apathetic slumber should make a simple demand: the government must ask Americans to share more fully in the costs of these wars. The Civil War generation sure the hell did, and we have been reaping the benefits, and paying the consequences, ever since.

27. Abraham Lincoln: Man vs. Myth

I almost share a birthday with Abraham Lincoln. When I was young, this was very convenient because I often got a day off from school. For Lincoln, unlike myself, is one of the most beloved and mythologized men in American history. When you visit the Lincoln Memorial, you feel like you are in some kind of a Greek temple. Except with Lincoln, you want to sit on his statue's lap and tell him your problems. People like Washington, Jefferson, and Franklin are deeply respected. Lincoln is loved, revered by many as a sort of political saint. It's not every president, after all, who has had a national holiday commemorating his birthday.

Lincoln, however, was more human (and interesting) than his statue. Lincoln, as the legends say, did work his way up from virtually nothing to become a successful lawyer, assemblyman, one-term congressman, and eventually president. His father could hardly write, which caused Lincoln to be ashamed of him. He did not even attend his father's funeral. Lincoln himself had a little more than a year of formal schooling. While we have had many presidents in recent years that came from humble backgrounds, it's hard to imagine a man of his education, upbringing, and limited political experience reaching the oval office today.

Lincoln loved telling jokes, some of which would be considered a bit dirty by his society's standards. But he would also suffer from intense bouts of depression where he would go into self-imposed isolation for long periods of time. Some believe that he may have had bipolar disorder or suffered from manic depression. His family life could also be stormy, with his wife Mary suffering from even more serious mental issues than he. These became even more serious after the death of one of their sons, with Mary sometimes conducting séances in hopes of speaking once again to her lost child. Imagine if a story like this

124

leaked out about the current first lady in our current political and media environment. The Lincolns would hardly be seen as good promoters of family values. The fact that Lincoln did not attend church and did not fit any conventional description of a Christian would not help either.

Of course, you could argue that it is unfair to judge him by his personal life or background. Instead, he should be judged by his behavior in the political arena. But even as a public figure and politician, some faults can easily be found. Throughout the political career of this "Great Emancipator," he would make public statements indicating that he did not necessarily believe in racial equality. He once famously said that his opposition to slavery's expansion to the West did not mean that he supported the idea of interracial marriage. When he started laying out reconstruction plans toward the end of the war, these plans did not include much in the way of aid for the former slaves he is given so much credit for setting free. When he first became president, a job he would have never dreamed of getting just a few years earlier, he was somewhat indecisive and insecure at times. When his generals during the early years of the Civil War often failed to take decisive and effective action, Lincoln did not feel confident enough to take more direct charge of the war. He was not particularly popular through much of his presidency, and he was nervous about his prospects for winning reelection in 1864. It was only after his assassination, along with the successful result of the Civil War, that he started to become one of the most beloved men in our history.

My goal is not to trash this man with whom I almost share a birthday. He definitely grew into the job of president, and many historians rank him as the greatest chief executive in our nation's history. No president of the future is likely to have a resume that includes achievements as impressive as abolishing slavery and saving the Union. He was also a man who showed the capacity to evolve. (Karl Rove would have labeled him a "flip-flopper.") He grew from a man who believed that abolishing slavery was impractical to the president who pushed through the 13th Amendment. This man with no military experience, who was subject to torturous bouts of depression, was also willing to stay the course until the war's bitter end, leading the nation through the most deadly conflict in its history.

If he had lived to see Reconstruction through, would he have eventually supported plans to help ex-slaves transition more effectively to their new lives? Would he have evolved in the same way as he did with the abolition issue, learning through experience that more needed to be done to help the ex-slaves? Or would he have realized that his goal of peacefully reconstructing the Union could only be achieved if the South was not pushed too hard toward accepting real racial equality? Unfortunately, his presidency was ended by an assassin's bullet, and he never had the chance to finish the process that he started. Lincoln is therefore frozen in time, revered for the Northern victory and the end of slavery, but not held responsible for the problems involved in transitioning to a post-Civil War America.

No man could ever live up to the Lincoln legend. Like all presidents, he was a flawed human being living in flawed times. Sometimes he had to say things to attract votes, and he was compelled to settle for the practical instead of the ideal. Still, he was one of those rare political figures who rose to the occasion, evolved, and was able in some cases to rise above his society's (and his own) limitations and prejudices. His imperfections, rather than tarnishing his saintly image, make his achievements more impressive. If a flawed person like him could have moments of greatness, maybe there is hope for our current politicians and, more importantly, for ourselves.

28. Reconstruction: Success or Failure?

It's hard to imagine what it must have been like to be a slave freed at the end of the Civil War. Suddenly, your entire life was no longer dictated by the whims of your master. Family and friends would no longer be sold, never to be seen again. There was finally a possibility that your future could hold more than backbreaking work with the fruits of your labor going to someone else. For the first time in your life, you knew what it meant to have hope.

But this initial euphoria, I suspect, would not last for long. Freedom brought new opportunities, but it also came with new questions and responsibilities. Most likely you had no money, no place to live, little or no education, and limited job skills. You also lived in the South, a region thoroughly disrupted and sometimes devastated by the Civil War. And as bad as slavery was, you were at least protected by the fact that your owner considered you a valuable piece of property. Now, if you were the victim of violence, or if you had no way to meet your basic needs, it is likely that no one would care. Southerners, bitter about their defeat and the complete disruption of their way of life, were likely to view ex-slaves as convenient scapegoats.

Clearly, ex-slaves needed some help if they were to successfully transition to their new lives as "freedmen." Part of what they needed was basic legal and police protections. A political faction nicknamed the "Radical Republicans," who controlled both the federal and Southern state governments in the years immediately following the war, was able to pass some laws and amendments designed to give ex-slaves basic rights. Enforcement of these legal protections, of course, was another matter. Union soldiers occupying the South could not be everywhere, and they could not continue to police the South forever.

But even if the rules on paper were completely translated into reality, ex-slaves faced a fundamental economic problem.

They needed to know where their next meal was coming from. The federal government could have provided adequate economic assistance in order to get them started. For instance, they could have provided each ex-slave with a certain amount of cash in order to get by for a while. Convincing enough Northerners to go along with this policy, however, would be difficult. At this point in history, federal welfare of any kind was essentially nonexistent. Those dollars would have to come from somewhere, and Northerners were already exhausted by the unprecedented levels of taxation that took place during the war. Expecting white Northerners to finance significant amounts of federal aid to ex-slaves would be quite a stretch in the late 1860's. Asking Southern state governments to do the same would create even more anger, and many of these states lacked resources anyway. Just like today, it was much cheaper to pass laws than it was to provide economic aid. But as anyone experiencing extreme poverty knows, theoretical civil rights don't mean very much when you are hungry.

There was, however, a simpler solution. Since slaves were often very experienced working the land, why not divide up some of the land of the South and distribute it to ex-slaves. As people who worked the land for generations without reaping the benefits, it was only fair that they should get a cut of the plantation owner's wealth that they did so much to create. It would also be more of a long-term solution than government handouts, and it would cost the United States government little or nothing in terms of cash. Just provide them with some seed, and let them work to support themselves.

There was a fundamental problem with this land reform plan, a problem that prevented it from being carried out on any significant scale. If you divide up some of the land and hand it out to ex-slaves, the previous owners, who were angry enough about the outcome of the war, were going to be completely livid. The Civil War, which had been won by the United States with such a tremendous cost, might start all over again. And this time, it would be more of a guerilla war, with Southerners possibly utilizing some of the tactics reminiscent of the insurgents of Vietnam, Iraq, and Afghanistan.

If you asked Abraham Lincoln what he was fighting for during the Civil War, the answer was simple: save the Union. To Lincoln and the overwhelming majority of Americans, slaves were of secondary concern. The decision to free the slaves was only carried out in order to achieve victory. Initially, President Lincoln was reluctant to make this decision. It was not a particularly popular option, largely because most Northerners feared the aftermath. Where are these people going to go? How are they going to support themselves? What will happen to Northern businesses that profit either directly or indirectly from slavery? They never really resolved these questions. Laws and amendments that looked nice on paper would require a large investment from the North in order to actually carry them out, an investment that would likely antagonize the South. And any significant effort to deal with the fundamental economic problems of ex-slaves would either cost too much in terms of Northern wealth or completely embitter the South. If the rights of ex-slaves were made the priority, then the goal of saving the Union would not be realized.

Many historians view the era of Reconstruction as a failure. In terms of the efforts made to help ex-slaves, it is hard to disagree with them. And after a short time, these efforts that were never adequate came to an end. As white Southerners began participating politically in larger numbers, Republicans lost their hold on Southern states. The Democratic Party in the South, at this point in history, was the white superiority party. In the North, many Americans grew tired of military forces occupying the South and of efforts to promote civil rights. Other priorities – settling the West, promoting further industrial growth – took precedence over aid to ex-slaves. Civil rights for African-Americans, after all, were never a high priority for most Northerners. The North was not exactly a place that had anything resembling racial equality.

So as the Republican Party declined in the face of a resurgent south and Democratic Party, ex-slaves began losing whatever friends they had in government. In 1876, after a disputed election in which the Republican Rutherford B. Hayes was declared the winner even though he lost, a deal was cut in order to gain Democratic acceptance of this "election." Once Hayes was inaugurated, whatever was left of the United States army withdrew from the South, and from that point forward, the federal

129

government essentially left the South alone. Segregation, voting restrictions, lynching of ex-slaves, and sharecropping would follow. Because of their lack of economic resources, large numbers of ex-slaves found themselves renting from the white landowning class. Black sharecroppers, along with many whites in the same situation, were often stuck in a cycle of debt that would last for generations. Some ex-slaves left the South, but most preferred sharecropping to the dangers and difficulties of traveling through the South toward an uncertain future in the North or the West.

Calling Reconstruction a failure, however, is only a half-truth. Because the South was allowed to once again control its own destiny and set up a new system of racial superiority, the nation was able to reconcile (more or less) and avoid any future civil wars. In the end, the country had to make a choice: you could either put the country back together, or you could push hard to help ex-slaves transition to their new lives. For most white Americans, this was a relatively easy choice. President Lincoln, who was assassinated shortly before the war officially ended, did not live to see Reconstruction. Had he lived, he would have most likely led the country toward achieving his primary goal: saving the Union. When the war was winding down, after all, Lincoln was clearly promoting a "forgive and forget" philosophy, and he proposed little that specifically addressed the rights and needs of ex-slaves. It is nice to think that Lincoln may have evolved, just as he had when eventually becoming an abolitionist. Maybe he would have realized that more needed to be done to help ex-slaves, and that these actions were worth the cost. We will never know.

It would be eighty years before we would see another push for African-American civil rights. In the 1950's and 1960's, the Supreme Court and Congress would overturn past decisions and policies, declaring segregation and racial discrimination unconstitutional. But when you consider the level of Southern hostility toward these actions that existed in the mid-twentieth century, you can understand why the federal government backed away from civil rights in the years right after the Civil War, a time when Southern resistance would have been even more intense. So the South was able to hang on to white racial superiority for decades.

Unfortunately for the South, it would also languish far behind the North economically for many decades. This was partly the result of the damage inflicted by the Civil War, and by the fact that the North began the process of industrialization decades before the South. It is my belief, however, that the South blew a tremendous opportunity. Millions of black Southerners had never been given the opportunity to build a better life for themselves. After the war, they finally had that chance. But instead of tapping into this potential economic resource, the South largely snuffed it out in the name of white racial superiority. Racism, in addition to being unjust, is just plain stupid. It can be, however, a terrific instrument for maintaining social stability. By keeping poor black and white Southerners divided along racial lines, what had previously been the plantation owning class could maintain their dominance over the rural south. It makes me wonder what opportunities our society may be squandering, and what injustices we may be tolerating, in the name of maintaining stability and protecting the status quo.

Part Six: Reform Movements of the Late 19th – Early 20th Centuries

29. From Housewife to Reformer to Feminist

The term "housewife" is a relatively modern concept. Back when most people were farmers, there was no distinction between housework and other forms of work. Everyone in the family had certain tasks to complete around the farm. But as the industrial revolution developed and spread, men increasingly left the home environment in order to work for money and purchase the things that in the past were often produced at home. And for America's growing middle class, the ideal situation was for a man to make enough income so that his wife could focus on parenting and his kids could acquire the education necessary to be middle class (or better) themselves someday. So in this middle class ideal, a woman's place was "in the home."

With the feminist movement of the 1960's, many women aspired to be more than "just" a housewife. Instead of finding fulfillment primarily through family, many felt that they, like men, should have the opportunity to gain a sense of achievement, independence, and meaning by building successful careers. The "housewife" seemed to be an archaic leftover from an age in which women were kept oppressed, ignorant, and dependent on men. Cleaning house and caring for children did not lead to either income or power, so if women wanted to be more than second-class citizens, then they needed to succeed in what had previously been a man's world.

But when the concept of the middle-class "housewife" evolved in the early to mid-19th century, people did not see it as a second-class vocation. Instead, men and women believed that good mothers were of vital importance. Without good mothers, children would not grow up developing the freedom-loving, democratic, (protestant) Christian values that were crucial to our new nation's future. So if people had the economic means to do so, women were expected to invest themselves fully into parenting.

Paradoxically, the pressure put on women to fulfill this housewife role would eventually increase their involvement in the public sphere. When most people were farmers living in fairly isolated, rural areas, parenting was largely a task performed at home. There were, after all, a limited number of people and social forces that could impact children in rural areas. But as increasing numbers of people found themselves over time living in towns and cities, and as children in these areas spent considerable time away from home attending school, children were now exposed to so much more than rural kids. And particularly in big cities, which became increasingly common by the mid-19th century, they were surrounded by a host of social problems: crowding, pollution, poor sanitation, crime, etc. To be a good parent, you could not merely wait at home until the children returned, hoping that they came back both safe and free of too much influence from the sins of the city. In order to protect and properly raise children, parents needed to step out of the home and work to clean up these urban environments. And since so much of the parenting responsibility was placed on women, they increasingly became involved in social reform movements, essentially playing the role of the "mother of society."

In becoming pioneers for reform, however, women were not only fulfilling their role as responsible parents. They were also responding to moral standards that were much higher for women than those for men. For if a woman "sinned" in certain ways – drinking, extramarital sex, gambling, foul language, etc. – society viewed her actions much more harshly than it would with men. To a certain degree, men were almost expected to do these things. "Boys will be boys," after all. But if someone ever used the equivalent phrase "girls will be girls" in response to a woman who was "sowing her wild oats," people would respond in shock. Even today, in our post-feminist era, double standards still exist to a certain degree. These social expectations are even embedded into our language. For example, if a woman is known for "sleeping around," Americans have a host of terms for this person: slut, tramp, whore, loose, skank, etc. With men, however, the language has no equivalent terms. Sometimes, because of the lack of negative terms for a promiscuous man, we simply place the word man in front of the negative terms used for women, such as "man slut," "man whore," or whatever the term of choice. For while women are expected to protect their feminine virtue, men are expected to pursue women in an attempt to give their male virtue away at the first opportunity.

Given the higher moral expectations for women, it is not surprising that they would often take it upon themselves to do something about the evils of society. Many 19th century reform movements, in fact, can be traced back to the early 1800's religious revivalism that swept through evangelical churches, institutions in which women participated in higher numbers than men. So whether the issue was alcohol abuse, slavery, public health, poverty, or the many social ills in the increasingly populated cities, women played a central role. And since poor women were often busy working, and rich women were more sheltered from society's social problems, it was often middle-class women, society's full-time parents, who were pioneers for reform.

Over time, through their efforts to alleviate this variety of problems, women came to realize that they also needed to fight for themselves. The seeds for the first women's rights convention, in fact, can be traced back to an anti-slavery convention a few years before. As active abolitionists, some American women attempted to be seated as delegates at the "World's Anti-Slavery Convention" in London in 1840. But instead of being welcomed as fellow soldiers for the cause, many of the supposedly noble-minded, abolitionist men from England and other European nations objected to these women participating. Some men, however, disagreed, recognizing the irony of holding a convention to eliminate slavery while relegating women to a second-class status. For days, these women were forced to listen as the men debated the question of whether or not women should be seated. As they sat there listening to these men decide their fate, it became increasingly obvious what had to be done. In 1848, the first Women's Rights Convention was held in Seneca Falls, New York. At this convention, these women activists drafted the "Declaration of Sentiments," a document modeled after the American Declaration of Independence. Only in this document, men were inserted in place of the British king, and women replaced the American colonists as the objects of oppression. And all that they essentially asked for were the same basic legal rights enjoyed by men, including the rights to own property when married, have equal employment and education opportunities, be free from physical abuse, and vote.

It would be decades before significant progress was made in many of these areas. In the late 19th - early 20th centuries, even as women continued to involve themselves in a variety of reform movements, including the fight for their basic rights, the battle for women's suffrage often received the most attention. Without a political voice, there were limitations on what women could ultimately achieve. And as the role of government grew, particularly during the Progressive Era of the early 20th century, the desire to vote only grew stronger. Finally, in 1920, more than 70 years after that first women's rights convention, the 19th Amendment was ratified. After decades of women contributing so greatly to social reform movements and engaging in political activism, the male-controlled government and society finally officially recognized that women had a role to play in the public sphere.

Over the next forty-five years, the roles and status of women would fluctuate depending on circumstances. In the 1920's, after gaining the right to vote and contributing in so many important ways to American efforts in World War I, the so-called "New Woman," or "flapper," emerged among the urban middle-class. These women openly challenged the social conventions and double standards of earlier eras, openly joining the "Roaring '20's" lifestyle by drinking and smoking in public, dancing to the "wild" jazz music, and cutting their hair and skirts short. They also challenged the notion that women should get married and start raising children as quickly as possible. In the 1930's, survival took precedence over challenging social norms, but when World War II began, women entered the workforce in even higher numbers than World War I, with women actively recruited to perform jobs typically filled by men. But when the war ended, the propaganda campaign shifted, with women strongly encouraged to stop working and focus their attention on home and family. People feared that if the women did not leave the workforce, the country would have a wave of unemployed ex-soldiers, triggering memories of the Great Depression. The 1950's sitcom housewife replaced "Rosie the Riveter" as the cultural ideal. It seemed that the 19th century notion of the middle-class housewife was making another comeback.

But in the 1960's, as part of a wave of social protest sweeping the country, women began challenging the notion that they should all find fulfillment in the traditional role of wife and mother. By the end of the decade, the federal government formally declared that the same rules protecting ethnic minorities from racial discrimination also protected women from gender discrimination. And as society over the ensuing decades has become more comfortable with the notion of female doctors, lawyers, politicians, business owners, police officers, executives, engineers, professors, and scientists, we have become closer to the ideal laid out in that first Women's Rights Convention more than 160 years ago. As has been demonstrated repeatedly throughout history, efforts to bring about social reform can often take decades, or even centuries, to reap any lasting benefits.

I am glad that my two daughters have been born into a country where they have the opportunity to fulfill their dreams. I also recognize, however, that history does not always go in a straight line, and that periods of reform can be followed by eras of regression. Human rights do not necessarily improve steadily over time, and old prejudices can die hard. History is also filled with examples of men actively engaged in screwing up the world and women left to deal with the mess. This is why I hope that as time passes, women continue to increase their presence in vital positions of political and economic leadership. Since women have more than proven that they are capable, and many of us men have consistently proven our incompetence, how could it hurt to have more women in charge?

So if my daughters seek to become the leaders of the future, more power to them. But if they decide to focus their attention on raising children or finding that right mix of family life and career, my wife and I will do our best to be supportive as well. There is definitely something to be said for having a parent at home with young kids. (Although there is no reason why that has to be the mom and not the dad.) Whatever they choose, we will encourage them to develop the capacity to stand on their own two feet and make their own decisions. The last thing that we want is for them to find themselves someday overly dependent on a man and judging themselves by chauvinistic standards. I also have no desire to see the United States, or any other country for that matter, degenerate back into a place where women are severely limited in their choices.

30. Is it Time for a Third Party?

Whenever elections draw near in the United States, I often find myself trying to care. Like many Americans who are not blinded by extreme partisanship, I am a bit disillusioned by both of the major parties. Neither seems willing to propose the specific, concrete measures necessary to get our country back on a firm foundation for the future. Asking for real, significant sacrifices - infrastructure investment; spending cuts on big budget programs such as defense, Medicare, and Social Security; and/or tax hikes - does not win elections.

So at times like these, I daydream about having an option beyond same-old versus same-old. There is no reason, after all, why Americans should feel obligated to vote for candidates from the two dominant parties. At times in the past, third party movements have had a certain amount of success. In the 1890's, for example, struggling farmers from western states became fed up with the two major parties that took little interest in their problems. So they decided to form a party for the people, the Populist Party, to elect representatives who would support policies designed to help average people, namely farmers and the industrial working class. In 1892, they had some success in local elections, particularly in western states. Their presidential candidate came nowhere close to winning, but he was able to win almost 10% of the popular vote and even get a handful of electoral votes. This was not bad for a new party, and they hoped to have even more success in 1896.

But then something happened to put a damper on their plans. The Democrats nominated a man named William Jennings Bryan as their presidential candidate. He was by no means a Populist, but the persona that he presented and his campaign style made it seem that he was an advocate for the little people. He even took one of the Populist Party's big issues, increasing the money supply through the coinage of silver (in addition to gold), and made it his own. So now the Populists were in a bind. Should they nominate their own candidate who supported all of their policies but was also guaranteed to lose? Or should they back up Bryan because he was at least better than the Republican alternative, a "same-old" candidate named William McKinley? Putting up a separate Populist candidate, after all, would take away more votes from Bryan than McKinley. So they backed up Bryan, and, as you might expect, he lost by a wide margin. As is often the case, the big corporations did whatever they could to assure the victory of the candidate perceived as more friendly toward business.

If you are instinctively a fan of the little guy, this is one of many sad stories in which the average people were crushed by the powers that be. If a third party starts to have some success, the major parties will co-opt one or more of their ideas in order to draw their members away. The prospect of having a chance of victory is often too tempting for third party members to resist, and they go back to choosing the lesser of the two evils. The story, however, is neither so simple nor depressing. The Populist Party may have died out as a political party, but many of the ideas in its platform lived on. So if you look up the Populist Party platform in a history book or on Wikipedia, you will find that all of their policy proposals, to a certain degree, were implemented during the early 20th century. They may have lost the electoral battles of the late 1800's, but in some significant ways, they eventually won some wars.

The Populist Party has some important lessons to teach us today. First, they demonstrated that real political change can take a long time, and there will be inevitable setbacks. If you allow yourself to get discouraged by a few years (or decades) of failure, then you will not survive in politics for very long. They also showed that politics is about more than winning elections. As a political party, an organization whose primary purpose is to get its people into political office, the Populists were a miserable failure. But as a movement to bring about changes in political policy, they would eventually achieve some success. Third parties, if they are able to muster enough support, will get the attention of the major parties and consequently bring some grassroots ideas into the political mainstream. And in the end, implementing policies that improve the nation is what politics is supposed to be about. Too often, people obsess about the electoral success of their political party. But if you think that political responsibility ends when you vote, and that the world will become a significantly better place by simply replacing one major party's political officials with the other, then you have two options. You can delude yourself and filter out information that challenges your unshakeable faith in your political party, or you can face up to reality and become increasingly disillusioned over time.

Finally, the Populist Party is a reminder that social change generally comes from the grassroots. If you study the history of most of the major social movements in history – abolitionism, women's rights, labor unions, civil rights, etc. – you will find that they generally started with average people. So often, we think that average citizens do not have the ability to transform the world. History teaches, however, that average people are generally the only ones who push for change; then, eventually, leaders might act when they feel enough pressure.

The time is ripe for a third party movement. In our digital, social networking age, it is easy to get a message out to massive numbers of people without spending too much money. And the masters of the information age, America's youth, are the ones who have the most reason to be angry. They are the ones who will have to pay the mounting debts that neither major party wants to take steps to remedy. They are also the ones who tend to get the least attention from the government. As spending on Social Security and Medicare continue to mount, the youth of America receive from our government a public university system of class cuts, teacher furlough days, and rising tuitions. So young people have both the technological tools and the potential motivation to shake up the political system. A modern day youth party may not win any elections, but they might get the major parties to pay a little more attention to them.

31. Predictable Disasters

In my Modern American History courses, we read a few primary source documents related to the "Triangle Shirtwaist Company Fire" of 1911. It's the story of a factory in New York City that produced textiles on the eighth, ninth, and tenth floors of a fireproof building. Because safety codes for factories were virtually nonexistent, the building did not have adequate fire escapes or enough working elevators. Many of the doors were also typically locked in order to stop workers from taking breaks or from organizing any type of labor unrest. So when the fire started, many had nowhere to go, and the city's fire engines did not have ladders tall enough to reach these upper floors. The building's fireproof walls acted like an oven, holding in the heat and feeding the flames. Due to the heroic efforts of some, certain workers were able to escape. Others, however, burned, choked, or jumped to death. Some of the people who jumped out of the windows were writhing on the ground for a short time before they died. In all, 146 people were killed. (The story has an eerie resemblance to a larger scale disaster: the destruction of the twin towers on 9/11. The fact that people would jump from such enormous heights shows how scary the prospect of burning to death must be.) The disaster, of course, was predictable and preventable. What kinds of heartless bastards would have people working with flammable materials on those upper floors without providing a means of escape? What kind of a city, state, or national government would allow this to happen? The enormous publicity generated by this fire contributed to an already growing movement for workplace regulation and workman's compensation laws. A disaster, after all, is a terrible thing to waste.

Today, most of us take for granted the various safety codes for which people a century ago were forced to sacrifice and struggle. Yet while our safety codes have improved, we still have a tremendous capacity for allowing preventable tragedies. The past decade, in fact, could be labeled the age of the predictable disaster. For years, people voiced concern about poor airline security, and others argued that more attention and resources should be devoted toward combating a group called Al Qaeda that had already conducted major terrorist attacks against American embassies in Africa and the USS Battleship Cole. One of the most amazing things about 9/11 was the fact that it somehow managed to catch so many Americans by surprise. Prior to Hurricane Katrina, some argued that a major hurricane might put New Orleans under water due to an insufficient system of levies. Others thought this was ridiculous. We all know who was right. Prior to the financial meltdown of 2008, some worried about a looming foreclosure crisis due to the large number of insane loans that had been issued in previous years. A few even recognized that a shadow economy of unusual financial instruments based on these bad mortgages could cause a complete financial collapse. Others thought that housing prices would keep rising and the good times would never end. As has happened multiple times in American history, the bubble eventually popped. Before the major 2010 oil spill in the Gulf of Mexico, British Petroleum had a less than stellar record on both environmental and workplace safety. Memories of the Exxon Valdez spill in Alaska quickly reemerged, renewing the same old concerns about the wisdom of offshore oil drilling.

What is the next looming disaster? For some, recent earthquakes in China, Haiti, Chile, and Japan may serve as a wake up call to better prepare for the next American "big one." Being a resident of Southern California, I have been told my entire life that the only question in our state is not if the big one is coming but when. In spite of this, most Californians, like most Americans in potential disaster zones, are woefully unprepared. (How many of us have adequate earthquake kits?) And if we are so unprepared for such an obvious looming catastrophe, imagine the shock that will come when we are hit by something that we are currently choosing to not see coming.

Horrible disasters can sometimes cause something that you rarely see in the United States any more: rapid government action. After 9/11, Democrats and Republicans temporarily realized that they loved each other and rallied together to take decisive action. The effectiveness of these actions – invading Iraq, "enhanced interrogation techniques," unwarranted surveillance activities - was, to put it lightly, questionable, but these actions were definitely drastic and decisive. Drastic actions were also taken when the economy seemed at the brink of going over a cliff. Enormous sums of money were pumped into financial institutions, businesses were nationalized, and hundreds of billions more were set aside (we thought) to buy up "toxic assets." Unfortunately, most analysts that I have heard argue that the Dodd / Frank financial reform bill is far too weak to prevent future financial meltdowns. For the moment, however, we seem to have averted a complete disaster. Hurricane Katrina, of course, did not provoke as rapid a reaction as many would expect in this country. Aid did eventually come, but it truly was a national embarrassment. Even now, I have heard it reported that a big hurricane could devastate the city once again. And for some, the private and public response to the BP oil spill was similar to what occurred with Katrina. How could a company be conducting deep-water oil drilling with no proven plan for plugging the hole should something go wrong?

It is encouraging to look back and see that the government has the capacity to sometimes act decisively (and occasionally even competently) in the face of a sudden crisis. The problem, however, is that many of the biggest problems of our time will never hit us as a sudden, cataclysmic event; instead, they are creeping up on us. For years, we have known that Social Security, Medicare, and Medicaid are unsustainable programs in their current form. The looming retirement of the baby boomers and the rising cost of health care will soon make these programs insolvent. If the climate change people are right, a gradual warming trend will continue over the coming decades and may eventually have drastic effects. Because this change is gradual, many will not notice and others will continue to deny that it is caused by human activity. By the time human-induced climate change becomes an obvious reality, it may be too late to do very much about it. (I just hope that the "Global Warming Deniers" are right.) Gradually depleting supplies of fossil fuels, possible fresh water shortages, and looming budget deficits are other problems creeping up on us, and the temptation for politicians is to put them off until another day. At what point, however, will we reach a crisis point for these issues, and if (or more likely, when) we do, will enough of us realize it?

32. The First Progressives: Liberal / Conservative Hybrids

When people hear the word progressive today, different concepts might flash through their minds. Some might think of an auto insurance company with advertisements involving a hyper, slightly annoying "agent." Others might think of cutting edge people open to new ideas that can create a better world. But those who are a bit more politically astute will recognize the term as a modern substitute for the word liberal. Because conservatives have done such a great job in recent years of demonizing the "L" word, liberals in recent years started calling themselves progressives. But about a hundred years ago, when the term progressive first came into common political use, it was a reference to reformers who saw the need for major changes in American society. And while they had some liberal traits, they also had a bit of the modern conservative in them.

In the late 1800's, the American industrial revolution went into full swing. And while technological innovation brought some major benefits, it also brought some new problems. Working conditions in factories were often terrible, significant parts of cities were crowded cesspools, powerful corporations increasingly dominated economic life at the expense of smaller operators, and mass produced goods could be low quality or downright dangerous. Government at all levels, rather than offering solutions, seemed to be part of the problem, with incompetence and corruption being the order of the day. As these problems developed and festered over the course of a few decades, many people concluded that reform was absolutely necessary. In their minds, one of the fundamental problems of this new, unprecedented industrial world was the lack of any significant planning or regulation. Since this modern world had simply burst on the scene, it was not surprising that such earth-shattering changes would bring some negative, unforeseen consequences. And what worked in a largely rural, small-town society might not cut it in this new and modern age. When we were mostly a nation of independent farmers, there was no need for government to regulate most people's work conditions or the quality of the food that they ate. Unless a person was masochistic, they were not going to mistreat themselves or their families in their work environment or feed themselves garbage. People were largely on their own, and if they worked as hard as they should, then they could at least survive. And if they faced some hard times, neighbors and friends could provide sufficient, temporary help. If they could just hold on to the land, then they could make it through. But in this new world where people were interconnected in so many complex ways, and increasing numbers of people were dependent on powerful forces that they could neither understand nor control, private charity, individual hard work, and a hands-off, "laissez faire" government might not cut it any more.

Progressives, however, did not by and large advocate a government takeover of society, and they did not generally see capitalism and corporations as completely evil. Instead, they recognized the benefits that the modern world was bringing, and they wanted a society that would continue to produce these blessings. But they also believed it was possible to clean up a few of the negative byproducts of modern industrial life, and they planned to use the cutting edge, scientific techniques of the new age to get there. As much as possible, they wanted to fill the more active, regulatory governments that they planned to create with competent, scientifically trained people. This way, government would be filled with people able to bring some order to the chaos. So a big part of the Progressive program was government reform, clearing out the incompetent idiots who received jobs through their participation in the political machines and replacing them with a trained bureaucracy of professionals. They also thought that if you gave more power to the voters, then political officials would be held more accountable. So it was during the Progressive era that the 17th Amendment was passed giving the voters the power to elect their two state senators. Many states also created initiative, referendum, and recall procedures in order to give voters more of a direct say in the making of laws and the selection of officials. If the power of government was going to be increased, then they needed to take steps that would improve the quality of that government.

So Progressives admired the innovative, efficient, productive qualities of big business, but they also recognized that unregulated corporations were doing some nasty things. Private businesses could have chosen on their own to improve work conditions and maintain the quality and safety of the products that they produced. But in the name of maximizing profits, they did not generally take these steps, so government began stepping in to impose regulations on them. During the Progressive era, usually starting at the local government level, many of the first laws in American history were passed to provide workman's compensation, ban child labor, and set limits on workdays. They did not establish all of the workers' "rights" that we enjoy today, but these were some of the first significant steps away from the laissez faire policies of the past. In addition, the FDA was created in the early 1900's in order to ensure the safety of food and drugs. And to limit the abuses of power by some of the largest corporations in the country, the federal government for the first time began enforcing anti-trust legislation, with a few monopolies broken up in the name of promoting competition and protecting consumers. In their attitudes and actions toward big business, they sound very much like liberals / progressives today.

Big business, however, was not the only aspect of society that they intended to regulate. In the minds of Progressives, immoral behavior by the general public was as big of a problem as greedy corporations. So just as they wanted to use the power of government to impose rules on business, they intended to pass tough laws that would stamp out alcohol abuse, gambling, prostitution, and sexual immorality in general. In this sense, they sound more like hard-core social conservatives than secular, liberal, modern day progressives. And just as we see with modern conservatives, they did not see the decline of family values as the only threat to American culture. Early 20th century Progressives were also concerned about the impact of the millions of immigrants who were pouring into the United States. If these immigrants were not quickly Americanized, they posed a threat to the American way of life. Public education, which had largely emerged in order to train a workforce for a modern industrial society, would also play a vital role in assimilating the children of immigrants. As always, teaching values was as big of a part of the school system as helping kids learn to read, write, and do math. In the end, these Progressives were subject to the same nostalgia for the past that is an inherent part of a conservative outlook, looking fondly to a time when people supposedly had good, traditional values and most of them were "real Americans."

To both modern conservatives and liberals, these Progressives must sound rather strange. How could anyone be so conservative on some issues but liberal on others, trying to reconcile beliefs from the two ideological extremes? Personally, I don't see any contradiction. Whether the issue was public morality or corporate behavior, early 20th century Progressives had the same basic answer: government regulation. What I find strange is the modern notion that there is any inherent connection between issues like abortion and tax rates, health care and gun rights. Why must a person who opposes abortion be against strong environmental regulations? Why must someone who supports gay marriage be in favor of a strong safety net? The logical thing is to look at each issue separately, not to accept blindly the so-called conservative and liberal agendas as a whole. In my mind, those who are either liberal or conservative on everything are the walking contradictions. On some issues – economic regulation in particular – liberals are in favor of a strong government, but on social issues, they are more in favor of a "live and let live" policy. Conservatives, on the other hand, tend to support big government when it comes to national security and defending traditional values while opposing strong regulation of business. So the question is not which side supports big government. They just disagree on the specific situations in which a strong government is necessary.

Early 20th century Progressives definitely had their weaknesses. They could be arrogant, intolerant, and narrow-minded when it came to people who did not share their traditional, protestant, middle-class, and "American" values. Like many people today, they could also romanticize a mythological past, editing out aspects of history inconsistent with their ideology. In addition, they had an excessive faith in government's ability to impose its will on the American people and to improve their lives. Because their experiences demonstrated the dangers of a government that did not do much of anything, they did not foresee the problems that excessive government could bring: stifling regulations, increasing taxes, abuse of power, etc. Because we have experienced decades of big government in one form or another, many today have concluded that government is more of a problem than an answer. But even today, few want to go back to the late 1800's era of virtually no government regulation at all.

Those first self-proclaimed Progressives managed to incorporate within a single philosophy the distinct weaknesses of modern people on both sides of the ideological spectrum. But if nothing else, they were consistent. They admitted to believing that government regulation was the answer to America's problems, and in some ways, these policies brought some measurable improvements. They also demonstrated that seemingly contradictory ideas are not in as much conflict as we may often assume. And if they were able to reconcile some of what is the best and the worst in all of us into a single philosophy, then maybe compromise is still possible today.

Part Seven: The 1920's and the Great Depression

33. Car Culture

I have mixed feelings about automobiles. On the one hand, I love the convenience of owning my own car. It's the only form of mechanized transportation where you have complete control. You are not required to follow any pre-set schedule in order to get around, and you can blast whatever music or news program you want from the radio as you travel. When the car breaks down, I am truly reminded of how completely dependent I am on this (generally reliable) traveling machine.

I am not, however, one of those people who has a deep relationship with his car. I don't treat it as some sort of a pampered pet, washing and waxing the thing every other day. Car maintenance and alteration are also not hobbies, so you will never find me buying some fancy accessories or tinkering with it under the hood. If you ever have car issues, I am the last place where you would want to go for mechanical advice. I also feel no need or desire to go out and get the latest thing in order to make a statement about my social class, personality, or sexual prowess. My long-term plan is to drive my current thirteen-year old car into the dirt, avoiding car salesmen, payments, and jacked up insurance rates for as long as possible. It is a good thing that I am already married. Rather than being a "chick magnet," my car probably functions more as a female repellant.

As a resident of Southern California, I also find cars at times to be a major annoyance. For one thing, cars are the only mechanized transportation devices that they will let anybody operate. This is a scary scenario when you consider the significant percentage of morons that make up the human species. And even when the drivers around me operate their vehicles in a relatively competent fashion, the sheer volume of cars can be very irritating, particularly if I find myself on a freeway between the hours of 7-10 AM and 3-7 PM on a weekday. In this traffic capitol of the United States, there are times when a car feels more like a trap than the ultimate source of freedom and mobility. The landscape in Southern California is also in many cases not particularly attractive. Asphalt is everywhere, with more physical space

151

devoted to parking lots than just about anything else. No other form of transportation has ever come close to competing with automobiles in terms of impact on the physical terrain. In order to have the luxury of driving to any location and parking relatively close to where we want to end up, pavement must be virtually everywhere. Sometimes, it's easy to forget what nature actually looks like. For the modern urban American, cars and asphalt are as much of a part of the natural world as the sun, moon, and stars. And for a person in Los Angeles, the sky is a hazy, grayish color, and the air is not always conducive to breathing.

It's easy to forget what a recent development our car society really is. Prior to World War I, cars were basically a luxury item for the wealthy. Even if you owned one, there were limited places where you could actually take the thing. But after the war, with the advent of Henry Ford's assembly lines, car ownership was more in reach for the average American. Soon, the car would become one of many technologies over history that quickly transitioned from luxury to necessity. The 1920's, with its economic boom and flowering consumer culture, is impossible to imagine without cars at the center. On so many levels, the explosion of the auto industry stimulated economic development. The industry's need for roads, raw materials, repair shops, gas stations, replacement parts, insurance companies, car loans, and other goods and services became integral to modern industrial life. If cars suddenly ceased to exist, countless industries would cease to function and jobs would be lost. To this day, millions of Americans owe their survival to the continued existence of this one technology.

Some believed in those early days that the car would help to resolve somewhat urban problems such as congestion and pollution. People could now spread out, no longer required to cluster homes and businesses near the public transportation lines. It did not take long to get over this delusion. Over time, suburbs evolved more into full-fledged cities, and the downtown areas that were once the economic hub of urban areas fell into decline. And while suburbs were often more car friendly than older urban areas since they were designed with automobiles in mind, they became distinctly less rural looking over time. With this, the idea that you could live in a neighborhood resembling the country and shop, work, and be entertained in the city also faded. Southern

California, for instance, is a giant sprawling mass of a city, with the distinction between so-called suburbs of Los Angeles and the downtown neighborhoods blurred over time.

Henry Ford, the man who helped make much of this possible, eventually became a bit outdated. He viewed the car as a machine designed to take you from point A to point B. General Motors, however, realized that cars could be so much more. Through their various car divisions and models, they began offering different cars for different types of people, including (among many brands and divisions) Cadillacs for the rich, Buicks for the not quite rich, and Chevrolets for the working class. They also frequently came out with new models, encouraging consumers to go out and buy the latest thing. Cars became a combination of a status symbol, pet, friend, hobby, and roving house. I can think of no other machine that holds a place in the heart of Americans comparable to an automobile. Even for a non-car fanatic like me, there is an emotional connection to my car. Whenever I sell a car and watch it drive off for the last time, I find myself holding back the tears.

Like everything else in modern industrial life, we are in uncharted territory when it comes to our transportation system. There is no way to know how long our car society with its dependence on petroleum can last. If the global warming people are right, there will come a time in the not so distant future when the reality of climate change is undeniable, and we will be forced out of necessity to use alternatives to the internal combustion engine. And even if they are wrong about the devastating effects of climate change, fossil fuels are a finite resource, and new techniques for oil extraction may not be sufficient to meet global demand. Whether the future will see an increased reliance on public transport or cars fueled by lithium batteries, hydrogen fuel cells, or some other energy source/technology is anybody's guess. Of course, there are many forces out there that are resistant to change. Because so much has been invested into the infrastructure of fueling and producing cars, alternative types of vehicles still find it difficult to compete. Because cars are so convenient, public transportation feels like a sacrifice. And because cars are so integrated into our very existence, many of us can hardly conceive of a world without them. But as always, change is inevitable. It's just a question of when. In the long run, our 90-year-old (and counting) car society may become a historical footnote, with petroleum dependent cars seeming as archaic to future generations as horse drawn carriages seem today.

34. The Creation / Evolution Debate and Public Education

I do not claim to have much in the way of scientific knowledge. I took a fair amount of anthropology and geography courses in my day and managed to fulfill the general education requirements for science, but I will make no attempt here to present any theories about the origins of life or of the universe. I suspect that the answers to these great questions are more interesting and complicated than anything that we humans have managed to develop, and there is a good chance that forces we define as natural and supernatural are both involved. In my mind, expecting humans to figure everything out is like waiting for an ant to figure out what the heck a human being might be. There are certain things beyond our capacity. But what do I know. To me, existence itself is the greatest mystery.

As a history teacher, however, I am forced from time to time to confront questions about the origins of human beings and of existence in general. In my Early World Civilizations course, these issues come up when we read and discuss the creation stories of different cultures. Now for all of these stories, I present them in essentially the same way: as mythological stories designed to communicate certain basic truths. In most cases, people are fine with this perspective. But when you present the stories in the book of Genesis in this way, this may rub a lot of people in our Judeo/Christian culture the wrong way.

These potential objections, however, are based on a misunderstanding of the term "myth." For many people, the word myth means "an untrue story," an oversimplification of the term. Instead, a myth is a means of communicating truth that has been used by various cultures for centuries. In fact, our method of communicating history – the type of dry expository writing that you find in textbooks – is a modern and historically unusual way to write about the past. Legends and myths have been the norm, and the people composing and listening to the stories understood this.

After all, they generally did not have the option of writing history in the way that we do. People in the past did not have access to the mass of information that is at the disposal of modern historians. So they told stories that were orally passed down and altered through succeeding generations until they might eventually be written down. Certain aspects of the stories might be loosely based on actual events, and other elements were based on what people wanted the past to be. Whatever the case, the goals were to present certain individuals of the past as role models (for good or bad), explain mysterious aspects of life, and instill the culture's values, beliefs, and traditions into the listeners.

Many Jews and Christians have no problem with this interpretation. They understand that the stories are not meant to be taken literally. They acknowledge that the world is probably more than a few thousand years old and that all life forms – including, possibly, human beings – were not created fully intact in an instant. For fundamentalists who take the Genesis stories literally, however, the theories and conclusions of scientists, archaeologists, and historians are potential threats to their worldview. So the battle rages and has been given different labels: faith vs. reason, creation vs. evolution, or science vs. scripture.

In my Modern American History course, we confront these questions and their educational implications very directly when we discuss the "Scopes Trial" of the 1920's. In this event that was one of many so-called "trials of the century," a science teacher named John Scopes was arrested for teaching that mankind descended from a lower order of animals. His behavior conflicted with a Tennessee state law, a law that was also on the books of a few other states, which stated that teaching evolution in a public school was illegal. This law, however, had not been enforced until opponents of this measure asked John Scopes if he would like to be arrested. After some hesitation, he agreed. They could now use his case to attack this anti-evolution law that they considered to be ridiculous.

So the trial had little to do with John Scopes himself. It should have been pretty straightforward. Scopes should have been asked if he taught evolution. He would then say yes. Trial over. Instead, it turned into this great media circus and entertainment event in which talented, prominent lawyers went back and forth discussing not just the merits of this law but of the whole creationist perspective. (Lots of monkey related items also went on sale in the town of Dayton, Tennessee.) The question of who won this short-term battle is subject to debate. Like all political and religious debates, most people came out believing that their side had made the better case. Over the long haul, however, many would say that the scientific perspective has won the battle in the public schools. Today, the evolutionary perspective is dominant, and people who want to bring back supernatural explanations are on the outside looking in.

Several years ago, people who called themselves "Scientific Creationists" argued that there was scientific evidence to support the fundamentalist Christian perspective. They also argued that there were holes in evolutionary theory, and these holes should not simply be glossed over. Forcing students to listen only to the evolutionary perspective was no different than banning evolution back in the 1920's. If scientists really believe in free thought, they should not be threatened by the idea of presenting alternative theories in public school science classrooms.

There were a couple of major problems with Scientific Creationism, however. First, as I mentioned earlier, there are many Christians who do not take Genesis literally, and they would argue, like most scientists, that evidence for a literal interpretation is pretty flimsy at best. A second, even greater difficulty in my mind was the First Amendment. Because Scientific Creationism was so blatantly pushing the perspective of a specific religion, it would seem to violate the provision banning the government from promoting the "establishment of religion."

People eventually found a way, it seemed, to get around both of these problems. Today, "Intelligent Design" is the new movement to bring the supernatural back into the science classroom. Advocates of Intelligent Design argue that evolutionary theory, which credits the random process of natural selection with creating the world as we know it, is unable to explain certain things, particularly the existence of life itself. In their minds, highly complex life forms originating and evolving into such a wide variety of species could not have possibly happened by pure chance. There must be some kind of a supernatural designer guiding the process. This perspective has two major advantages

157

over Scientific Creationism. First, you are not limited to providing evidence for a fundamentalist interpretation of the book of Genesis. You can now bring in both Christians and members of other religious faiths who might believe that the earth is billions of years old and who accept a certain amount of evolution. They would argue that evolution, instead of being purely random, has been guided by a "designer" working "behind the scenes." Now, by bringing in people from many different religious perspectives, you can claim that you are in compliance with the First Amendment. Intelligent Design, by not promoting a specific religious faith, can be accepted by all people who believe in anyone or anything supernatural.

Intelligent Design supporters make a good case. Teachers in science classes should point out the things that scientists are unable to explain. It would also be legitimate to point out that many people turn to spirituality when dealing with things not yet explainable. Inserting an intelligent designer (or designers) to fill these gaps in knowledge, however, goes beyond the scope of science. Science, by definition, is a discipline in which people seek knowledge through experiment and observation. An Intelligent Designer, by definition, is supernatural, which means that he (or she, or it, or they) is not subject to physical observation. Theories beyond the scope of scientific observation do not belong in a science class.

This does not mean, however, that religious explanations should be kept entirely out of public schools. What the Scientific Creationist and Intelligent Design theories demonstrate, more than anything else, is the degree to which the scientific perspective has become dominant. People feel that if an idea is to be considered credible, it must be backed by scientific evidence. What we have forgotten is that science is only one path to knowledge. Philosophy, mysticism, and the use of metaphor are also approaches one can take when trying to answer life's great questions. These also happen to be approaches that have been in wider use throughout history than the scientific method. If we overemphasize science, we lose touch with a part of our nature. I would argue, then, that religious ideas should be presented and discussed in public school literature, humanities, philosophy, religious studies and art classes as legitimate options. (Although no single religious option should be emphasized or promoted in any way.) Of course, it would be necessary to offer these subjects in grammar and secondary schools in order to make these ideas known, something that I also think should be done in our overly "practical" educational system.

In my Modern American History class, I always end our discussion of the Scopes Trial with two simple questions: Why did people care so much about this case, and why are people still so passionate about the creation vs. evolution issue? There may be several valid explanations for this phenomenon, but I think it largely comes down to something very simple. When the Scopes Trial occurred in the 1920's, the country was going through a period of major social change. "Flappers" challenging traditional rules of behavior for women, an emerging youth culture, and the growing influence of a mass media seemed to threaten traditional values. Excessive drinking (in spite of Prohibition), "wild" jazz music, and reckless spending on new consumer goods made it seem that people were seeking nothing but pleasure. Concerns about the influence of communists and foreigners, fears leftover from the World War I era, made people wonder if American culture itself was under siege. (Sound familiar?) During times of fear and change, people often cling to traditional values. Seemingly, if scientists had their way, then the Christian belief system that was such a central part of traditional American culture would be wiped out. And if people lose the fear of God, then the rampant immorality of the 1920's would only get worse. After all, if there is no promise of a reward in heaven or threat of a punishment in hell, then what's the point of being good?

The human race is in a sorry state if the only reason that people are good is the prospect of getting a reward or avoiding punishment. On some level, maybe we all know that the things labeled as bad are actually good, and we would all go out and experience all the sex, alcohol, and gambling binges that we could if we knew that there were no eternal consequences. There may not be enough atheists in the world to conduct a case study in order to determine if this is true. If it is true, however, then the Christians may be right about human nature. Maybe we are inherently sinful, and we have a limited capacity to figure things out. Whatever the case, the creation/evolution struggle will rage on into the foreseeable future. In the mean time, I will try to focus on becoming a better and a wiser human being (just for the hell of it).

35. Herbert Hoover vs. Franklin Roosevelt: The Ongoing Struggle

In 1928, Herbert Hoover won the presidential election in a landslide, taking 58% of the popular vote and winning all but eight states. As Secretary of Commerce in the previous administration, Hoover, along with the Republican Party in general, was rewarded for the unprecedented economic prosperity of the 1920's. Their "laissez faire" style of governing, guided by the philosophy that whatever was good for business was good for America, seemed to be working very well. And when times are good, the public is happy to have government stay out of their lives, keeping taxes low, regulations lax, and allowing capitalism to thrive and prosper.

But all was not well during this so-called new era of permanent prosperity. The nation as a whole was wealthier than ever before, but much of this wealth was concentrated in the hands of the richest people. With not enough wealth trickling down to the masses in the form of higher wages, and both ethnic minorities and rural Americans cut off from much of this prosperity, purchasing power for average Americans was somewhat limited. For a while, increased access to credit through installment buying made up for some of this lack of income, but excessive borrowing would eventually put financial institutions at risk. The stock market, which had grown by the 1920's into a more significant economic institution, reached record highs partly through the same kind of risky borrowing. Corporations, protected by high tariffs and a government no longer interested in breaking up monopolies, had less incentive to be more efficient or make goods somewhat more affordable. And in this era of unprecedented optimism, companies kept expanding production under the assumption that the following year would be even better than the last.

The country was set up for a fall, a collapse that was triggered by the stock market meltdown of October 1929. But this was just the beginning. During that initial crash, the Dow Jones Industrial Average dropped by about 40%. By the summer of 1932, it had dropped approximately 85% from its 1929 peak. The disintegration of the stock market and the U.S. economy, therefore, did not happen virtually overnight. And most economists would agree that the initial financial crisis did not have to turn into a general depression. What ultimately killed the economy was the collapse of the banking sector, a collapse only partially caused by the initial stock market disaster. Because of risky lending, and panic from a general public that wanted to pull their money out of banks before their savings were all gone, banks began to go under. And in an era before the existence of the Federal Deposit Insurance Corporation, a failure of a bank ruined its depositors. So once this process of collapsing banks started, the dominoes started to fall. People lost their savings, and less money was available to lend to consumers, leading to less spending. Companies had inventory that they could not sell, so they scaled back production and laid people off. Unemployed people could not buy much, and some had loans that they could not repay, triggering more problems for banks and producers of goods. This feedback loop then repeated itself over and over, and the economy spiraled downward.

Drastic action was needed immediately after the initial stock market crash in order to stop the implosion of the financial sector. Unfortunately, Herbert Hoover and the Republican dominated Congress were ideologically opposed to drastic government action. Hoover, however, was not the do-nothing caricature of a president that so many people grew to hate. He sat down with business leaders and tried to get them to refrain voluntarily from layoffs, pushed through a program for loaning money to the financial sector and railroad companies, and even started programs of public works and limited direct aid. But these actions were not nearly enough to stop the bleeding, and some of his policies, such as raising tariffs to an even higher level and supporting income tax increases in 1932, made the situation even worse. And the Federal Reserve, which played such a huge role in trying to stave off a 2008-2009 depression, was too worried about maintaining a stable currency to infuse the economy with a massive amount of cash. Even in the face of this disaster, balanced budgets and a stable dollar were seen as more important than rising unemployment and the suffering that went with it. And because Hoover was convinced that government aid led people to a state of lazy dependence and government regulation hindered economic growth, he focused most of his limited government interventions on stimulating business in the hope that the economy would ultimately correct itself. Needless to say, it didn't work.

So in 1932, Hoover was handed a defeat in the presidential election as decisive as his victory four years before. Franklin D. Roosevelt took 57% of the popular vote and won all but five states. Fed up with Hoover, much of the American public hoped that Roosevelt would be the savior. Philosophically, at least in the beginning of Roosevelt's presidency, the two men were not significantly different. Like Hoover, Roosevelt wanted to get the capitalist system back to normal, not to fundamentally change it. But as a practical politician, Roosevelt proved willing to take more drastic steps to get the economy stabilized and then moving forward again.

Much of the legislation passed during the first two years of Roosevelt's presidency was focused on stabilizing and regulating the parts of the economy that had failed most spectacularly: banking, the stock exchange, and agriculture. These were designed to increase public confidence in the financial sectors, get food prices up, and help prevent future catastrophes. After another frenzy of bank runs shortly before his inauguration, these measures were able to bring some stability, and the number of banks in existence remained fairly stable through the rest of the 1930's. But unemployment remained very high, and things were not improving fast enough. So beginning in 1935, the New Deal began to shift more heavily toward direct aid: increased relief, an expansion of public works projects, and Social Security. If people could get money in their pockets, increased consumer spending would hopefully kick start the economy and then government spending could be scaled back. Through most of the 1930's, the economy gradually grew and unemployment came down. But New Deal programs never brought the economy close to the levels before the depression started. To this day, economists and historians argue about how much these programs may have helped, hindered, or did little to affect economic growth. And during Roosevelt's time and ever since, some resented the government deficits and high tax rates on the rich that were required to pay for these programs.

Roosevelt's most impressive achievements, however, were more political than economic. For while people may disagree on his merits as a president, it is impossible to deny that he was an effective politician. Remarkably, this president who came into power during a horrible economic crisis managed to win four consecutive presidential elections. He also laid the groundwork for decades of dominance by the Democratic Party, forming a coalition of groups who tended to lean Democrat – women, ethnic minorities, the poor, and the working class – that is still somewhat intact. From 1932-1968, there was only one Republican in the White House, Dwight Eisenhower, who served for eight years. From 1932-1980, Democrats controlled the Senate and House of Representatives for 44 of the 48 years. (They continued to control the House until 1995.) Due to the improvement of the 1930's and the relative prosperity of the 1940's through the 1960's, many were convinced that Roosevelt's combination of regulation and government aid had discredited the laissez faire approach of Herbert Hoover. Even Republicans had come to accept certain aspects of the Roosevelt approach. Under Dwight Eisenhower, the interstate highway system began to be constructed, and the tax rate for the highest income bracket was 91%. Richard Nixon, who in 1968 became the second Republican president elected in 36 years, signed more liberal legislation than any president since. And few politicians considered the idea of radically changing or dismantling programs such as Social Security, the FDIC, or the Securities Exchange Commission.

But cracks in the Roosevelt approach began to show by the late 1960's and 1970's. Inflation spiraled out of control; deficits began to rise, particularly with the expansion of aid programs under Lyndon Johnson; American companies struggled to compete against upstarts in Japan and western Europe, with many blaming stifling regulations and strong labor unions for their troubles; and around the world, the United States did not seem quite as powerful as before. By the late 1970's, the time was ripe for an ex-actor and governor named Ronald Reagan to come to the rescue, a man who seemed to be straight out of the 1920's. He argued that the government was more of a problem than a solution, holding back the American economy with high taxes, excessive regulation, handouts to non-working people, and an unwillingness to combat inflation. Reagan's crushing defeat of Jimmy Carter in 1980 was reminiscent of Roosevelt's rise to power in 1932. Herbert Hoover would have felt proud and, I imagine, somewhat vindicated.

The first two years of Reagan's presidency were terrible economically. Fed chairman Paul Volcker decided to raise interest rates through the roof in order to trigger a recession and defeat inflation once and for all. It was brutal, but the policy eventually worked. And to Reagan's credit, he publicly supported the policy in spite of the damage that it did to him politically. Eventually, it was determined that inflation was under control, so interest rates were brought back down, and by 1983, the economy was turning the corner. The next twenty-five years were largely a period of economic growth, with only a couple of relatively minor recessions mixed in. And to this day, many conservatives give the "Reagan Revolution" of reduced taxes and business deregulation credit for the prosperity. In addition, they give Reagan credit for finishing off the Soviet Union through a military buildup and aid to Afghanistan, both of which helped lead to the exhaustion and ultimate disintegration of our Cold War enemy.

Critics, however, might point out that technological innovation and the expansion of global trade had more to do with our prosperity than Hoover-style "supply-side economics." Much of the so-called "Reagan Revolution" was also more rhetoric than reality. Government spending steadily increased during the Reagan years, and this symbol of fiscal conservatism oversaw an administration that never came close to balancing a budget. In addition, the prosperity of the last three decades has not been evenly spread – just like the 1920's – with increasing amounts of wealth concentrated in the hands of the richest people and a weaker safety net to help out those who are poor and/or down on their luck.

Like Franklin Roosevelt, it is difficult to determine the exact economic impact of Reagan's policies, and the debate between liberals and conservatives rages on. The political impact, however, was clear. From 1980-2008, Republicans controlled the White House for twenty of those years, the Senate for sixteen, and in 1994, they controlled the majority in the House of Representatives for the first time since 1955, maintaining that control for twelve straight years. Just a few decades before, it would have been hard to believe that a disciple of the reviled Herbert Hoover could have led such a political sea change.

But in 2008, it looked like the country might be going through another political shift. When the financial system imploded shortly before the election, many people pointed at factors similar to those that caused the 1929 crash: wealth inequality; reckless lending; a big fat bubble, this time primarily in real estate; and a government that allowed a financial free-for-all to take place with little or no regulatory oversight. So when Barack Obama easily defeated John McCain and Democrats achieved major gains in Congress, he seemed to channel Franklin Roosevelt in attempting to combat the crisis. Massive aid (which started under President Bush) was pumped into the banking sector to prevent a Depression-style financial freefall; a stimulus package combining Roosevelt-style public works projects with money to prop up various social programs; a health care reform bill designed to expand insurance coverage; and a financial reform bill which was supposed to prevent future abuses like those that caused the crisis. If Roosevelt had been around, he may have been proud of some of these measures, and the 2008 crash would probably have seemed quite familiar, vindicating his approach to governing.

But the early years of the Obama presidency were not necessarily Roosevelt circa 2000's. Many liberals complained that the stimulus package was not big enough, financial regulation was too weak, and the health care reform bill left out too many people. Many had also hoped that the new president would use his public mandate to push through tougher environmental regulations after years of Republican attempts to weaken or prevent the passage of efforts to combat climate change. The president, however, was facing some basic political difficulties. When Roosevelt became president, the country had already gone through three years of an economic meltdown that only grew worse, so it was easy to dump all of the blame on Hoover and push for drastic action. Obama, on the other hand, came to the White House before the full effects of the crisis had been felt. So Republicans could gain traction by dumping the blame for the struggling economy on him. And unlike those who tried to paint Roosevelt as a socialist in the 1930's, they had a public more receptive to the idea that Obama was a liberal, free-spending radical who wanted a government takeover of the economy. It is also important to note that the recent (and still current) crisis, as bad as it may be, has not come close (thus far) to the misery of the Great Depression. So there have been fewer desperately poor people than in the 1930's crying out for government aid.

Ultimately, for whatever reason, the failure of the deregulated financial sector did not lead to a major ideological shift in the country, and we did not see the same level of anger directed at the wealthy "fat cats" who screwed over the economy as was evident in the 1930's. Roosevelt "soaked the rich" with higher taxes to help pay for New Deal programs. Meanwhile, about one-third of the 2009 economic stimulus package consisted of temporary decreases in taxes, and the Bush era tax cuts were maintained. Clearly, as even President Obama on some level recognized, the Reagan ideology was stronger than some people thought. In 2010, Republicans regained control of the House of Representatives, and in 2011, the government spent more time talking about balancing budgets than creating jobs and stimulating economic growth. Herbert Hoover would feel right at home. (Although history indicates that he may have gone along with some tax increases as part of a deficit reduction passage.)

If Hoover and Roosevelt were around today, I am sure that they would be able to find much in the past eighty years to support their political ideology. In the case of Roosevelt, who was less fixed to an ideology than Hoover, he may have recognized some mistakes and modified his beliefs somewhat. But one thing seems certain. If they ran against each other again in either 2012 or 2016, it would be much closer than it was in 1932.

36. So You Think We Have Problems

As I write this in the fall of 2011, it is clear that we live in some difficult times. The United States, Japan, and much of western Europe are feeling the burden of government debt and the lingering effects of the global economic crisis. Meanwhile, there are many countries throughout Africa, Asia, and parts of Latin America that would gladly trade their economic situations with those of Greece, Italy, or Portugal. And even in the booming economies of China, India, and Brazil, major problems remain: environmental destruction, large populations, and huge disparities of wealth. Globally, threats such as terrorism, climate change, energy shortages, and overpopulation unify us all. It is no wonder that many people believe we are living in the "end times," and predictions regarding the exact date of Armageddon are able to gain some traction.

It may be human nature to assume that we are living in unique times with unprecedented problems. In the modern world, there is some truth to this point of view. Past generations did not have to worry about problems such as climate change, nuclear proliferation, or rising oil prices. But in most cases, the problems that we face are nothing new, with generations of human beings dealing with war, ethnic conflict, famine, disease, substance abuse, habitat destruction, and a host of other "modern" concerns. And as a general rule, most of these problems were much worse in the past. Modern technological advances in the areas of medicine, communication, production, and transportation have lessened the impact of certain types of suffering. But due to historical amnesia, along with our natural tendency to fixate on the present, it is easy to feel overwhelmed by current events and fearful about the future.

Take the United States for instance, a nation that is remarkably pessimistic these days in spite of its relative wealth and power. At the moment, unemployment hovers at around 9%, economic growth is relatively anemic, and we are seemingly facing deficits until the end of time. But while I recognize that there are a lot of Americans struggling out there, our current situation is nothing compared to financial crises of the past. During the worst of these, the Great Depression, low-end estimates for unemployment at its peak are 25%. So in other words, imagine our current financial situation with all of its problems, and then multiply them by three times. But even then, this will not fully measure the gravity of their situation. Because when the crisis started in the late 1920's, the limited, modern American social safety net – Social Security, Medicare and Medicaid, unemployment benefits, food stamps, etc. – did not yet exist. So if people lost their jobs or their banks failed, they were basically on their own, and there was no FDIC to back up their deposits. And from late 1929-1933, the crisis only grew worse. It was not until the Roosevelt administration that you saw an aggressive response from the federal government, with the beginnings of the modern welfare state resulting from these desperate times. The New Deal, however, was never able to get the country close to pre-Depression economic levels.

Due to our recent financial crisis, the Great Depression has been on a lot of people's minds. The discussion, however, has tended to focus on the causes of the mess and the effectiveness of the government response. For obvious reasons, our leaders did not want to repeat some of the same mistakes of the early 1930's. But while this is a vitally important discussion, the Great Depression must never become just an economic case study. I always tell my students that the only way to get a grasp on what the Depression was like is to hear or read the firsthand accounts of the people who lived through it. Once you hear enough stories, or possibly look at enough heartbreaking photographs from the era, it might start to sink in. Either that or you can visit or read about the current situation in nations throughout the world where people face situations that are markedly worse. In historical terms, even bad times in the United States were relatively good.

Fortunately, the Great Depression eventually came to an end. Unfortunately, it took the worst war in human history to do it. By 1943, federal spending was almost ten times higher than it was just a few years before, and this massive influx of cash and activity finally kick started the economy out of its lull. Compared to World

War II spending, the New Deal was microscopic. After years of high unemployment, there was actually a labor shortage in the United States, creating opportunities for women and ethnic minorities to perform jobs typically filled by white men. But with wartime rationing, certain consumer goods could be in short supply, and Americans were compelled to save more money than they normally would. When the war ended, after an economic downturn caused by the transition to a peacetime economy, people began to spend that money. With the United States sitting on top of the world and consumer spending high, the United States entered an era of unprecedented prosperity. In the mid-1950's, it must have been hard to believe that the Great Depression had only been fifteen years before.

That was the good news. All of that government spending created a mountain of debt even larger (as a percentage of GDP) than we face today. High taxes (particularly for the wealthy) would be in place for decades in order to pay off this debt and sustain the newly formed welfare state and defense establishment. And more importantly, approximately 420,000 Americans died in World War II, hundreds of thousands more were wounded, and countless others were psychologically scarred. Friends, parents, children, and siblings were either lost or changed for life. And these American casualties represented a small percentage of the global carnage. World War II, unlike many other "conventional" wars, involved civilians on a level rarely seen before. Cities were bombed, civilians were massacred by the millions, and many nations sustained heavy property damage. This was not just a war between soldiers on battlefields. And when it all finally ended with two atomic blasts in Japan, people must have had a sense that no person or place was completely safe anymore.

When the war finally ended, Americans did not even get a break. The Soviet Union, a nation that was our ally in World War II because we shared a common enemy, quickly became the new threat. On every level, the Soviet empire seemed to represent the opposite of what our nation stood for. The Cold War would rage for decades, with Korea, Vietnam and other battles in the not so distant future.

Today, the United States faces economic hard times, has some dangerous enemies, and finds itself at war. But on every level, our current struggles pale in comparison to those who lived through the Great Depression and World War II. Bin Laden was not Hitler, Ahmadinejad is no Stalin, modern China is not Mao's China, and the Great Recession (so far) has not evolved into anything like the Great Depression. And anyone who thinks that modern catastrophes and villains must be signs of the "end times" has apparently never cracked open a history book or talked to the (soon to be gone) people who personally experienced the Depression and World War II. (If anyone ever fit the description of the antichrist, it was Hitler.) History can be a depressing subject, but it can also give you a sense of perspective. With all of our modern troubles, I feel lucky to be living in the 21st century United States. Life could sure be a hell of a lot worse.

Part Eight: American Foreign Policy (Late 1800's – 1945)

37. Impact of the United States on the World

In the late 19th - early 20th centuries, many Americans believed in a concept called "The White Man's Burden." This was the belief that the people of Western civilization, due to their blessed civilized status, had the responsibility of helping the "non-white" people of the world advance toward civilization.

In my history classes, I show my students a classic cartoon from this era that depicts this concept. In this cartoon, you see two men, one looking like Uncle Sam and the other some type of British authority figure. Each has a basket on his back that is filled with non-white people of various societies, all of whom are drawn in a very racist fashion. These two are both climbing a mountain, and on the top of this mountain that shines like gold, you see the word "civilization." On the bottom of the mountain you see more negative words like vice, superstition, and ignorance. There they are, these symbols of the most advanced societies of the time, carrying out their duty of helping the less fortunate.

Then, immediately after showing this first cartoon, I put up a second cartoon that is clearly a parody of the first. In this second cartoon, you once again see Uncle Sam and that British authority figure. Only this time, they are sitting in the baskets, and underneath them you see non-white people carrying them forward. In this cartoon, rather than accepting a burden of responsibility, these symbols of civilization are placing a burden on the "less civilized" peoples of the world. The true "White Man's Burden" is exploitation, not selfless laboring on behalf of the less fortunate.

Today, the debate still rages over the proper meaning of the phrase "White Man's Burden." Does the United States, the most powerful "white" nation on earth, have a positive effect on the world, or does our nation inflict mostly harm? Do we help to lift up poorer nations, or do we primarily exploit them? As anyone who pays attention to current events knows, the United States is not particularly popular in the world these days. Some Americans would argue that this is the direct result of our tremendous wealth and power. The top dog is always resented, particularly when it feels compelled to exercise some of its power. Others would say that the people of other nations, especially from poorer countries, have good reason to resent the United States. The United States, like all nations, primarily looks out for its own political and economic interests. It is no coincidence, after all, that the United States became increasingly interested in the outside world at the same time that the industrial revolution increased its need for foreign raw materials and markets. Americans, however, like to think of themselves as members of a nation committed to noble principles, not a country simply looking to enrich itself. People of other nations, who directly feel the impact of the policies of our government and corporations, can see through this hypocrisy.

So in which camp do I belong? Am I a "flag-waving conservative" singing the praises of our noble nation, or am I an "America-hating liberal" ranting and raving about our country's many sins? When confronted with this question, I find myself unable to answer. In my mind, the question is fundamentally flawed. In my view, there is no such thing as a single entity called the United States of America. Instead, our nation, like all nations, is a collection of individuals, and in our case, we are talking about more than 300,000,000 people. We Americans disagree on many things, as the deep partisan divide in our country shows. Political policies and corporate actions that benefit certain Americans may anger others and possibly even harm them. Certain Americans may be fundamentally good and wise, some are bad and foolish, and most are a mixture of positive and negative qualities. We are also participants in various institutions that have varying effects on the world. When discussing America's impact, it is important to clarify if you are talking about our government, military, corporations, charitable organizations, tourists, media, or universities. With all of this diversity in terms of individual citizens and institutions, how can anyone make general statements about our country's impact?

It is important to keep in mind that everything I have just said about the United States applies to other nations as well. Nations are collections of individuals, and we must try to avoid making generalizations and assuming that the actions and opinions of these nations' governments reflect those of all their people. Too often, we, like many people of other countries I assume, demonize entire nations because of the views or behavior of their governments or the evil actions of a few of their citizens. Iraq was not a nation of Saddam Husseins before the American invasion. All of the people of Venezuela, Cuba, or Iran do not necessarily agree with their "anti-American" governments. And believe it or not, most of the citizens of other countries do not sit around all of the time obsessing about the United States. When they think about politics at all, they are, like us, primarily thinking about events in their own countries.

I have heard it argued several times that in many countries, the citizens' opinions about the United States are often the opposite of their governments' stance toward America. In countries that have more America-friendly governments, people tend to be more anti-American. Because people often, for good reason, dislike their own governments, their government's relationship to the United States plays a big part in their feelings toward Americans. Of course, some citizens of other countries are able to make a distinction between powerful American institutions like our government and the American people themselves. We would be wise to do the same with them.

Having said all of this, you still may wonder which way I lean on the question posed in this essay's title. Unfortunately, I will have to disappoint and say that I am not quite sure. Our country is significantly flawed in many ways, but every country past and present has been imperfect. As countries go, we are a pretty good one in a lot of ways. Our common mistake, however, is to confuse the principles that our country is supposed to be founded upon with the reality. The problem is not that we are unusually bad; instead, it is that many of us like to think that we are unusually good. Expressions of humility could be the first baby steps toward improving our relations with the world.

38. World War I: A Series of Bad Decisions

If you tried to compile a book about the dumbest moments in human history, you would have a wealth of material to choose from. In just the last few years, we have seen several good case studies of human incompetence. But if I ever took on this massive project, World War I would be somewhere near the top of the list. Whether you talk about its causes, battle tactics, death toll, or peace settlement, this supposed "war to end all wars" revealed much of the worst that humanity has to offer.

Almost all of us (I hope) recognize that wars are horrible things. But with the exception of the hard-core pacifists, we also acknowledge that they may sometimes be necessary. Sometimes, the cost of not fighting is higher than that of taking up arms, and there are certain ideals worth fighting for. The trouble with World War I is that it is hard to identify any noble causes, and you would be hard-pressed to explain how this was an unavoidable, necessary evil. Instead of being a struggle of good against bad, it was a battle between a bunch of stupid nations who found themselves at war.

In the end, World War I was just one in a long line of power struggles between different European nations. European history, in fact, reads like a war game that goes on for centuries, with alliances shifting and the balance of power changing over time. The late 19th – early 20th century was an era when the competition between European nations was particularly intense as many countries were engaged in a colonial land grab throughout Africa and Asia. It was also a time when modern systems of public education and mass media began to take shape, creating new means by which the public could be conditioned to love the homeland and, even more importantly, hate the enemy. Young people raised in this environment would be particularly easy to recruit as they sought to prove their loyalty, bravery, and devotion.

In 1871, Germany became truly unified for the first time, and it quickly began to emerge as the dominant power in Europe. The emergence of this new power made other nations nervous, and they began to come together in order to counteract Germany. This fear of Germany was even strong enough to cause the traditional enemies of Britain and France to become somewhat friendlier. Meanwhile Germany, which did not want to be standing alone if a future conflict occurred, sought out allies of its own. Eventually, you had two sets of alliances that were more or less equally matched. That was part of the idea. If the two sides were balanced, war would be less likely because one side could not be guaranteed of overwhelming the other. The only problem was that a small-scale conflict between two countries on opposing sides could snowball into a war that involved just about everyone. A metaphorical fuse was set up, and the only question was whether or not a spark would eventually set off the explosion.

That spark ended up being a terrorist attack. In 1914, a member of a Serbian nationalist group assassinated Archduke Ferdinand of Austria-Hungary, nephew of the emperor and next in line to the throne, and his wife Sophie. This nationalist group was angry that Austria-Hungary ruled over Serbians living in territory that, in their minds, should have been part of Serbia. Austria-Hungary, which had tenuous control over a hodgepodge of people from different ethnicities and backgrounds, decided that a display of strength was necessary to maintain order. So instead of viewing this assassination as a criminal act carried out by a terrorist organization, they interpreted it as an act of war carried out by Serbia. And by interpreting this as an act of war, the only plausible response was war.

Ten years ago, the United States was in a somewhat similar situation. The 9/11 attacks could have easily been interpreted as a mass murder carried out by nineteen criminals. But instead, almost immediately, it was described as an act of war. So like Austria-Hungary almost a century ago, the United States declared war against the enemy. Only in this case, there was no single country to declare war against. This was to be a war against people who engaged in a certain behavior. Unfortunately, since the United States immediately framed this as a war, the natural response was to conduct military operations. First Afghanistan and then Iraq were invaded and occupied as a part of this War on Terror. But when you are dealing with an "enemy" that is not a single, united force and does not represent a particular country, invading countries and toppling governments may not be particularly productive. The most important task is finding the potential enemies, and to get this done, criminal investigation techniques may often be more effective than conventional military operations.

Now to be fair to the United States and its many citizens who have supported the War on Terror, the destruction of massive buildings and the murder of over 3,000 people is a very different scenario than the assassination of a major political figure. Thousands of deaths feel much more like a military attack than the murder of a single person. But in both the cases of the United States and Austria-Hungary, the decisions to turn to war began a string of events that are playing out to this day. The ultimate costs to the United States in terms of money, lives, and international prestige are yet to be fully calculated. A good case can already be made, however, that the military components of the War on Terror have done more harm than good. And since this is a "war" against a behavior, it is hard to imagine a scenario in which the United States can ever declare a final victory.

In the case of Austria-Hungary, the decision of its leaders helped turn this single act of violence into the spark that lit the fuse. Austria-Hungary, however, did not make the only fateful decision. As Russia decided to mobilize in defense of its ally Serbia, Germany, Austria-Hungary's most important ally, realized that a European-wide war might be coming. For years, Germany had made contingency plans based on the assumption that any war would involve all of the countries tied into the two competing alliance systems. If war was coming anyway, it made sense for Germany to implement the plan that would give it the best chance of winning: blast quickly into France (by way of neutral Belgium) before it was fully mobilized, making it then possible to shift more forces to the east in order to deal with Russia. In other words, try to avoid fighting a two-front war. So in order to increase its chances at a quick victory, it was Germany who ultimately made the decision that brought on a four-year nightmare. In a nutshell, a Serbian killed an Austro-Hungarian prince, so Germany attacked France. Although there is a certain logic to this chain of events, you can see why I would characterize this as one of the stupidest events in human history.

When the war started, the United States had no obligation to get involved. Since the early days of the republic, the United States had made a concerted effort to stay out of European conflicts. Still, there were more Americans who rooted for the British than the Germans. For various reasons, ties with the British were particularly close. In addition to the United States' historical roots and the many aspects of its political system that were derived from Great Britain, there was also the crucial economic connection. By far, The British were the Americans largest trading partner. So when Germany tried to cut off foreign access to their enemies, this could cause some significant economic pain in the United States. And when Germany was compelled to turn to submarine attacks to scare people away from Britain and France, it created the impression that Germany was more of the bad guy. In relative terms, Britain's similar policy of cutting off access to the Germans seemed like a minor inconvenience. With the largest navy in the world and a relatively small German coastline to worry about, Britain could run a more conventional blockade. (It was hard for the Germans, on the other hand, to blockade an island.) And if a ship were turned away from Germany's shores, at least the crewmembers were still alive.

Still, the United States stayed out of the war for its first three years. But due to its economic connection to Britain, which grew even more significant as the war progressed, the United States was not technically neutral. In 1915, in fact, the United States came close to entering the war after the sinking of a British cruise ship, the Lusitania, which had more than one hundred Americans on board. Germany, however, fearful that the United States might declare war, agreed to suspend submarine attacks. But almost two years later, Germany decided to step up submarine attacks once again in a desperate gamble to finish off its enemies before the United States was compelled to enter the fight. Ultimately, the German gamble failed, and the United States, through its supply of fresh troops and weapons, tipped the scales in favor of the Allies. After four years of hurling bodies at one another and mowing millions of people down with machine guns, artillery fire, and chemical weapons, the "Great War" was finally over.

It is unfortunate that anybody won. The best result would have been a draw, with both sides eventually saying, "Boy, that was stupid. Let's not do that again." By bringing the United States into the war, President Wilson hoped to help make the world "safe for democracy." France, Britain, and the other victors, however, were more interested in gaining something for their victory. Germany, which was utterly defeated, was stripped of some territory, forced to pay billions of dollars in reparations, and compelled to acknowledge that the war was its fault. The seeds were then sown for a future German movement that would seek to get revenge for World War I and offer scapegoats for Germany's economic troubles. If the war had ended in a tie, or if the Germans had managed to win, I doubt that any of us would have ever heard of Adolf Hitler. It's even possible that a future fascist movement would have taken over the defeated nations of Britain and/or France. Of course, a different peace settlement could have also averted the even more disastrous war that started only 20 years later. Some of the provisions of the Versailles Peace Conference, therefore, would represent the last of the bad decisions associated with World War I.

The European theater of World War II was not the only eventual consequence of World War I. The Russian government collapsed before the war ended. After handing over territory (temporarily) to Germany and going through a brief civil war, a faction of socialists took over the country, and the Soviet Union was born. The Cold War conflict between the United States and the Soviet Union, between capitalism and communism, would define the latter half of the 20th century. Many countries around the world are still trying to recover from their recent experiences as Cold War battlefields.

The Ottoman Empire, another loser in World War I, was broken up, with only the nation of Turkey remaining from this ancient and once glorious empire. The Middle East was temporarily split up between Britain and France, much to the chagrin of many of the local people who had helped fight against the Ottoman Turks. By the 1930's, the nations of Syria, Lebanon, Iraq, Jordan, Kuwait, and Saudi Arabia emerged, with borders that did not necessarily reflect the ethnic makeup of the various people who lived there. And the region of Palestine remained a British mandate until after World War II, with a growing number of Jewish people from various parts of the world migrating to what they saw as their traditional homeland. Palestinians who had lived there for centuries, of course, saw things differently.

For so many reasons, you can make a good case that World War I was the central event of the past century. After this conflict, the world as we know it began to take shape, making it impossible to imagine the history of the past century without the "Great War" a part of it. Because we know how the story goes, it is easy to assume that this conflict, and the world that arose from it, was inevitable. And if the assassination of an Archduke had not been the spark, then something else would have eventually started the war. The human element, however, must never be discounted, and there are moments when decisions can really matter. Simply writing off events as inevitable can be a means of abdicating individual humans of responsibility.

Often, I find myself thinking that leadership does not really matter, and the political system is going to plow forward as it always does regardless of elections, the current fortunes of political parties, or much of anything else. There are times, however, when big decisions have to be made, and leaders cannot simply apply their political ideologies to the situation. Hopefully, when these moments come in the future, we will have leaders with strong characters, wisdom, and a working knowledge of history. For once these big choices are made, they will initiate a string of events, for better or for worse, which can never be completely unraveled.

39. World War II, Appeasement, and Hindsight

Ever since World War II, "appeasement" has been a dirty word in foreign policy, particularly in the United States. Instead of stepping up and strongly opposing Adolf Hitler when he began to ignore past treaties and invade neighboring countries, weak, naïve European leaders hoped that they could avoid war by appeasing Germany. It was only when Germany invaded Poland, more than six years after Hitler had come to power, that the British and French finally stepped up. By then, a German military machine had been built that was unleashed on France. In a matter of weeks, France fell, and Britain would barely hang on in the face of heavy air attacks. (To this day, the French are stereotyped in the United States as people that retreat and/or surrender before the fighting even starts.) But if European nations had taken decisive action the first time that Germany had broken the rules, then maybe things could have been different. And if the Soviet Union had not selfishly and stupidly signed a non-aggression pact with the Germans in 1939, and if western democracies and communist Russia could have looked beyond their differences in reaction to a common enemy, then the Soviet Union could have possibly saved themselves some future devastation.

In hindsight, it is clear that major efforts should have been taken to stop Hitler early. If war was inevitable due to Hitler's ambitions, then why wait until he was powerful to start fighting? Today and ever since, Americans who support military action to deal with dangerous leaders and/or nations can use the simple argument that the bad guy(s) must be stopped before becoming "another Hitler." This argument was particularly common in the buildups to the campaigns against Iraq in both 1991 and 2003. And if a European nation like France was not supportive of these necessary measures, then it was obviously playing its standard role as an appeaser. (Can you believe that those damn French actually believed that Saddam Hussein had no weapons of mass destruction?)

This line of reasoning, however, is not entirely fair. Because we know how the story ends, it is easy to look back and say what should have been done. But if you were living in the middle of these unfolding events, your perspective would likely be different. Only 15-20 years earlier, the worst war in human history, the supposed "war to end all wars," had taken place. Rational, humane people did not want to live through something like that again. So the natural tendency was to take every possible step before resorting to another nightmare. The problem was that Hitler was not a rational person. He and his followers could therefore behave more recklessly than others, not worrying so much about the possible violent repercussions. World War I, after all, had been the one time in Hitler's life that he had the opportunity to be something other than a loser. But when Germany and Austria-Hungary were defeated, his world was shattered once again. So the Nazi movement, at its core, was more than an attempt to build a German empire and eradicate the inferior races. It was also a quest for revenge and an attempt to recapture the glory that had been sought and lost with Germany's previous defeat. Sometimes, it pays off to be irrational, ruthless, and bitter. You are not held back by ethics, compassion, and a desire to keep peace. Negative qualities are the stuff that dictators are made of, and brutal leaders often view what most of us see as positive qualities as signs of weakness.

The lack of a crystal ball that could accurately tell the future also caused many to underestimate Hitler, especially during his early years in power. Some assumed that a radical, right wing movement such as the Nazis could not last. Others thought that Hitler could be controlled and manipulated. When Hitler was appointed Chancellor in 1933, some of his initial supporters in the business community and in political office thought that he and the Nazis could be used to weaken labor unions and communists. Meanwhile, the people on the left, the Social Democrats and the communists, were more worried about each other than the Nazis, so they failed to unify against the more serious right wing threat. Apparently, Stalin thought that Hitler would bring about the final death of capitalism in Europe. Meanwhile Hitler, backed by his loyal followers, took whatever steps necessary to consolidate his power, easily defeating potential opposition forces that were less united and ruthless than the Nazis. And so long as you were not one of those "inferior" races or opposition groups, the Nazi program of public works and military spending brought amazing economic improvement, further solidifying Hitler's power and causing many Germans to go along with the program.

But Hitler's ability to create a dictatorship was not the only thing that people underestimated in the 1930's. Many also failed to see the Nazi capacity for unspeakable cruelty. Looking back, there were plenty of signs in the 1930's of the Holocaust to come. But even today, knowing what we know, it is hard to believe that the mass murder of millions of people could have actually happened. And to a person who lived before the Holocaust occurred, harshly anti-Semitic, racist, homophobic statements would not be particularly unusual. Even practices such as vandalizing Synagogues and rounding up Jewish people into ghettoes were common throughout European history. This was particularly true during times of economic strife. And as horrifying as it may sound today, there were likely many "true" Germans who recognized that the persecution of those "inferior" peoples could create opportunities for them. If these German, non-Nazis had known about the slaughter to come, maybe more would have stood up to defend the victims of this persecution. Or then again, given the prejudices of the time, the economic strife, and the biological compulsion to survive, many may have stayed silent anyway as the devoted Nazis took the first steps toward what would eventually become the "final solution."

Still, these excuses do not completely exonerate the people of this era. But at least the people of the United States can feel less guilt about the behavior of our past countrymen. The British, French, and Russians, after all, were the ones who were too soft and/or foolish to deal with a problem that originated in their neighborhood. Personally, I find this line of reasoning to be rather hypocritical. For as the German threat emerged in the 1930's, the United States did not do anything to stop it. And even after Germany invaded Poland, the United States did not officially enter the conflict for two more years, and it took an attack on the other side of the world to make this happen. Maybe the United States should be added to the list of appeasers.

Now to be fair to American leaders, there are some perfectly reasonable explanations for the United States' initial lack of involvement in World War II. Many Americans were still disillusioned by what happened in World War I, feeling that their country had been manipulated into believing that it was fighting on the side of the good guys. The treatment of Germany after the war, however, made it clear that the United States had simply taken sides in a power struggle. Also, as Hitler rose to power, the United States was in the midst of the Great Depression, and most Americans felt that the focus and resources of the government should be on the problems at home. The United States also had a long tradition of isolationism, believing that faraway political problems, particularly those in Europe, were not its responsibility, and being bordered by two large oceans would keep the nation safe. With its eventual entry into World War I, the United States went against this traditional policy, and it did not turn out as most Americans hoped. The desire to stick with isolationism in the future, therefore, became very strong. And in the early days of Nazi Germany, when Americans heard stories about Germans doing horrible things, they may have been reminded of World War I propaganda that portrayed Germans as barbaric savages. This time, they were going to take these reports with a grain of salt. Pearl Harbor, of course, changed the American point of view. And today, given the United States' involvement just about everywhere, it is hard to imagine that we once had such a strong, isolationist tradition. With the end of World War II and the transition to the Cold War, it became clear that the United States could not simply stick its head in the sand.

Clearly, there are valuable lessons to learn from the events leading up to World War II. The rise of Adolf Hitler is a great case study demonstrating the process by which dictators come to power. These years also show that there may be times when strong, preemptive action can reduce violence over the long run. In addition, they demonstrate that all forms of prejudice must be taken seriously, and in times of strife, people living in sophisticated, industrial countries can be receptive to crazy ideas. The danger, however, is that you might overly generalize and see future Hitlers everywhere. Today, as at all times in the history of civilization, the world is filled with lousy dictators. As the United States' recent experiences in Iraq and Afghanistan have demonstrated, no country, no matter how powerful, can easily topple them all and replace them with something better. It takes a great deal of both insight and courage to separate the future Hitlers of the world from the run-of-the-mill dictators that will someday be long forgotten. Sometimes, military action is the easy path for a politician to take, and maintaining peace takes more courage than declaring war. And whatever path a leader takes, he or she will be labeled by some as either a weak appeaser or a violent warmonger. But we should all do our best to cut people of the past and present some slack. These are tough decisions, and simplistic labels and generalizations don't cut it in a complex world where no one knows the future. For even if a leader is stopped from becoming the next Hitler, we won't know it.

40. World War II Fascination

In terms of best-selling books written, films made, and board games inspired, World War II is probably the most popular topic in American history. Only the American Revolution, the Civil War, and the Old West can compete. Some of this is a symptom of Americans' general fascination with violence. When you take into consideration the movies and video games that rake in the most money, it should not be surprising that war is one of the few historical topics that can catch some Americans' interest. And no conflict in history quite lives up to World War II in terms of sheer size, scope, and carnage.

But this fascination is based on more than just the size of World War II. For some, it is also the new technology that was in play: tanks, air power, mobile assault rifles, heavy artillery, carriers, radar, nuclear weapons, etc. I have met many people over the years that are fascinated by every minute detail of some or all of these various killing toys. Others are more interested in how this technology was utilized, and they pour over every detail of the major battles and general strategies. World War I was still essentially a foot soldier's war. But in World War II, many of the tactics utilized throughout world history were out the window. The war in the Pacific, in particular, is impossible to imagine without the new tools that were necessary for achieving dominance of the sea and air.

Due to the fusion of these new technologies and tactics, World War II is a board game maker's dream. Of the World War II games that I know, "Axis and Allies" was always my favorite. To win, you have to both make good attack decisions and use your resources properly in order to produce the right balance of the various types of military equipment. The only problem with the game is that it takes about a weekend to play, which can be a bit of a hassle if you have even a semblance of a life.

But it is not just the violence, technology, and battles that make the topic appealing. World War II was also one of those rare conflicts that seemed to be a clear struggle of good versus evil.

Unlike World War I, a conflict in which a bunch of countries fell into a pointless war, it was clear in World War II that Japan and Germany were the aggressors. And from the American perspective, we were involved in response to a direct attack. This was not the type of murky situation that you had with wars such as the Mexican War, Spanish-American War, Vietnam, and Iraq. The cause was noble, and Americans were ready to make tremendous sacrifices in order to achieve victory. It was probably the last time, in fact, that nearly all Americans were unified around a military cause. And they rose to the occasion in a way that is in profound contrast to current conflicts that have wavering public support and in which most Americans have not been asked to sacrifice much of anything (in the short term, at least).

Japan and especially Germany, however, were not just your run-of-the-mill conquerors. Japan could be brutal in its treatment of conquered civilian populations or prisoners of war, but Germany took brutality to another level. When I was a kid, I remember watching an episode of "The Family Feud." In this game show, people try to guess the most common answers given to a survey question. In the episode that I remember, the question was, "Name people most likely to be in hell." Adolf Hitler was the top answer; Satan came in second. When a person can out-bad Satan, then you know that this person has come to symbolize the epitome of evil.

Hitler, in fact, sounds like a villain straight out of a science fiction novel or Disney film. Voldemort, the most famous fantasy villain of the last fifteen years, is essentially modeled after Hitler. Harry Potter's nemesis is basically a Nazi wizard trying to eradicate those who do not have pure wizard blood. And when I was a kid, Darth Vader and "The Empire" was our story of evil dictatorship trying to snuff out democratic resistance. In both cases, the storytellers ultimately spent a lot of time explaining how these villains turned evil. For whatever reason, it is inherently fascinating to study the psychology of those who are profoundly bad. Because we tend to assume that good is the norm, figuring out what makes a hero tick is not nearly so interesting. But there are also few things more gratifying than watching that not so interesting hero slay the ultimate villains. And when you know that the story is actually true, it can be more compelling than the greatest fiction. Historians, of course, would argue that things are never that simple. The Soviet Union, our ally of convenience, was led by a man as murderous as Hitler, and the United States resorted to some brutal tactics in order to achieve victory. But in spite of these unsettling facts, World War II seems as noble of a cause as a war could be.

The war was also undeniably important in shaping the last 66 years of United States and world history. For the first time, the United States emerged as a military superpower, a position it is yet to relinquish. Its only rival was the Soviet Union, a nation that the United States would compete with around the planet for the next forty-five years. We are still feeling the lingering effects of these Cold War struggles in various countries. Before World War II, many of the countries that became the battlefield during the Cold War were still European colonies. But the devastation in Europe caused by the war laid some of the groundwork for independence movements throughout Asia and Africa. By the late 1960's, the map of the planet bore little resemblance to how it looked before the war.

After years of struggling through the Great Depression, World War II initiated a period of American economic prosperity that had never been seen in world history. For the first time, the middle-class American lifestyle became the norm, with half of Americans living in suburban neighborhoods by 1960. There was also a population explosion, and this baby boom generation, the most economically privileged in American history, would eventually become the driving force in shaping post-war American culture. Without the post-war prosperity of the late 1940's and 1950's, and the huge generational differences between the baby boomers and their parents, it is impossible to imagine the social changes of the 1960's. And without the changes of the 1960's, it is difficult to imagine the modern conservative movement and the so-called "culture wars" that rage today. For better and for worse, World War II is arguably the defining transitional event of the past century of American history. It therefore deserves the attention that it gets.

I just hope that when certain people obsess about the details of World War II, they will never forget to step back and see this event as more than a compelling, entertaining story. When talking about the tactics, the weapons, and the characters, it can be easy to lose sight of the human element. Unspeakable, horrific atrocities were committed in this conflict that cost tens of millions of lives. In many ways, there were Americans and other people worldwide that performed heroically, and they deserve our respect. There is always a danger, however, that in celebrating past heroic acts we can get caught up in glorifying war itself. And as we reflect on the actions of this "greatest generation," there may be some people out there looking for the opportunity to be equally heroic. War is sometimes a necessary evil. But we must be careful to ensure that it does not become entertainment, a simplistic means of stamping out "evil," or a means of trying to prove ourselves.

I suspect that people who have seen war firsthand have less of a tendency to glorify it. Inevitably, as time has passed, the number of World War II veterans has steadily decreased. By the year 2025, almost all will be gone. Hopefully, the lessons that they learned will not die with them, and they will continue to be more than characters in a compelling story.

Part Nine: Post-War America (1945-1970's)

41. The Cost of Stability

It's hard to imagine what it must have been like to be an average twenty-five year-old American in 1945. Much of your childhood consisted of the Great Depression. Then, after more than a decade of economic troubles, the crisis finally came to an end with the worst war in human history, a war that you were likely to have experienced firsthand. After fifteen years of economic distress and unimaginable violence, people wanted peace and stability. For many people, this must have been a desire close to an obsession.

So where do people get any sense of security in this crazy world? What keeps us from waking up in the morning and saying, "Oh my God, I'm going to die!" When I ask my students this question, they will often mention things like police departments and military forces as important factors in making them feel safe. But while I agree that it is nice to have providers of order and protection around, these security forces are not the most important factors in keeping me from going into a frequent panic. Most of the time, cops and soldiers are actually in the back of my mind, largely taken for granted. Instead, I feel relatively secure if I have a stable job, decent income, nice house (in a safe neighborhood), and family and friends around. If these basic elements are in place, then life is basically good. But if any of these foundations for my security are shaken or threatened, then the forces of law and order do not provide a great deal of comfort. I doubt that a homeless, jobless, socially isolated American wakes up each morning and says, "Thank God that we have plenty of cops on the streets and the most powerful military force in the world!"

Because I have had a relatively sheltered life, it does not take too much to get me stressed out. So in some ways, I am sure that the post-World War II generation consisted of people who were often tougher and more resilient than I. But because they had personally experienced so much suffering and insecurity, their longing to possess those basic elements of the "American Dream"

192

– a good job, house, family, yard, white fence, dog, etc. – may have been even stronger than mine. And because of the unprecedented general prosperity of the late 1940's and 1950's, government aid through the GI bill, and/or the prevalence of affordable housing, more Americans than ever before got their chance.

For many, home ownership was the ultimate symbol of prosperity and stability. But people did not just want any old home. They wanted a place that was somewhat isolated from the hustle and bustle of city life, a place with enough space, serenity, and security for kids to go out and play and for parents to take a relaxing nap in the backyard. They also wanted a home surrounded by neighbors with similar values and goals who would not drag the neighborhood down. A country, small town life may have been appealing to many, but in this increasingly urbanized society, the high salary, stable jobs tended to be in the city. So how could people have the economic benefits of the city without living among the crowds, crime, and people who just did not quite look and act like them? Ever since the early 20th century, the answer had been the suburbs. Only now, in a society where the middle class increasingly became the norm and mass-produced housing tracts helped keep down the cost of real estate, the suburbs were no longer an escape for only the elites.

Suburban housing tracts were more than just places. They came to symbolize an entire way of life. The values emphasized in the suburbs – conformity, materialism, sexual restraint (especially for women), the male as "breadwinner" and female as "housewife" – became the American mainstream. And the overriding theme of these values was an emphasis on security. In this land of plenty where people knew their roles and did not rock the boat too much, people could find that stable, peaceful life that many lacked growing up. And when parents dumped that classic guilt line on their kids – "I want you to have all of the things that I never had as a child" – it really meant something.

But even as they strove to create this little bubble world, plenty of fears remained. The Soviet Union quickly replaced Nazi Germany and imperial Japan as the new bitter enemy, and communism replaced fascism as the ultimate evil in the world. And in some ways, this new enemy was even scarier. As of 1949, the Soviet Union possessed the atomic bomb, and it was not long before it was possible for the Soviets to launch long-range missiles that could do major damage to any U.S. city. And since communism was an inherently revolutionary ideology directly opposed to capitalism, there were likely communist spies and infiltrators living within the United States who were trying to undermine the American way of life. Bomb drills were conducted in schools, with kids apparently taught that ducking under a desk would repel the impact of a nuclear attack. Or, as a more plausible explanation, these drills were designed to scare the hell out of kids and keep them constantly reminded of that evil force that might incinerate them someday. Senator Joseph McCarthy tried to root out communists from the government while the House Un-American Activities Committee focused on supposed communist influence in the entertainment industry. The sacrifice of innocent people's reputations was a small price to pay in the name of security, and the ideal of "innocent until proven guilty" did not apply apparently to suspected communists. It was better to be safe than sorry.

Some people today have that same attitude toward suspected terrorists. But as scary as the people we label terrorists may be, they do not represent a threat comparable to what the Soviet Union once posed. We have not yet resurrected the bomb drills, and I am not aware of anyone building a bomb shelter in the backyard. Suburban housing tracts, however, are alive and well. And in some ways, they have gotten a little weirder. Newer housing tracts seem to have even less variety in terms of design and house color than the ones built decades ago. And in the gated communities with housing associations, life is even more tightly regulated. Some places have strict rules regarding how long one's garage door can be left open, how tall the grass can be, and what kinds of tacky lawn decorations – gnomes, windmills, basketball hoops – can be placed in the front (or even back) yard. It's not enough to have clone homes. These are also worlds of clone landscaping, and it makes one wonder if people living there will also become clone families, driving to the same soccer practices, riding in the same minivans, and raising kids to be just like them.

Fortunately, you can no longer get away with the kind of blatant racial discrimination that you could in the late 1940's and

1950's. But still, if you drive around an area like Southern California, a state considered rather liberal, you will notice some clear demographic patterns. The ethnic makeup of Irvine, California, land of the tightly regulated housing tracts, for instance, is quite different from South Central Los Angeles. This segregation is not backed by any legal ordinance, but it is still very real. Of course, if people are honest, they will admit that this is one of the attractions of Irvine. People feel secure when surrounded by others similar to them. And to be fair to Irvine, it has one of the lowest per capita crime rates in the United States. Sure, you have to paint your house a certain color, and you are on some level helping to maintain a system of de facto segregation, but at least you and your family feel safe.

When I was younger, I used to mock the "sell-outs" living the suburban American Dream even more than I do today. I was going to be different. I was going to maintain my youthful idealism and go out there as a missionary or Peace Corps volunteer and help people living in the so-called Third World. I recognized the injustice of inequality, and I knew how superficial the happiness that came from material prosperity really was. But then I grew up. And now, here I am in my mid-40s with a house, wife, two kids, and a reasonably well manicured front lawn. (I keep resisting my kid's requests for a dog, however.) This is no Irvine, but it's a nice, reasonably safe housing tract with four or five basic house layouts and middle-class Americans somewhat similar to us. So what happened? First, I reached a point in life where I was expected to pay my own bills. And when that day comes, a bit of that youthful idealism can fade away. You realize that the basics of life that you have become accustomed to enjoying are not cheap. You also realize that there are some definite benefits to family life, and being alone can get old after a while. On some level, we are biologically programmed to leave the nest, find a mate, and start our own nest. I may not be as obsessed with the necessity of family life as Americans fifty years ago, but I recognize that there are some definite benefits to security.

Still, that idealism is not entirely dead. I still have the opportunity to rant and rave about the importance of history and the injustices of the world in my writing and in the classroom. I may not be the one venturing off to change or save the world. But

195

maybe through my words, I can inspire a few people to go out into the world and have a more significant, positive effect than I. And in the meantime, I can enjoy hanging out with family, admiring my backyard, playing racquetball at the health club, and watching my new flat screen. There is something to be said for the "American Dream," so long as we remember those who are not so well off, and we do not let our desire for security make us a little nutty.

42. Defending the 1960's

When people of the conservative persuasion think of the 1960's, negative images often come to mind. They think of drugged out, irresponsible "hippies" having various forms of extramarital sex, listening to crazy music, and dabbling in eastern mysticism. Other common images may be anti-war (some would say anti-American) protesters, race riots, gay rights parades, and/or Lyndon Johnson's big government, "Great Society" programs. This narrative that demonizes the "liberals" of the 1960's has been a powerful story for decades, galvanizing conservatives in their fight against the "liberal agenda." Some analysts may have viewed the success of President Obama and the Democrats in 2008 as a sign that this modern conservative version of history had lost its political effectiveness. The mid-term elections of 2010, however, along with the types of attacks unleashed against President Obama since his inauguration, proved that this version of history is alive and well.

While largely demonizing the 1960's, this conservative version of history tends to glorify the eras immediately before and after the "hippy generation." The 1950's are often remembered by conservatives as years similar to the old sitcoms that were satirized so effectively in the movie *Pleasantville*. In this narrative, Americans were increasingly living in a suburban, *Leave it to Beaver* kind of world. Neighborhoods were clean and safe. Neighbors knew each other, and every adult participated in helping to monitor the whole neighborhood's kids. Kids were well behaved, dads worked hard, and moms made sure that the houses stayed clean and that dinners were cooked on time. People also went to church and tried to maintain traditional, wholesome "family values."

Then, according to this conservative narrative, the previously mentioned liberals and "hippies" came along and messed everything up. Consensus was replaced by disagreement and strife. Stability turned into chaos. Young people became rebellious spoiled brats dying from overdoses, contracting venereal diseases, having unwanted pregnancies, and protesting in the streets instead of getting real jobs. And if is this wasn't bad enough, the federal government in the 1960's and early 1970's became increasingly large and obtrusive, creating wasteful social programs, regulating business too much, imposing affirmative action measures, and creating the stagnant, inflation ridden economy of the mid-to-late 1970's.

Conservatives needed a savior, so like Californians when they turned to the "governator," they looked to an optimistic, Republican actor. Ronald Reagan seemed to embody an earlier era, and he called for America to go back to a time before government had become so bloated, taxes had been so high, and traditional values had been so recklessly abandoned. He also argued that America had to grow strong again by building up its military and being willing to use it. In a country stinging from humiliations like the Vietnam War and the Iranian Hostage Crisis, his hopeful message of regaining strength struck a chord with many people. In a country with a stagnating economy facing rampant inflation and increasing foreign competition, his message that government needed to get out of the way and allow business to succeed also rang true. He was the right guy for the right time (no puns intended), and many conservatives have been singing his praises ever since.

The question of whether or not Ronald Reagan was truly a savior is a matter of intense debate. But what I want to question here is the conservative premise that the 1960's had a primarily negative impact on the United States. In my view, this premise only works for people who have a selective memory. Life in the 1950's, after all, was hardly *Pleasantville*. Sure, on the surface, an unparalleled number of Americans seemed to be living the "American Dream." Many of those suburban families, however, had some "issues." After living through the Great Depression and World War II, many parents probably suffered from some degree of post-traumatic stress disorder. This helps explain why their kids would grow up feeling disconnected from the parents who tried to buy them happiness. With the rock and roll listening, leather jacket wearing, drag racing "greasers" of the late 1950's, there were already clear signs of the massive 1960's youth rebellion to come.

Also, the family values that were projected in the suburbs were not always being practiced in private. When Alfred Kinsey published his studies of late 1940's – early 1950's sexual behavior, many were shocked by what he had found. If you read and accept his findings, then people in the 1950's sound a lot like those sex-crazed "hippies." In addition, the happy housewives seen in 1950's TV shows and commercials did not necessarily reflect reality. Many women were dissatisfied, a feeling that only intensified their burden of guilt as society pressured them to fulfill their motherly duty. If they chose to work outside the home, they were expected to do so-called women's work: teaching, nursing, domestic service, secretarial work, etc. There were few women, after all, in high status occupations such as management, medicine, law, science, and engineering.

Outside of the suburbs, things were even worse. The United States, after all, was still a thoroughly segregated, racist society, and I am not just talking about the South. Informal segregation and racial stereotyping were rampant throughout the general culture, forming barriers that limited the opportunities of ethnic minorities to rise up. The suburbs, by their very nature, were racially exclusionary. After years of depression and war, people flocked to the suburbs to feel safe, and part of this sense of safety came from knowing that only other white people lived there. It is no wonder, therefore, that the Civil Rights Movement, which is often associated with the 1960's, hit the streets in the middle of the 1950's.

Because of the Civil Rights Movement and other movements for social change and reform that accelerated in the 1960's, the United States has become a much better place for the majority of its citizens. Most Americans, after all, do not share all three of the traits that are possessed by the traditionally dominant demographic: white, male, and heterosexual. I can guarantee you that there are few women, ethnic minorities, and homosexuals who would like to go back to life before the 1960's. So how do conservatives who demonize the 1960's manage to brush aside this simple truth? I get the sense that many view the positive, post-1960's social changes as inevitable products of progress that reflect our nation's noble values. Others, whether they are willing to admit it or not, see the rise of traditionally oppressed groups as more negative than positive, and they would prefer to go back to the "good old days." Either way, they are able to discount and/or discredit the liberals who helped to bring about these changes. But for people who recognize the history of these social changes and want them to continue, it's crucial to remember that people had to organize and fight for things that are largely taken for granted today, and we need to keep fighting.

Sixties "liberals," without a doubt, had their flaws, most of which I mentioned in summarizing the conservative critique. At their worst, they could be naïve, irresponsible, overly rebellious people who had too much faith in government. At their best, however, they were engaged in what was happening in the world and were willing to make selfless sacrifices for the betterment of society. Our often apathetic, self-absorbed, cynical, materialistic population could probably use more people with some "hippy" in them.

43.   Were Old People Always Old?

I originally wrote this shortly before the rock band "The Who" was playing the Super Bowl Halftime Show in 2010. It was an ironic moment for a band that had sung in the early 1960's, "I hope I die before I get old."

I've seen a few advertisements recently for this Sunday's Super Bowl Halftime show. Apparently, one of my favorite rock bands of all time, The Who, is getting together again for this year's extravaganza. I had a few different reactions when I first learned of this. First of all, I was surprised that they had not gone into permanent retirement. After all, they have to be well past the age where many start collecting Social Security. The fact that they are getting up there in age also makes me worried about both their musical abilities and their personal safety. I remember hearing years ago that Pete Townshend was practically deaf from years of playing really loud concerts. Will he still be able to hear well enough to stay in sync with his band mates? Also, if he breaks into one of his windmill guitar moves, is there a danger that his shoulder will come out of its socket? And at the end of "Won't Get Fooled Again," when he attempts to smash his guitar into pieces, will he still be able to generate enough force to carry this out?

After some reflection, the logic of booking The Who became clear. Ever since Janet Jackson terrorized the world by flashing one of her breasts a few years ago, the organizers of the Super Bowl have been booking older, seemingly safer artists for their halftime shows: Paul McCartney, Bruce Springsteen, Tom Petty, The Rolling Stones, and now, The Who. (You know that the world has changed when The Who and The Rolling Stones are considered to be "safe" acts.) These older artists, whose status is based on the quality of their music and not stunts like a "wardrobe malfunction," seem less likely to offend anyone. So if God forbid they accidentally flash some private body part to the world, the

201

emotional reaction of the audience is more likely to be repulsion than arousal. And let's face it; repulsion offends far fewer people than arousal.

I also wonder about the oncoming reaction of the younger audience to these old men rocking out at the Super Bowl. I am sure that some of them are familiar with The Who. Classic rock still gets the attention of some young folks. Some unfamiliar with the band may also be impressed with what these guys can do. In their heyday, after all, The Who played stuff that was louder, harder, and more powerful than just about anything out there today. Still, I think that most of the youth will see some old guys doing old people music, something that is, by its very nature, uncool. Old people can't do real rock music. Good music, after all, is played by people who know how to be bad.

There is a disturbing moment that all children must go through when they learn about the "birds and the bees." When the concept sinks in that certain body parts must be placed into certain locations in order to produce children, an image pops into their head that is unavoidable: "If I am standing here, then my parents must have had sex." Then, if they have the guts to follow this line of reasoning, there is an even more disturbing insight: "My grandparents also must have had sex." Then, if they have healthy imaginations, other questions follow: "Is it possible that mom, dad, grandma, or grandpa had sex with other people before they got married. I wonder how experimental they were in exploring different ways to..." and then their brain shuts down due to psychological trauma, and they may possibly lose their lunch. It is probably best at that point for kids to convince themselves that mom and dad and grandma and grandpa only did it enough times to produce the kids that they had. It also lasted for a very short time and was not very good.

It is very difficult for young people to picture old people doing all of the fun things that society tells them are bad, whether it is playing wild music or having a good time "doing the nasty." (My Uncle once told me that his kids thought that they invented sex.) This is partly because it is hard for young people to picture older people as ever being young. It is almost like they live under the delusion that older people came out of birthing pods as fully mature adults. The reality, of course, is that their parents and grandparents were young once, and their behavior was not all that different from modern day young people. They may have had moments where they drank too much, drove in an unwise fashion, accidentally set fire to their parents' garage, or, God forbid, repeatedly disobeyed their parents.

Parents are partly to blame for this delusion. We recognize that we are role models for our kids, so we want to present the best image that we can. This includes, of course, giving them at times a somewhat edited version of our own personal history. In essay/chapter seven of this book, I discussed the dangers of feeding kids a romanticized version of American history. Do these same truths apply when we give our kids a romanticized personal history?

Whatever the case, through the course of writing this essay, I have thought of another good reason for kids to study history. As I have said, it is difficult for us parents to be honest with our kids about our own past (or present). So instead of introducing kids to the fact that the world and the people in it are often messed up through the example of our own lives, maybe they could get used to what the world is really like by studying history. That way, when we as parents inevitably disappoint them, they won't be so surprised. Sometimes, the opportunity to get a dose of reality about both their families and society in general might come up for kids simultaneously. I can imagine a situation where a kid is watching the movie documentary about the Woodstock Festival of 1969. There, in the front row, they might see grandma and grandpa half (or more) naked, smoking something that looks illegal, and having a great time listening to The Who.

44. Comparing Vietnam to Iraq & Afghanistan

When it became clear that the conflicts in Iraq and Afghanistan were going to drag on for a while, the inevitable comparisons to Vietnam began. In some basic ways, however, these wars have borne little resemblance to Vietnam. The rugged terrains of Iraq and Afghanistan are nothing like the tropical rainforests of Vietnam. Insurgents in these recent conflicts seem to have far less domestic and international support than the Vietcong once had, and they have not been organized as single, united forces. Also, the number of American deaths in Iraq and Afghanistan combined are only 1/10 (so far) of those killed in Vietnam.

Still, there are some eerie similarities. Like in Vietnam, the United States has been fighting against enemies who can be very difficult to locate and properly identify. These insurgents, like the Vietcong, recognize that they cannot take on the United States military in a "conventional" war. So they infiltrate communities, blend in with the civilian population, and are content to harass American soldiers (and the population in general) with quick hit-and-run strikes and booby traps. They know that they do not have to win in a conventional sense. They also know that when Americans kill civilians, it plays into the insurgents' hands. So all that they need to do is inflict enough casualties and drag these conflicts out long enough to convince the United States that the costs are too high. In other words, they have to do the same thing that the Vietcong was able to accomplish.

This is why some would say that continued U.S. operations in Iraq and Afghanistan are ultimately pointless. Like Vietnam, these conflicts cannot be won. Others, however, disagree. Part of the reason that our efforts in Vietnam failed, they would argue, was that the American public did not adequately support the efforts of the military. And this lack of support went beyond the efforts of the liberal media and of those anti-war hippies. The federal government, partly out of fear of public opinion, asked the military to fight this war with "one hand tied behind its back." For fear of inflicting excessive civilian casualties, soldiers could not root out and destroy communists as aggressively as necessary. Also, due to concerns about possible domestic and international reactions, restrictions were placed on bombing targets, with the North Vietnamese capital of Hanoi being a particularly important "off-limits" potential site. If enough of the public had recognized that "war is hell," but you must fight to win, then the results may have been different. To those who maintain this view that Vietnam was winnable, history may be repeating itself in Iraq and Afghanistan.

I agree with those who say that lack of public support was a big part of America's failure in Vietnam. Anti-war protestors, in fact, would take this as a compliment. In theory, it is also possible that more aggressive action could have led to a different result. This is assuming, of course, that over a half million troops, double the tonnage of explosives that were dropped in all of World War II, and the extensive use of chemical agents were just not enough. Still, there is an even more fundamental problem with this line of reasoning, a problem that also applies to the conflicts in Iraq and Afghanistan. In Vietnam, the United States' basic justification for involvement was to stop the spread of communism. Part of this effort, like the Cold War in general, was to protect and promote American interests. (A world full of communist nations, after all, is bad for business.) The United States also claimed, however, that defending South Vietnam from communism would make that country a better place. So there was a humanitarian component to this war, a component that can lead to big trouble. The more damage that the United States did in South Vietnam, the harder it was to argue that these efforts were helping the people of that nation. In a sense, the United States, through its stated policy objective, doomed itself to failure. At some point, the infliction of excessive death and destruction would make it impossible to declare any legitimate victory.

In World War II, the United States was not fighting against Japanese and German soldiers in an effort to make those countries better places. The goal was to defeat their military forces and destroy their capacity to continue fighting. World War II was unimaginably horrific, but it was also much simpler than a war like Vietnam. The enemy's military forces were more easily identified, and the United States felt justified in targeting their civilian populations and using all of the firepower at its disposal.

The wars in Iraq and Afghanistan resemble Vietnam much more than World War II. In both places, like in Vietnam, the United States initially used national security as the justification for fighting. Afghanistan had terrorist training camps that were harbored by the Taliban government, and Saddam Hussein (supposedly) had "weapons of mass destruction." Over time, however, particularly in Iraq, the United States justified its efforts with humanitarian language: liberation, promoting democracy, etc. Now, like in Vietnam, the United States is trying to win wars while appearing to help people, fighting against insurgents who are difficult to distinguish from civilians. With such unrealistic stated goals, it may already be impossible to ever declare victory.

45. Watergate, Conspiracy Theories, and the Information Age

To understand fully the impact of the Watergate scandal, you have to place it in its historical context. In the years before and during this scandal that unfolded between 1972-1974, the United States was going through some tough times: Vietnam, race riots, assassinations, inflation, rising gas prices, and worst of all, out of control hippies. Vietnam, a war that led to tens of thousands of American deaths and a strong anti-war movement, created the perception among many that the federal government could not be trusted. So when Nixon finally resigned as a result of his obvious involvement in attempts to cover up the Watergate break-in, along with the other "dirty tricks" carried out by his staff, it merely confirmed what many had already suspected. The increased cynicism that resulted from this era lingers to this day.

But some would argue that there is a less negative, cynical angle to the story. Watergate, in addition to being a national embarrassment, also demonstrated what is great about this country. It showed that even the president is not above the law, and the system of checks and balances created by the Founding Fathers could work. When Nixon resigned, articles of impeachment were being drawn up in the House of Representatives. And ultimately, Nixon's fate was sealed when the Supreme Court ordered him to turn over his personal tapes. Because Nixon knew what was on those tapes, he decided to resign in order to avoid being thrown out. I'm sure that in many other nations - the Soviet Union in particular - political leaders saw this whole episode as rather strange. Nixon, after all, was driven from power due to actions that were commonplace in the Soviet Union. As violations of personal privacy and human rights go, what Nixon and his aids did was pretty minor in comparison to communist governments and political dictators everywhere. But thankfully, his downfall proved that the United States is different.

Personally, I do not entirely buy this more hopeful hypothesis. Sure, Nixon was ultimately driven from power. But were it not for the efforts of Bob Woodward and Carl Bernstein, and their willingness to pursue and report on a story that many initially thought was a wild conspiracy theory, this story of a break-in at the Democratic headquarters would have faded away rather quickly. And if Richard Nixon had not been stupid enough to record himself while discussing cover-up plans and other illegal activities, then he would have probably been let off the hook. Sure, many Nixon aids would have paid the price, and his administration would have sustained some heavy damage. But his claim to have no personal knowledge of the behavior of his subordinates could have held up with no proof to the contrary. Ultimately, to bring Nixon down, it took some gutsy reporting and a foolish, arguably paranoid, self-absorbed president. So maybe the main lesson that future presidents took to heart was to cover their tracks more carefully, not necessarily to always abide by the law. As many people have argued over the years, maybe Nixon's biggest crime was being dumb enough to get caught.

In the 222 years that the United States has been governed under the Constitution, only two presidents have ever been impeached. Andrew Johnson was impeached and nearly thrown out of office in 1868 because he tried to stand in the way of the Reconstruction program that was being implemented by Congress. And more recently, Bill Clinton, in one of the more obvious smear campaigns in American history, was impeached for lying under oath about his sex life. To the surprise of no one, the Senate had nowhere near the votes necessary to throw him out. Other than the Clinton scandal, there have been some episodes since Watergate in which presidents were accused by some of potentially impeachable offenses. President Reagan was able to convince enough people in Congress that he was not personally involved in the Iran-Contra scandal, and I know of no serious talk of impeaching him. Under George W. Bush, government officials were involved in questionable – and some would say illegal – interrogation techniques of suspected insurgents and surveillance of Americans' international phone calls. It was obvious, however, that any talk of impeachment was nothing but talk. So either Nixon was the only president in history who deserved to be thrown out of office for illegal behavior, or the American impeachment system is very weak.

In the current political environment, in fact, it is almost impossible for me to imagine a president being thrown out of office. He would practically have to kill or rape someone on video in order to get tossed out, or he would have to pull a Nixon and leave some evidence of illegal behavior lying around. For if less verifiable information came to light about a president's illegal activities, members of his political party would rise to his defense, claiming that the allegations were a partisan attack. Then, since neither party is close to a 2/3 majority in the Senate, the prospects of actually deposing the leader are extremely remote. And since so much of the public is convinced that its political party is constantly under attack by forces from the other side, there will always be a significant percentage of the population that will reject outright any of its opponent's "partisan conspiracy theories." They know, after all, that people who disagree with their ideology are not just misguided. They are also ethically inferior, so they cannot be trusted. And major media outlets, unfortunately, are either blatantly biased or are bending over backwards in an attempt to be politically "balanced." So for every accusation, self-proclaimed non-partisan news sources must give equal time to the defense. In this battle of political spin, truth is secondary to the maintenance of so-called "objectivity," and one party's "truth" is as valid as the other.

So if a president engages in some shady behavior, do we have modern versions of Woodward and Bernstein to bring this stuff to light? Some would argue that in the internet age, this question is out-of-date. In Nixon's time, the government may have believed that it could put the lid on things and prevent information from coming to light. You just had to make sure that troublemaking reporters did not find out what was going on. But today, in a world where an army of bloggers can get information out as easily as major news outlets, it may be impossible to keep everything secret. As governments in North Africa and the Middle East have recently been finding out, it is difficult to cut off the flow of information in a world of smart phones, Facebook, and Twitter. But in a way, this army of conspiracy theorists from all parts of the political spectrum may be a tremendous ally for American government officials. Because of the constant wave of conspiracy theories flying around the blogosphere, it is very difficult to recognize those claims and stories that actually reveal some truth. Since people are "crying wolf" all of the time, it is very hard in the information age to know when the wolf will actually show up. Paradoxically, information overload may do as much or more to keep truth from coming to light as excessive secrecy ever did. Nixon may have been better off now than he was in the 1970's. And had he recorded all of those conversations on his personal hard drive or some IPODs, they may have been easier to unload than a pile of giant cassette tapes.) LOL

Part Ten: Modern Times
(1980's – Present)

46. 1980-2011: A Quick Overview

Several times, I have taught a class that covers all of United States History, from Columbus to Obama, in nine weeks (six hours per week). This is an unusual format for me. At the three other schools where I teach, the classes either cover Early American History (before 1877) or Modern American History (post-1877). Plus, classes usually last for sixteen weeks and meet for three hours per week. So students in this "unusual" format are expected to absorb 500 years of history in half of the normal time.

By cutting out some material and moving faster than I normally do, I have been able to get through all of this information when I have taught with this hectic format. I am always worried, however, that if I don't pace myself properly, I could end up being forced to cover the last thirty years of American history in about a half an hour. So should that ever occur, here is how I might go about covering the years from 1980-2011 during those last precious minutes of class time:

So in 1980, things were not looking too good for our country. Inflation was out of control, Americans were starting to buy lots of things from other countries (especially Japan), and circumstances such as the Iranian Hostage Crisis made us look weaker around the world. So many Americans turned to a conservative ex-actor named Ronald Reagan to be our savior. He had the right plan for the right time: to get government out of our lives – cut taxes, roll back regulations, cut expensive social programs - and to build up the military so that we could once again take on communists and other evildoers. After a couple of bad years, the economy started to turn around, and inflation was brought under control. As the economy grew, many Americans went back to our good old-fashioned heritage of materialism and individualism. Even some TV preachers used channels on a phenomenon called cable television to tell people that God would make his devoted followers rich. After all, what did years of that hippy, anti-materialist, liberal, secular, "peace and love" crap get us? We rediscovered what Americans always knew: that money makes you happy. There were some problems, however, that would come back to haunt us. The federal government was running big budget deficits, wealth was more concentrated toward the top, and the push toward deregulation may have eventually gone too far.

Then George W. Bush's dad became president, and an amazing thing happened. The Soviet Union, and their puppet governments in Eastern Europe, collapsed. To the shock of almost everyone, the Cold War was over. This was fantastic, but there was one big problem: what would guide our foreign policy now? For forty-five years, U.S. actions were consistently guided by a desire to defeat communism. Without the big bad guy, what would be the plan? At first, Saddam Hussein stepped into the role of bad guy when Iraq invaded Kuwait. Here was a chance to use that big military that Reagan built up in the 1980's, and in a matter of days, the Iraqi army was annihilated. Suddenly, Americans were waving flags again and celebrating a military victory. For many, this was a sign that the embarrassment of Vietnam was being put behind us. "Bush the first" seemed like a lock to win re-election.

But when the economy went bad for a while in the early 1990's, and a quirky businessman named Ross Perot decided to run for president, the door was open for an unknown governor named Bill Clinton to become our next president. And conveniently for him, the economy took off on the longest ride of sustained economic growth in American history. Much of this was due to the increasing integration of the global economy, the growing sophistication of personal computers, and the expanding use of something called the internet (which Clinton's vice president had apparently "invented"). And as many Americans gorged themselves on all of this wealth and invested into new high-tech products and industries, politics was of limited interest. O.J., Monica, and Y2K kept us distracted, and it wasn't like politicians were getting much done anyway. We had a Democratic president and a Republican Congress, and as the two parties

213

became increasingly hostile, they seemed to spend more time talking about Clinton's sex life than proposing effective policies. Things seemed to be going remarkably well anyway – the federal government actually ran a surplus for a while - so the lack of political achievements did not seem like a big problem. Also, our newfound status as the world's only remaining superpower created a sense of safety from foreign threats.

But due to Clinton's "sexual issues," Al Gore's lack of political charisma, a spoiler named Ralph Nader, our ridiculous system for choosing presidents, and the beginnings of a mild recession triggered somewhat by the bursting of a high-tech investing bubble, "Bush II" became president in one of the stranger elections in history. George W. Bush immediately began to push the Reagan agenda. Then, within a matter of months, the growing terrorist threat that most Americans had spent years ignoring and neglecting hit our country on 9/11/2001. Suddenly, we had a big, scary enemy again, and as you are well aware, the War on Terror has been proceeding ever since. Most Americans were terrified and ready to "kick ass" for a while, but it did not take long for many people to become distracted once again by good old-fashioned materialism and the wonders of modern technology: smart phones, high speed internet, social networking, reality TV, "Tivo," etc. They were also distracted by a new bubble in real estate that began to form after the previous internet bubble had burst. Housing prices rose rapidly, fueled largely by insane loans packaged together into strange, unregulated financial instruments that few understood. Then, toward the end of the Bush presidency, the financial system crashed and burned, and government came running to the rescue.

This collapse laid the groundwork for an amazing event: the election of the first non-white man to the presidency. Unfortunately for President Obama, he came into office at a time of several crises: conflict dragging on in Iraq and Afghanistan, economic recession, the rising cost of health care, and an intensifying level of partisan bitterness that can be traced back to the Clinton years. To a large degree, our nation is beginning to pay the price for past foolishness. Unsustainable spending on Medicare, Social Security, and defense has caused ballooning budget deficits now that the economy has slowed down. Reckless borrowing and spending over the course of many years brought us to the brink of disaster, although the government, at a very high cost, has apparently managed to ward off a huge crisis. The housing sector, however, continues to struggle, creating a steady drag on an economy still yet to recover fully. President Obama, ironically enough, may be swept from power by the same financial crisis that played a major part in making him president in the first place.

Has the time finally come where we have to face reality? Have we started to realize that our political and economic systems as they currently stand are unsustainable? Or will self-centered special interest groups and partisan bickering continue to hold back meaningful reform? Every generation must ask itself how the people of the future will judge them. I have a feeling that the last 30 years will be remembered for a couple of things. First, it will be remembered as the beginning of a technological revolution comparable to the invention of agriculture or to the industrial revolution of the early nineteenth century. It is still too early to tell where this change will ultimately lead us. Second, it will be remembered as a period of reckless borrowing and spending – in both the private and public sectors - fueled by the belief that happiness comes from accumulating the stuff that every American has a God-given right to have. And as Americans were distracted by their desire for things, tough decisions have been put off by politicians (of both parties) who are afraid of telling American voters the truth: taxes on all Americans must inevitably be raised, significant spending cuts on big budget programs must be made, the health care system must become more financially efficient, and we must begin the initially painful process of moving toward an economy that is not based on fossil fuels. In short, Americans must make sacrifices. These tough decisions have been put off for too long, and my grandkids might look at me someday and ask me what the hell we were thinking.

47. Was Jesus a Conservative?

Christianity, as far as I can tell, is basically an apolitical religion. Jesus did not really talk about politics in the gospels, and his early followers did not seem to take much interest in the subject either. There is a simple explanation for this lack of interest. Christianity teaches that the world is hopelessly sinful. Satan is the ruler of "the world" – a term repeatedly used in the New Testament - and at some point in the very near future, Jesus is supposed to come back to bring a new world order. There is no point, therefore, in concerning yourself with political questions. Government, a key institution in this hopelessly sinful world, will either be too corrupt or too powerless to do anything about a world that is so evil.

The Religious Right, however, seems to believe that there are certain political opinions that are more in line with Christian teachings than others. Followers of this movement don't always agree on everything, but they tend to support the basic Republican platform: the right to bear arms, low taxes, a strong military, limited business regulations, restrictions on welfare, etc. Now the problem with all of these positions is that the New Testament never addresses these issues directly. I don't recall, for instance, Jesus or the apostles taking positions on the "right to bear arms." (Can you imagine Jesus as an NRA member?) The "Sermon on the Mount" did not include, as far as I know, a quick lesson on politics and economics that sung the praises of a laissez faire, free market economy. I also cannot remember any New Testament writers discussing the importance of a powerful military. (I do recall something, however, about "turning the other cheek.") You could actually make a pretty good case that the positions of the Religious Right on welfare, the military, and free market capitalism are not particularly Christian. Jesus does, after all, say some things that seem downright pacifist, and he talks a lot about the importance of not loving money and of sharing the wealth. Of course, you could also argue that Jesus' words on these topics do not directly relate to politics, a topic that was clearly not his main interest. So the positions of the Religious Right are not necessarily anti-Christian, but they are not necessarily Christian either.

You could make a better case, however, that the positions of the Religious Right on so-called "social issues" - abortion, homosexuality, and sex in general – have stronger support in the Bible. Yet even with these issues, things are a bit hazy. As far as I know, abortion as we define it is not directly addressed. They did not, after all, have doctors that were as sophisticated as ours in Biblical times. Of course, if abortion is understood as murder, then the Bible is pretty clear. Negative statements regarding homosexuality can also be found in the Bible, although not as often as some might think. It is mentioned a few times in Old Testament law, but it only appears once in the New Testament (in the book of "Romans"). Jesus never directly mentions it. So while the Religious Right may be correct in interpreting the Christian view of homosexuality and of sexual immorality in general, they clearly spend a lot more time talking about this stuff than Jesus and his followers were inclined to do. In the gospels, Jesus spends most of his time healing the sick, casting out demons, talking about himself and the kingdom he was implementing, and preaching to the "sinners" with whom he often spent his time. Sometimes, the Religious Right seems fixated on talking about things that you should not do. I guess that it is easier to criticize behavior than it is to propose constructive solutions to problems.

While the positions and behavior of the Religious Right are questionable in my mind, the "Health and Wealth Gospel," a message attractive to some in the Religious Right, is downright wrong. The preachers of this message, which became increasingly popular in the 1980's and lives on somewhat today, argue that people who follow Jesus will be rewarded with health, wealth, and general prosperity. Now I can understand why this movement caught on with some. In the 1980's, materialism was back in style as people moved away from the "hippy liberalism" of the 1960's and '70's. Plus, it is such a nice, easy to follow message. Just avoid blatant immorality, believe in the right stuff, and send some money to the televangelist, and you can then experience prosperity on earth and in heaven. You've got it all. The only problem is that this was not the message of the founder of the faith that you claim to believe. Jesus said that if you follow him, you will end up like him: penniless, persecuted, and ultimately dead on a cross. In a

217

hopelessly sinful world, followers of Jesus are going to suffer because they are going against the grain. Material prosperity is not a sign of holiness; it is a sign that a person is "of the world." A Christian is rewarded with spiritual - not material - blessings and will receive his or her ultimate reward in the next life.

It's amazing to see the disconnect between the message of the "Health and Wealth Gospel" and the gospel preached by the early Christians. But in the United States, a wealthy and powerful country that celebrates materialism, you can see why people would "tweak" the Christian message a bit. Many, but not all, of the people attracted to the political ideology of the Religious Right are also drawn to the Health and Wealth gospel. So if you put the two together, what you get is a new, modern American Jesus. He becomes a hybrid of Ronald Reagan, Charlton Heston, Jerry Falwell, Warren Buffett, and a touch of the Jesus of the gospels.

I strongly emphasize to my class when criticizing these modern American religious trends that I am not making statements about Christianity in general. Many Christians, in fact, would agree with my critiques. I remember going to a conference over twenty years ago where a Christian preacher tore apart the materialistic Christianity so common in the 1980's. I also had a Christian student shout "amen" in the middle of my class one time after I did my little mini-sermon criticizing the Health and Wealth Gospel. Still, there may be students who are offended by my criticism. Then, since their worldview has now been challenged, or they have become downright angry, they may even start studying the Bible in more depth in order to see if my criticism is justified. If this happens, then I know that I have done my job. Sometimes people need to get personally shaken in some way before they will do some independent learning, and in the end, pushing students to study on their own should be the ultimate goal of every teacher. They are not going to remember most of the facts and ideas presented in my class, but if they develop the impulse to start learning on their own, they will go much further then I could ever dream to take them. And if I have to occasionally piss a few people off in order to make that happen, then so be it (amen).

48. 9/11, Terrorism, and Understanding Your Enemy

Every once in a while, an event will take place within the United States or around the world that grabs the attention of the American people. The ultimate, recent examples of this were the terrorist attacks of September 11, 2001. So as people sat transfixed in front of their TV screens watching 24-hour news coverage of 9/11, there was a tremendous opportunity to educate the American public. Many Americans, after all, were caught completely off guard by these events, a fact which revealed our remarkable ignorance. Who the hell were Al Qaeda and Osama Bin Laden? Why would they attack the United States? What is it that these terrorists were trying to accomplish?

After watching some of this news coverage and talking to many students and other Americans over the years, I have concluded that the media largely blew this teaching opportunity. In my Modern American History and World Civilizations courses, I always ask students the simple questions listed at the end of the preceding paragraph. Too often, I either hear simplistic answers or no answers at all. When I ask them about the possible motives of the various Islamic extremist groups that we generally label as terrorists, some students say that these groups are trying to convert everyone to Islam. Others say that they hate the United States because of our secular, sinful, feminist, and freedom loving culture. Others might simply say that these are crazy, evil, religious fanatics who feel that they are carrying out the will of Allah.

Now I am not going to argue that these common responses are completely wrong. The motives for terrorist attacks may vary, and many who resort to these kinds of activities probably do see the United States as a sinful, mostly non-Muslim place that deserves to be attacked. It's also difficult to dispute the idea that a suicide bomber trying to kill as many people as possible is messed up in the head and/or evil. These simplistic explanations, however, are incomplete and therefore not particularly helpful.

My primary hope, and hopefully the goal of all Americans, is that the terrorist threat can be minimized as much as possible. I am not primarily motivated by a desire to punish terrorists or to exercise vengeance. Now to achieve this goal effectively, it is important to consider as many strategies as possible. Military action and the training of security forces may be appropriate at times, but these are not the only possible approaches. In formulating this comprehensive strategy, it is important to gain a deep understanding of your enemies. If you don't understand your enemies, and the forces that helped to create them, you might do some things that are counterproductive.

So let's start with the simple assumption that terrorists are evil. The next obvious question should be, "So how did they become so evil?" Are certain people just born with the evil gene that eventually leads them to become suicide bombers? Most would argue, I hope, that people in general are not born evil (although some might be biologically inclined toward mental illness). Instead, they might eventually turn to evil acts due to the influence of their upbringing, environment, and/or other circumstances of their lives. So what kind of an environment produces these "evildoers"? Are there things that the United States can do to alleviate the negative environmental conditions that may produce future terrorists? Are there things that the United States has done in the past (and present) that may have played a role in producing more terrorists?

Some Americans would object to this final question. Others might object to this entire line of reasoning. If you try to describe the circumstances that are likely to produce terrorists, isn't this a form of justifying what the terrorist has done? And if you say that the United States has made some mistakes in the past that may have incited the growth of terrorist movements, then you are essentially blaming America for terrorism. The only people to blame for a terrorist act are the terrorists themselves. It's not our fault that they hate America. We are just culturally different from them, and they are too messed up in the head to accept this simple fact.

I understand these objections, and I agree that terrorism is ultimately the fault of terrorists. I disagree with the notion, however, that trying to understand a terrorist is a form of justifying his or her behavior. Instead, it is merely an attempt to gather as much information as possible. It is also foolish to live under the delusion that our country has never made mistakes that had negative repercussions. Refusing to recognize mistakes will lead a nation to repeat them.

So why do some people resort to terrorist acts, and why do Islamic extremists hate the United States? There is no single answer to this question. There are, after all, many different individuals and groups out there who we lump together under the term terrorists. But after ten years of listening to and reading the works of many experts on this subject, I think that some general statements can be made. Most importantly, Islamic extremist groups are primarily concerned with events within the Muslim world. Some are local groups trying to shape events within a particular country. Others are international organizations trying to fight a "global jihad." Their primary complaint is that the nations of the Muslim world have generally been ruled for decades by secular, corrupt dictators who do not adhere to either the ethical or legal principles – as these extremist groups interpret them – of Islam. Their goal, then, is to topple these governments and create what they consider to be truly Muslim societies that follow the legal and social system laid out in the Koran. Some even dream of a united Islamic world with a single caliph ruling as in the days shortly after Mohammed.

So what does this have to do with the United States? In the minds of these various extremist groups, the United States has played a role in installing and/or supporting these lousy governments. And like all western nations who have meddled in the affairs of North Africa, the Middle East, and South Asia, it has done this largely to promote American economic interests, namely secure access to oil. The extremists' main reason, therefore, for attacking the United States is not our American culture. What they primarily object to are American political policies. The United States, in their minds, stands in the way of their goals.

While disagreeing with the tactics of Islamic extremists, many people within the Muslim world have similar attitudes toward both American political policies and the Arab governments that the United States has a history of supporting. The Arab Spring of 2011 made it very clear that Islamic extremists were not the only ones who favored toppling Middle Eastern and North African despots. Their vision for the future, however, is generally more in line with western, liberal democracies than some sort of an Islamic theocracy. For the United States, this has created a tricky situation. While some Americans may celebrate this potential march toward democracy, others prefer the social order provided by dictators to the inevitable uncertainty associated with more open societies. Will democracies in the Muslim world be America-friendly? Will Islamic extremists increase their influence either through the ballot box or by taking advantage of a weaker central authority? At the moment, it is too early to know how the Arab Spring will turn out. But if countries such as Egypt and Tunisia become more democratic societies, public support for America-friendly politicians may not be particularly strong. People in these countries remember, after all, decades of American support for the dictators of the past.

What is taking place in the Muslim world is basically a civil war. On one side you have the more moderate, secular Muslims who want the same things that most people want: peace, security, good jobs, family, decent governance, etc. On the other side you have the Islamists who want a society based on their interpretation of the Koran. The most common victims of terrorist attacks, after all, are the moderate Muslims who constitute the majority of the population. From the beginning of the War on Terror, and arguably decades before, the United States should have actively sought out these potential allies. This is a simple fact that has apparently been lost on many Americans. Too often, we like to understand the world in simplistic terms. Often, generic words such as "Arabs," "Muslims," or "terrorists" are used as if there is some single group out there that we are fighting against. By failing to recognize the complexity and divisions that exist within the Muslim world, the United States has often found itself alienating, attacking, and fighting against the wrong people.

The Iraq invasion, in particular, is the ultimate example of a counterproductive war. By targeting the kind of a leader that Islamic extremist groups generally hate, we essentially did Al Qaeda a favor. We took out a lousy ruler without providing an effective replacement, and we created widespread anger that made it easier for terrorist recruiters. At least in the Arab Spring, revolutionary movements have risen from the domestic population. And as non-violent activists were able to do in some cases what terrorists have never accomplished, these movements for democracy have the potential to do more to weaken terrorist activity than United States' efforts to snuff it out by force. When governments have legitimacy, and people have a peaceful means of expressing grievances, the anger that fuels terrorism can be quelled somewhat. There are no guarantees, and dropping a bomb on some bad guys can provide more of a sense of control and a tangible measure of accomplishment than supporting unpredictable social change. The problem is that bombs can sometimes create as many (or more) enemies as they destroy, particularly when they hit the wrong people.

The Iraq War shows what can happen when you misunderstand and inaccurately identify your enemy. There are signs, however, that military leaders and policy makers have grown a bit wiser over the years. Efforts have been made in Iraq and Afghanistan to find people within these countries willing to work with Americans rather than fight them. I get the sense, however, that too many efforts are still focused on trying to snuff out terrorism through brute force. Presidents, after all, whether Republican or Democrat, do not want to be labeled as soft. I just hope that President Obama, a man who has stepped up military efforts in Afghanistan and in neighboring Pakistan, recognizes that fighting is not the only way to go. The focus should be on results, not displays of strength, attempts to establish a sense of control, or the administration of "justice." Of course, we live in a democracy. And in a nation with large numbers of uninformed voters, the wisest actions might not win elections.

49. We Need Investment, Not Speculation

If you want to know someone's political ideology, just ask him or her why the economy has been so bad (thus far) during President Obama's first three years in office. A conservative will be happy to complain about President Obama and his liberal, Democratic buddies. Because of these liberals, the economy is being held back by excessive taxes, regulations, and public debt. People are spooked both by the situation at the moment and by the future impact of health care reform, financial regulation, and a potential "cap and trade" energy policy. Consumers are afraid to spend, and private industry is nervous about investing in an unpredictable environment with a likely future of complicated, burdensome, government rules.

Those liberal Democrats, of course, tell a different story. They emphasize that President Obama inherited a complicated mess left over from the previous administration. Years of lax regulation and shortsighted tax policies that favored the rich led to a financial implosion, massive public debt, and an average American consumer with limited purchasing power. Immediately upon entering office, the president was compelled to propose, create, or inherit bank bailouts, a stimulus package, new financial regulations, and long overdue reforms of health care and energy policy. These drastic, necessary responses to a crisis have made it easy for Republicans to attack him as a promoter of big government. So for primarily political reasons, they say no to everything that he proposes. Clearly, it is unfair to blame a guy for not fixing an inherited problem when the opposition has done everything it can to block his proposed solutions.

There is something to be said for both of these perspectives. And while the liberal version of events seems more plausible to me, I am not particularly impressed with either political party. Our nation clearly faces systemic political problems that cannot be blamed on any one party. I also believe, however, that we give either too much credit or blame to politicians for the economic health of the nation. To a large degree, the economy has a life of its own. Policies can matter, but political success is often a question of luck. You just hope that your political party is in charge when the economy is in an upswing and out of power during the bad times.

I am not an economist, but I am forced to discuss economic issues frequently during the course of my history classes. This has been particularly true during these last few, extraordinary years. I have tried as best I can to make sense out of this current situation, and from what I can gather, the recent financial crisis and lingering economic troubles are largely the result of the decisions of both private industry and of individual Americans. Banks and other financial institutions made a lot of bad loans, and many Americans were more than willing to take those loans to get into homes that they could in no way afford. Neither political party denies this obvious truth. Republicans, however, tend to blame the borrowers for being foolish enough to take on risky loans and the government for aggressively promoting home ownership. Democrats, on the other hand, blame financial institutions for "predatory lending" and the government for its poor regulation of banks and the real estate industry. Whatever the case, the behavior of the years preceding the crisis demonstrate a problem that runs deeper than some bad home loans.

For many years, some of the greatest minds – and many lesser ones - in America have been drawn to the financial sector. They have gone there to apply their considerable intelligence and technical expertise to two activities: speculation and financial engineering. Some have studied the stock market using complex mathematical and statistical models in an attempt to "buy low and sell high." Others created complex financial products that they claimed could eliminate the risks from lending and investing. Pools of thousands of mortgages or other types of debt were compiled, and investors would theoretically get a consistent return from these "Mortgage Backed Securities" when borrowers made their payments. Since so many mortgages were lumped together, you could theoretically predict with some certainty how many borrowers were likely to default and therefore eliminate the risk. The problem was that the people originating the loans often did not

225

care if the borrowers had any hope of paying. These brokers, after all, planned to quickly sell the loans to the institutions creating the pools. Home prices became inflated by all of the easy credit, housing speculation became increasingly common, the real estate industry became overgrown, and a false illusion of prosperity resulted from the "bubble," leading people to spend beyond their actual means.

When many of these loans inevitably began to go bad, all sort of banks and financial institutions were stuck with these financial instruments, and no one knew what they were worth because few understood them. This ultimately led to mass panic, the financial bailouts, a decline in home prices, and lingering economic hardship. Now I don't know enough about derivatives trading to give advice on what should be done in this area. My gut tells me that it should either be outlawed or heavily regulated, but what the hell do I know. I can say with some confidence, however, that there are probably more productive things that great minds can be doing than inventing complicated instruments or models for turning money into more money.

What if more money was invested into the creation of actual goods and services instead of pure speculation? What if great minds were focused on innovative products rather than revolutionary investment strategies? To my simplistic economic mind, it seems that our nation would be better off. We live in an increasingly competitive world, and the winning nations will not be the ones that have the best financial engineers who create short-term profits for their investors and themselves. Bankers play a vital role in our economy, but in the end, great innovators and entrepreneurs have played the most significant role in our nation's prosperity. Americans either invented or played the dominant role in the development of the telephone, electric light, television, personal computer, internet, and countless other life-changing technologies that have produced massive wealth and job opportunities. So where will the next great innovations come from?

Right now, banks and many private companies are sitting on an enormous amount of money. Some of this is the result of improvements in efficiency, productivity, and efforts to scale back the quantity of goods and risky behavior from the inflated, "bubble" years. Consumers are also keeping their wallets shut somewhat due to fears about the uncertain future. In the end, productive investment from the private sector is the key to getting us out of the hole. The government is strapped, and it has historically shown little capacity to efficiently produce innovative goods and services that the public demands. If anything, politicians should be thinking of creative ideas for encouraging investment into the development of innovative products and ideas. When jobs in industries with long-term viability are created, then consumers will once again have money to spend. The trick is convincing banks and companies that it is time to start lending, investing, and expanding once again.

I recognize that the stock market and the real estate industry play vital roles in generating income, creating jobs, mobilizing capital, and improving our future prospects for retirement. It is unhealthy, however, to have an economy where too much investment goes into these potentially speculative activities. "Flipping" a house or selling stock transfers income; these actions do not produce wealth over the long haul. We need innovators who develop valuable goods and services and financial institutions that have the foresight to invest in them. Who will be the next Alexander Graham Bell, Thomas Edison, Henry Ford, or Steve Jobs? God help us if minds like these innovators get too busy analyzing the market or creating the successor to the "Collateralized Debt Obligation."

50. The Fall of Tiger Woods, and What it Reveals About Us

Tiger Woods is one of a handful of people who was able at one time to dominate his sport through sheer talent and/or force of personality, a list that includes larger-than-life sports figures such as Babe Ruth, Michael Jordan, Wayne Gretzky, Muhammad Ali, Jim Brown, and Roger Federer. In 2009, however, his name was added to a longer, less distinguished list of sports figures tarnished by scandal: OJ Simpson, Kobe Bryant, Michael Vick, Barry Bonds, Roger Clemens, Ben Roethlisberger, and the list goes on and on.

This story offended people on multiple levels. Some were obviously offended by his infidelity. (Many men, I suspect, were actually kind of jealous.) Others were more sympathetic toward Tiger and argued that his private life should remain private. Golfing skill earned him fame and respect, not the quality of his personal life. We should continue to focus on those skills that make him great – or, at least, that used to make him great - and leave the rest alone. Still others asked the question that I find to be the most interesting and important: Why do we care? There are so many things happening in the world that merit more attention than Tiger Woods' sex life and failed marriage. While I sympathize with this complaint, I also think that Tiger's story demonstrated some very important truths. His behavior, after all, was not the story. The story was the public reaction to his behavior.

The United States may be the most celebrity-obsessed nation of all time (although this is a trait that is not exclusively American in the modern world). Because people are trained from birth to constantly need some external source of entertainment, they end up worshipping entertainers. Now worship, some might say, is too strong of a word, but I find it very appropriate. Americans on average spend far more time, energy, and money on entertainment than they do on religious activities and institutions. They can often tell you more about sports statistics and contestants on *American*

Idol than they can tell you about the Bible, and in my mind, actions speak louder than words.

The problem, however, goes far beyond spending huge amounts of time and money on entertainment. Many Americans, from what I can tell, show as much interest in celebrities' personal lives as they do in the entertainment that these famous people provide. And in some cases, due to our modern obsession with "reality" TV, an individual's personal life is the entire basis of his or her fame. Personally, I try to avoid celebrity "news," and yet I often know which famous people are currently facing marital problems, struggling with weight issues, choosing the wrong fashion designer, or struggling to get pregnant. All that I have to do is go through the checkout stand at the supermarket to get a quick update. A while back, I was able to find out who had the best and worst beach bodies, and while I recognize the vital importance of this issue, those were some images that I (in some cases) really did not need to see.

So where does all of this interest in the personal lives of celebrities come from? One source may be the boredom and dissatisfaction that Americans feel with their own lives. By obsessing about celebrities, they get a chance to live vicariously through someone more beautiful and talented. In other cases, the problems celebrities face may actually cause average Americans to feel better about their lives. We may face marital problems, but at least we are not Tiger Woods. Finally, we may also be a society that is always on the lookout for idols and heroes. In an entertainment-crazed culture, this search naturally draws us to people with musical, acting, or athletic skills. But we want more. We want a human being that we can admire, so we are then unable to resist the desire to find out who this person is that entertains us so well. Unfortunately, idol worship directed toward entertainers will often lead to disappointment, and when it does, we make those celebrities pay in the tabloid press.

In addition to the tabloids and the public, certain companies also decided to punish Tiger Woods. I remember seeing a chart in a newspaper once that showed the highest paid athletes in the world, and Tiger Woods topped the list to the tune of approximately $100 million in a single year. He made a lot of money winning golf tournaments, but it mostly came from advertising dollars. So why do advertisers dish out that kind of money to a guy who is not necessarily an authority on many of the products – watches, razors, cars, etc. – that he endorses (or endorsed)? Part of the answer goes back to the celebrity worship mentioned earlier. I also believe, however, that famous people endorsing products, and advertising in general, is clear proof that the human race is not particularly rational. Because Tiger Woods or Michael Jordan is paid to tell us to buy something, does this improve the quality of the product? I hope that we will all answer no, and yet companies keep shelling out the big bucks. Are they that stupid? I doubt it. The truth is that we are apparently that stupid.

Advertising does not appeal to human reason. It appeals to subconscious desires. So apparently, on some subconscious level, we believe that buying a Buick or wearing Hanes Underwear will improve our golf game or enhance our vertical leap. Celebrities project an image which appeals to our subconscious desire to be successful "like Mike." This is why Tiger lost some endorsement deals. Tiger Woods' appeal to consumers was not simply his golf game; it was also the positive, "family values" image that he projected. Kobe Bryant ran into the same problem a few years ago when he had his own sex scandal. Kobe has shown, however, that you can eventually earn some of that reputation back. Will Tiger someday do the same?

Finally, in fairness to Tiger Woods, Kobe Bryant, Bill Clinton, Jonathan Edwards, and countless other famous, powerful men who were unable to resist "temptation" at some point in their lives, it is important to note that these celebrities have opportunities that few men (or women) can ever fully comprehend. It is easy to be faithful when opportunities to cheat are not falling into your lap (pun intended). But if you are famous in a world of people who find fame irresistible, it can be difficult to keep "fighting them off." To paraphrase Henry Kissinger – a guy who claimed to get a lot of sex – "power is the ultimate aphrodisiac." Ultimately, we humans are the same as all other animals, driven by the primal desires for food and sex. The desire for lots of sex, in the end (no pun intended), may be one of the biggest reasons why people want to be famous in the first place. One of the biggest costs of this fame, however, is the privacy that Tiger Woods and other fallen heroes consistently request from the public. Privacy, however, is one thing that he and other megastars gave up a long time ago.

Part Eleven: The Big Picture and the Future

51. The "Arab Spring" and American Foreign Policy

For the last several decades, there have been two consistent themes in American foreign policy. First and foremost, the United States has sought to promote its economic interests, seeking out foreign sources of raw materials, markets for American goods, and cheap overseas labor. It was not until the industrial revolution accelerated in the late 19th century, in fact, that the United States took much interest in foreign affairs at all. The second pattern, appearing particularly after World War II, has been to focus attention on a single, global, overriding threat. From the end of the war until about 1990, the United States was fixated on the other global superpower, the Soviet Union, and more generally, on the "evil" of communism.

It was impossible to separate these goals of fighting communism and promoting economic interests. If nations throughout the world adopted the Soviet economic system, it would close off opportunities for American businesses. States would assert control over economies, and American landowners and businesses operating there would be displaced. Protecting economic interests, however, was not the primary motive given for fighting the Cold War. Instead, the American public was told that communism was a threat to the principles that they held most dear: democracy, individual freedoms, and basic human rights.

But when the communist bloc collapsed about 20 years ago, the United States suddenly lacked direction now that the big "bad guy" was gone. The only coherent strategy left was the promotion of economic interests, a task that many Americans, especially the opponents of "globalization," did not find particularly noble. This situation changed, however, on September 11, 2001 when terrorists emerged as the new evil force that needed to be defeated. And with the invasions of Afghanistan and especially Iraq, a Bush doctrine emerged to help justify these actions. By establishing democratic systems in these nations, the threat of future terrorist attacks would supposedly be minimized. Democracy would provide a healthy outlet for people to express grievances, and governments more responsive to their people would evolve. Terrorist groups would therefore have a less angry population at their disposal as they recruited future attackers. Then, over the course of time, the Afghani and Iraqi governments would become role models for other predominantly Muslim nations, and the spread of democracies would reduce the threat of terrorism everywhere.

So in both the Cold War and the War on Terror, the United States argued that it was promoting democracy and basic human rights. The problem in both cases, however, was that the United States, to say the least, was highly selective in actually carrying out this task. During the Cold War, it was common practice for the United States to support anti-communist dictators in order to contain the "Soviet" threat. And during this so-called War on Terror, the United States, at the same time that it was "promoting democracy" in Afghanistan and Iraq, maintained its often long-term support of dictators and monarchs in nations such as Egypt, Jordan, Yemen, Bahrain, Saudi Arabia, Pakistan (under Musharraf), and Tunisia.

There are two general explanations for this discrepancy between American words and American actions. Some would emphasize that we live in a dangerous, less than ideal world, and in this "real world," you must sometimes support a "bad guy" to prevent the emergence of someone or something even worse. A leader that we support might be a son-of-a-bitch, but at least he is our son-of-a-bitch. If the United States was to only support leaders who upheld certain principles, or if it were to step back and let events unfold in another nation, then an evil, anti-American government might take hold, or you may end up with chaos in the streets. So in the name of American national security and general global stability, the U.S. government did what was necessary. Others, however, would argue that it is mostly a question of economics. If a leader or government serves American economic interests, whether it is banana plantations in Guatemala or oil produced in Saudi Arabia, then the United States will offer consistent support. A government's record on human rights and democracy is of secondary concern.

So as events in the "Arab Spring" continue to unfold, with insurrections spreading from Tunisia and Egypt to other nations in North Africa and the Middle East, our government has found itself in a tough spot. For decades, the United States operated under the assumption that tough dictators are generally better than the potential alternatives. As much of the world figured out a long time ago, American promotion of democracy has been mostly just words. So is it time for a real shift in policy? Can the United States run the risk of allowing events to unfold in a part of the world that is so economically vital and potentially dangerous? Have events already spiraled out of America's false sense of control?

Since the War on Terror began, the American public has been bombarded by images of explosions, angry religious fanatics, and rampant anti-Americanism. This has created the impression that all of the anger in the Muslim world is directed against the United States in the form of religious extremism. Once again, as in the Cold War, we have been fixated on a single, simplistically defined threat. Events in Tunisia, Egypt, Syria, Libya, Yemen, and Bahrain, however, have made it clear that there are plenty of angry people who are not Islamic fundamentalists, and their anger, believe it or not, is primarily directed against their own governments. Apparently, most of these people want the same basic things as we Americans: the right to express themselves, the rule of law, decent jobs, and governments not engaged in plunder. The protestors in the streets do not represent a single, coherent group, but I do not get the impression that "terrorists" have played a major role. So maybe the majority of people in these nations are not so foreign and dangerous after all. And unlike Iraq and Afghanistan, the people themselves have generated this push for democracy, not an outside invader. So if some form of democratic government emerges in Tunisia, Egypt or elsewhere, it will have a degree of legitimacy lacking in Iraq and Afghanistan. Maybe the Bush doctrine, an idea that many Americans ascribe to in theory, will get a chance to play itself out.

The rubber has met the road, and it's time to find out what our current policymakers actually believe. In the past, economic interests and stability have generally trumped human rights and democracy. It is easy to understand why. Democracy is such a messy, unpredictable process that often fails to take hold, so the only apparent alternative is to make friends with the best available dictator. Civil wars and coups, after all, tend to be more common ways that power is transferred than peaceful elections. And in the Muslim world, a region where the United States is not particularly popular, even a successfully established democracy could very well result in an anti-American government. The temptation, therefore, is to intervene in an attempt to shape and control events, a temptation that the United States has had trouble resisting for decades.

As the only remaining military superpower, the United States still views itself as the world's policeman. It outspends militarily the rest of the world combined, maintaining hundreds of bases throughout the planet. And while I am sure that these efforts provide a certain amount of security, I suspect that the United States is often investing into an illusion. With all of its power, the United States cannot predict or control events to the degree that it would like, and as Iraq and Afghanistan demonstrate, imposing its will can often do more harm than good. So as counterintuitive as it may seem, allowing events to unfold, along with nudging autocratic governments toward reform, could be the best way of promoting American security. After years of aid and intervention in the Muslim world, any United States government attempt to do more than nudge could harm the legitimacy of these movements. But if average citizens in the Muslim world are truly given the opportunity to shape their own destiny, there may be fewer of them with the energy and motivation to attack Americans. It's a gamble, but as we should have learned on 9/11, the world is an unpredictable place, and there is no way to guarantee absolute security.

52. Creating Jobs

Particularly during tough times, elections in the United States often boil down to one main issue: the economy. So in the course of long and monotonous presidential and congressional campaigns, we all get to hear a phrase that has been repeated countless times over the decades: "create jobs." Candidates will brag about jobs that they have created or will someday generate, and the political party that does not control the White House will blast the president for his seeming inability to bring enough of them into existence.

But what do politicians mean when they say, "create jobs"? The only direct way that government officials can create jobs is to hire people to perform some sort of a public service. If people are out of work, then the government can seemingly snap its fingers and go out and hire them. This will not only help people meet their basic needs, get something done, and go out and spend in order to stimulate the economy. It will also help them maintain a degree of dignity and personal responsibility that does not come from receiving a government handout. If the government is not going to just sit back and let people starve, then why not pay them to do something? It's better than handing out food stamps and unemployment checks.

There is a problem, however, with this simplistic approach. In the short term, public works can possibly be a way to boost the economy. But taken too far, it will inevitably lead to unproductive spending. The government will end up creating jobs for the sake of creating jobs, and people will be hired to do things that serve no vital need and meet no public demand. The government will spend more than it gets back in the form of economic growth, and it will be forced to finance this continued, inefficient spending with tax increases, borrowing, or the inflation of the currency.

At times in American history, the government has tried to spend its way toward job creation and economic growth. In the 1930's, at the height of the worst economic disaster in American history, Franklin Roosevelt tried to improve the situation through a combination of public works, social service spending, and increased government regulation. The economy generally improved over the course of the 1930's, but the country never came close to complete recovery. Unemployment remained high, and historians and economists still disagree on whether or not the New Deal helped, hindered, or did next to nothing to promote economic growth. In the 1960's, Lyndon B. Johnson embarked on his attempt to create a "Great Society" through government legislation. Medicare, housing programs, food stamps, and education spending, among other things, came out of this remarkable period of expanded government. Poverty and joblessness, however, remained, and many blame government efforts to create this so-called "Great Society" for the rampant inflation of the late 1960's and 1970's and some of our current budget deficits today. President Obama in 2009 was able to get through Congress an economic stimulus plan to deal with the nasty recession that he inherited, with about 2/3 of this three-year program consisting of public works and social service spending. (The rest of the "spending" consisted of tax cuts.) But while the economy started growing again shortly after he entered office, many saw these efforts as largely a failure, and like Johnson and Roosevelt before him, this spending added even more to government debt.

Conservatives would argue that this increasingly bloated public sector has drained away resources over the years from the private sector, the part of the economy that is much more productive and efficient when it comes to creating jobs. This is why they would argue that the best way for the government to encourage the creation of jobs is to get the hell out of the way. By cutting taxes, reducing business regulations, and scaling back this unproductive spending, businesses will have a better environment in which to succeed and compete in a global economy.

The only problem with this perfectly logical philosophy is that it does not seem necessarily to work. At the moment, both income and capital gains taxes are historically very low. And while corporate income taxes in the United States are high relative to many other countries, these tax rates are irrelevant for large corporations with the resources and accountants that make it possible to exploit the gaping loopholes in the system. Meanwhile, the economy sputters along, with corporate profits not necessarily translating into American jobs.

In fact, the story of the last thirty years of American history has largely been one of gradually decreasing taxes and business regulations, and conservative Republicans have done much better over the past forty years than they did in the previous forty. From 1933 to 1968, there was one Republican in the White House, Dwight Eisenhower, a man considered at the time to be a moderate. But from 1969 to 2008, Republicans controlled the White House for 28 of the 40 years. Democrats, however, still controlled Congress for much of this time. But from 1995 to 2007, Republicans held the majority in the House of Representatives for the first time since 1955, indicating that Bill Clinton's election had more to do with early 1990's circumstances and his political skills than the country's shift in a liberal direction. You could make a strong case, in fact, that the administrations of Bill Clinton and Barrack Obama (so far) were far more conservative than those of Lyndon Johnson and Richard Nixon. The country has shifted to the right, and many would argue (including myself) that if Ronald Reagan ran on his record today, he would face a great deal of opposition from within the Republican Party. His willingness to go along at times with tax increases, support of limited amnesty for illegal immigrants, and eventual decision to negotiate with the Soviet Union would be attacked by many of the party faithful as far too liberal.

But if you really want to test historically the ideology of limited government, you need to go back to the 19th century, a time when politicians of all parties supported a "laissez faire" policy. Income taxes (with the exception of the Civil War period) did not exist, labor unions had no guaranteed right to collectively bargain in order to improve their unregulated work conditions, environmental regulations were not even a consideration, and there were no social services at the federal level. It was a libertarian's dream. And while the period is characterized by spectacular industrial growth – just as the 1980's through the mid-2000's experienced tremendous technological growth - it also had periodic economic collapses. These came roughly every twenty years, and since the government did next to nothing to regulate financial activity or provide aid in times of crisis, the downturns could be particularly violent. Nine percent unemployment would sound very good to people in the mid-1870's or 1890's. Eventually, the Federal Reserve was created in the early 20th century in an attempt to prevent and mitigate these occasional crises. Increased social service spending over the course of the 20th century has also evolved, at least in part, to provide a stabilizing effect on the economy. So with the exceptions of 1929 and 2008, the last 100 years have not seen the kinds of financial panics and economic catastrophes that we had in the 1800's. It is important to note, however, that both the 1929 and 2008 crashes were preceded by periods of laissez faire policies regarding financial regulation. (The same can be said about the savings and loan crisis of the early 1990's.) Is this a coincidence? You can decide for yourself.

So what is the best way to create jobs and promote economic growth and stability? Should government be actively trying to improve our current situation, or should they be getting out of the way? If you look back over American history, it can be difficult to find patterns. We have had both good and bad times under liberals, and the same can be said for conservatives. To a large degree, the economy seems to have a life of its own, with factors such as technological innovation and events in foreign nations having a greater impact than politicians. Sure, political policies can matter. Massive government spending on Social Security, Medicare, and defense has a tremendous impact on the economy. Changing the highest progressive income tax rate from 70% to 35% has made some kind of a difference. But in our current environment, few politicians from either side are proposing that we completely dismantle entitlement programs or significantly change tax policies. And in a complex, $15 trillion economy with interconnections around the globe, no one can predict or measure the impact of relatively minor adjustments to spending and/or tax rates. A non-biased economist would tell you that tweaking the economy in these ways would likely have no impact at all.

I often envy certain political commentators or some of the people engaging in dialogues on Facebook. It would be nice to have all of the answers, to be able to interpret every event in a way consistent with one's political ideology. When trying to comprehend complex economic matters, however, I often find myself throwing my hands up in surrender. And when I hear people attributing all of the ebbs and flows of unemployment and economic growth to the actions of politicians, I automatically lose a certain amount of respect for their level of wisdom and objectivity.

Still, there are a few things that I can say with a fair amount of confidence. Regardless of recent election results, our economy would currently be struggling. No matter what Barack Obama, John McCain, or anyone else did or might have done, we would inevitably pay a heavy price for years of stupid lending, borrowing, and financial engineering. And the federal government would be facing massive debt right now from years of refusing to ask Americans to sacrifice in the form of higher taxes or significant cuts in government spending. The best time for the government to get its financial house in order is when times are relatively good. Instead, they have waited for a massive drop in government revenue to start talking seriously about spending cuts, tax increases, and/or balanced budgets. So the job picture remains bad, and government layoffs, especially at the state and local level, are making the situation even worse.

Anyone who is willing to take an objective, historical perspective will realize that it takes years to determine the effects of political and economic decisions. It is silly to hold any politicians fully responsible for the state of a complex economy. But it is even more ridiculous to hold any current leader fully responsible for the present. The inability of Americans, and most likely humans in general, to think about the long-term is one of our biggest weaknesses. It is always easier to focus on the present and to look for someone who claims to have an immediate, simple answer. This is why election results often hinge more on present circumstances than on history or even ideology. Changing leaders is unlikely to have much of an immediate effect on the economy. But it can be a nice way to vent.

53. Entertainment Addiction: A History

In recent years, the term "cell phone" has become increasingly out-of-date. The *Iphone, Blackberry, Android,* and other similar devices are more like miniature, full- service personal computers than phones. And since computers have enhanced my life in so many ways, it is very tempting to get my hands on a portable one that can always be with me. I can then use it for browsing the internet, taking pictures, listening to music and podcasts, getting directions, and god knows what else with the countless "apps" that are available. So why have I not taken this plunge? Part of the reason, believe it or not, is fear. Most practically, there is the fear of the cost, which is particularly strong for a part-time teacher living in tough economic times. There is also, however, my traditional fear of things that are new. A part of me does not want to go through the technological learning process again.

There is also, however, an even deeper fear. I know from past experience that I can easily become addicted to things. For instance, I have always loved playing games of all kinds, and the more complicated the strategy, the happier I am. If I allowed myself, I could easily spend all of my time playing various board games, card games, or computer and video games. There have been times, in fact, where I struggled to stop thinking about a game that I had been playing frequently. More recently, I have had trouble logging off of Facebook, HubPages, or music-downloading sites. If I had a mobile device that could do just about anything, would I be able to turn the thing off?

Part of this fear derives from the students that I see passing through my classes. So many of them, after all, cannot imagine life without one of these mobile devices, and from what I can gather, they are unable to turn the damn things off. When they had devices that were simply phones, this was not a big problem during class time. Students could not very well conduct conversations in the middle of class. But with the prevalence of text messaging and of the various apps that can be loaded onto these modern devices, it is pretty easy for a student to play with these things covertly during class. The problem, however, goes far beyond class time. It is when I see students walking around campus that it is clear just how pervasive these devices have become. It is increasingly rare these days to see a student hanging around campus who is not text messaging, playing some game, listening to headphones, or talking on the phone. But if they are doing this outside of my class, then why should I care?

First of all, it concerns me as an educator. If students are constantly distracted by these addictive devices, then how much time are they investing into my class or into any other educational activity? In addition, how can I as a teacher compete? Playing with these devices is so much more fun, and requires far less in terms of mental effort, than trying to learn history. My worries, however, extend far beyond the college campus. Anyone venturing out into the general public knows the degree to which Americans are addicted to their mobile devices.

Because these things are still relatively knew, it is currently difficult to determine their long-term social impact. One of the few things historians can count on is that attempts to predict the future are almost always, to a certain degree, wrong. But I believe that it is still possible to make some educated guesses that are based on the social impact of past innovations. These mobile devices, after all, are a culmination of long-term trends in how Americans access entertainment and information.

As the media revolution of the past 125 years has evolved, one can notice a few general trends. First, we have seen an increasing variety in the means by which a person can receive either entertainment or information. The development of telephones, radio, movie theaters, television, and video games created entertainment and information options that people in the not so distant past could hardly imagine. Until recently, however, these life-changing technologies had certain limitations. With radio, television, and movie theaters, people were limited to watching the programming that was being offered at a particular time. Telephones had to be plugged into a wall in order to operate them, so they were only available in limited locations. And video games, in addition to being far less sophisticated than today's options, allowed a person to only compete against a limited number of opponents who were physically connected to the same video game system.

As anyone who does not live under a rock knows, the limitations listed in the previous paragraph have ceased to exist, which brings me to a second major media trend to develop in recent history: personalization. The first small step in this direction was the increasing availability of recorded sound. Through record players, you could now listen to specific spoken or musical recordings at the time of your choice. You were not restricted to whatever the radio played or to the current live performances in town. When cassette tapes became readily available later in history, the listening experience could be even more personalized because individuals were able to create their own tapes and not be restricted to whatever compilations that the recording industry chose to produce. Video cassette recorders would later have the same impact on TV viewing, and when the movie industry began distributing videos for purchase or rental, the movie theater could now be brought into the home under the viewer's own terms. And whether you watched rentals or used your VCR to record your favorite shows, you were able to watch things when it was convenient. You no longer had to follow someone else's schedule.

These trends toward increased variety and personalization, of course, have rapidly accelerated in recent years due to the development of digital video recorders, the explosion of television channels due to cable and satellite TV, and, most importantly, the development of personal computers that were eventually connected to the World Wide Web. The personal computer and the internet, among other things, can pull together in a single device all of the past innovations for transmitting information and entertainment. A computer is a television, stereo, sound recorder, book, newspaper, magazine, video game system, telephone, and a sender of mail all wrapped up into one. And with the rapid development of the internet as an information and entertainment tool, the number of options in all of these various forms is seemingly infinite and instantly available.

Now if personal computers remained as fairly bulky objects that needed to be plugged into an outlet and a phone jack, they would still be life-changing devices. With increasingly sophisticated mobile computers, however, the last obstacle to endless entertainment and information access has been removed. Not only do we have seemingly infinite variety and personalization; now we can have every form of media ever developed by the human race with us at every moment of the day. So on the one hand, one could argue that the modern mobile device is simply a culmination, a pulling together, of past media developments. It is possible, therefore, that the long-term social impact of these mini-computers will be no greater than that of radio, television, video recorders, walkmans, or telephones.

I suspect, however, that we are dealing with something that is more than just an improvement of past forms of media. First, there is the issue of volume. The amount of information and entertainment available, and the ease of accessing all of these options, is something new in the human experience. And second, there is also the issue of mobility. In the past, it was nearly impossible to have continuous access to the television, radio, movie theater, or phone. (Unless, of course, you had no life at all.) Now, all of these are available on the spur of the moment virtually anywhere you go. This has never been true to such a degree before, and in ways that we can still not imagine, this technology has the potential to enhance our lives. But have we already reached a point, as I mentioned earlier, where people are unable to turn the things off? And if this is true, is that a problem?

One of the most common complaints of young people in our society is that they are bored, and I am sure that there are quite a few adults in America who would be bored too if they were not busy with working and/or parenting. Boredom may be a constant throughout human history, but I suspect that it has become a bigger problem in the modern world. Children in modern society are inundated with entertainment and information from birth, and because they are continually entertained, many never develop the capacity to entertain themselves. Creative play, which comes naturally to children, may have already become an increasingly lost art. And if kids conditioned in this way are not constantly receiving an external source of entertainment, boredom is the frequent result. In my mind, people who are easily bored are often boring people. It is not their fault. They were never given the opportunity to become interesting. It should be no surprise, therefore, that we have long been a society that worships entertainers. These entertainers provide the one thing that many Americans have most been taught to crave.

I am not only worried, however, about living in a society filled with people who are not particularly interesting. I also wonder if we will become a society filled with people who seldom take the time to stop and think, and when I say stop and think, I am not talking about reading blogs and discussing issues with their friends on Facebook. Self-reflection may become a lost art, and when people stop asking themselves why they think, feel, and act the way that they do, we will have a population of people that are easily controlled. Advertisers, particularly with the advent of television, have developed controlling others into an art form. At the moment, they are struggling to figure out how to operate in this new media environment. I have no doubt that they will improve their ability to get their message out through these mobile devices in the same way that they have done it through all previous forms of media. And if people struggle to turn the things off, and rarely stop to reflect on their own core beliefs and values, they are vulnerable to whatever forces are out there trying to program them. Corporate advertisers are the most powerful of these forces, but there are many other groups – political, economic, and cultural - who are also competing to get their message out.

Then again, maybe I am as paranoid as all of the conspiracy theorists preaching their message all over the internet. Time will tell. In the end, it all comes down to moderation. I have fallen more deeply in love with technology as time has passed, and I foresee this relationship only getting stronger in the future. I try to limit my exposure, however, to a reasonable amount of time because these new technologies make me more than a little nervous. My fear is that future generations who have never known a world without these technologies, and who will have access to things that I cannot yet imagine, will no longer be capable of seeing any reason to fear them.

54. Will You or I be Remembered?

It is a depressing but undeniable fact that the overwhelming majority of humans who have ever lived were forgotten shortly (in historical terms) after their deaths. For tens of thousands of years, all people lived in hunting and gathering societies. Since writing did not yet exist, a culture's memories were preserved through the telling of stories. These stories may have included important individuals from the past, but as they were told and altered through succeeding generations, direct connections to the individuals who inspired the stories faded. Stories originally told about actual people evolved into legends, and most people were not prominent enough to inspire any legends.

About five thousand years ago, the first civilization (we think) in history, the Sumerians, developed the earliest known writing system. One of the most important functions of writing is the preservation of a culture's memories and values. Because some of their writings were preserved, we know more about the Sumerians than we could ever know about ancient hunters and gatherers. The problem is that only a small percentage of Sumerians knew how to write, and these were people from the upper classes. So we only know about things that interested these classes of literate people. Most people, of course, were peasant farmers, and the literate classes did not say much about these "low-lifes." The voices of the majority of Sumerians, like most of the people living in past civilizations, will be forever silent.

The closer we get to the present, however, the more likely it is that records from a period have been preserved. With the development of the printing press first in China and later in Europe, there was a tremendous increase in the number of books produced. Still, literacy was a skill dominated by the upper classes, so books that were widely circulated and that survived until the present day were generally produced by and written about the rich and famous. The writings of average people, when they existed at all, largely disappeared over time. Eventually, of course, the skills of reading and writing began to spread beyond the upper classes, and today we have a fair amount of written resources produced by the average people who lived in the last few centuries. Many of us may even have some written documents from some of our own fairly distant ancestors. We may even have some photographs of ancestors who lived after about 1840. The further back you go, however, the scarcer these records become. But ff we had access to more information, would we spend more time learning about our ancestors?

Let's be honest. How often do any of us even think about relatives who lived before we were born? Even if we have some photographs or documents from these people, do we ever take the time to look at them? And if this is true of people today, will it be true of our future descendants when we are long gone? After all, young people today know very little about individuals who were famous not too long ago. How many people in their twenties can provide very much information about Frank Sinatra, Lyndon Johnson, C.S. Lewis, Clark Gable, or Howard Hughes? Even huge names like George Washington and Abraham Lincoln will elicit a blank stare from many Americans. So if many have forgotten the famous people of the past, and if even our own descendants are unlikely to be interested in our stories, are most of us destined to enter the same void as the billions who came before? Death is a hard enough fact of life. Realizing that the world will someday move on as if we were never here may be an even bigger slap in the face. The compulsion to write, paint, sculpt, build or do anything creative may be largely an attempt to leave behind some proof of our existence. Some would argue that religion also came into being to help us deal with our future annihilation.

There may be some hope, however, for people of the 21st century. (And I am not talking about technology that will soon help us live forever.) I have heard it argued that we are living through the third major media revolution in human history. The first was the invention of writing; the second, the development of printing; and the third, the digital age. Today, we have the ability to both access and store information in ways that people in the not so distant past could hardly imagine. We have digital cameras and video recorders that can take limitless images and store them on computer hard drives, flash drives and compact discs. The same, of course, is true of written records, as personal computers are increasingly making many types of physical documents obsolete. We can then if we so choose take these various digital records and share them on the World Wide Web, which essentially establishes another location for our stuff to be stored.

What will happen someday to our home movies, photos, and various other records that we have digitally backed up? What will happen in the future to blog entries, Facebook posts, uploaded Youtube videos, e-mails, or anything else that we have shared with others on the World Wide Web? Will these records be stored away into some type of super database for future generations to access? At the moment, there is no way to answer these questions because the digital information age is so young and unprecedented. This stuff may be well preserved for hundreds of years, or it could disappear into the void like so many of the memories and written records of the past.

When I was a child, my family's home movies were filmstrips. These were low quality, silent films that give some indication of what I used to look like and how I sometimes behaved. I will never quite know, however, the sound of my voice when I was four years old or some of my other distinct childhood mannerisms. In the 1980's, my parents bought one of those new video cameras that produced videotapes rather than filmstrips. Now we were able to stick a tape into a VCR immediately after filming and see (and hear) ourselves on TV. So if a person is about 25 years old or younger, they may have the opportunity to see themselves as a child in a way that I never will. We have, for instance, hours of digital footage of my kids. Someday, their great, great grandkids may have the opportunity to watch these home movies on whatever devices that their society will be using. For them, these 100-year-old movies will look like they were just filmed.

Future generations should have easy access to an enormous amount of information about their ancestors. These may be digitally stored as part of their personal records or they may be floating out there on the World Wide Web. The only question is whether or not they will care enough to look.

Sources

As stated at the beginning of this book, this is not a work of historical scholarship. My goal is not to produce anything new in terms of historical information. Instead, I have tried to present the basics of American history in a manner that is both understandable and relevant to people today. Much of the history presented, therefore, can be placed in the category of general historical knowledge. And like the lesson plans I present in my classes, my understanding of the material has evolved over the course of twenty-five years of taking history courses, reading books and articles, listening to NPR, watching documentaries, going to museums, and doing whatever else I could to increase my knowledge. So for most of what I have written, I cannot recall the exact, individual sources from where I derived the information. After so many years of teaching, I was able to write most of the essays off the "top of my head" without accessing any historical resources as I typed.

The only material that may be original would be the personal commentary that attempts to connect the American past to events today. These have evolved through my direct, personal experiences trying to make this stuff meaningful for my students. I do recognize, however, that some of my personal ideas and insights were drawn partially (or completely) from others. It is almost impossible, after all, to claim that any of our ideas are completely original.

Having said all this, I have included a list of sources – arranged, more or less, in chronological order - that I know had some direct influence over the essays written here. And if nothing else, this list will provide some resources for people who want to study specific topics in more depth than I have attempted to delve in this book. So with all of the authors listed here, I am thankful for their scholarship and unique insights.

Diamond, Jared. *Guns, Germs and Steel: The Fates of Human Societies.* New York: Norton, 1999.

Zinn, Howard. *A People's History of the United States.* New York: HarperPerennial, 1990.

Shenkman, Richard. *Legends, Lies, and Cherished Myths of American History.* New York: HarperPerennial, 1988.

Shenkman, Richard. *I Love Paul Revere, Whether He Rode or Not.* New York: HarperCollins, 1991.

Boyer, Paul and Stephen Nissenbaum. *Salem Possessed: The Social Origins of Witchcraft.* Harvard University Press, 1974.

Carlson, Laurie Winn. *A Fever in Salem.* Ivan R. Dee, 1999.

Morgan, Edmund S. "Slavery and Freedom: The American Paradox." *Journal of American History 59 (1972): pgs. 5-29.*

Keegan, John. *A History of Warfare.* New York: Vintage Books, 1993.

Morris, Richard B. *Witnesses at the Creation: Madison, Jay, and the Constitution,* pgs. 186-223. Henry Holt and Company, 1985.

Beard, Charles A. *An Economic Interpretation of the Constitution.* Macmillan Publishing Company, 1963.

Cowan, Ruth Schwartz. *A Social History of American Technology.* New York: Oxford University Press, 1997.

Beniger, James. *The Control Revolution: Technological and Economic Origins of the Information Society.* Harvard College, 1986.

Chandler, Alfred. *The Visible Hand: The Managerial Revolution in American Business.* Harvard University Press, 1993.

Sowell, Thomas. *Ethnic America.* New York: Basic Books, 1981.

The Confessions of Nat Turner, Leader of the Late Insurrection in Southampton, Virginia, as Fully and Voluntarily Made to Thomas Gray, pgs. 5-17. New York, 1964.

Oates, Stephen B. *With Malice Toward None: A Life of Abraham Lincoln.* New York: HarperCollins, 1994.

Trachtenberg, Alan. *The Incorporation of America.* New York: Hill and Wang, 1982.

Limerick, Patricia Nelson. *The Legacy of Conquest: The Unbroken Past of the American West.* New York: Norton, 1987.

Wrobel, David W. *The End of American Exceptionalism.* Lawrence: University Press of Kansas, 1993.

Cronon, William. *Nature's Metropolis: Chicago and the Great West.* New York: Norton, 1991.

Glad, Paul W. *Mckinley, Bryan, and the People.* Chicago: Elephant Paperbacks, 1964.

Beisner, Robert L. *From the Old Diplomacy to the New.* Arlington Heights: Harlan Davidson, 1986.

Galbraith, John Kenneth. *The Great Crash.* Boston: Houghton Mifflin, 1961.

Goldston, Robert. *The Great Depression: The United States in the Thirties.* New York: Fawcett World Library, 1968.

Halberstam, David. *The Fifties.* New York: Ballantine Books, 1993.

Weiner, Tim. *Legacy of Ashes:* The History of the CIA. New York: Anchor Books, 2008.

Reeves, Richard. *President Nixon: Alone in the White House.* New York: Touchstone, 2001.

Samuelson, Robert J. *The Great Inflation and its Aftermath.* New York: Random House, 2008.

Postman, Neil. *Amusing Ourselves to Death.* New York: Penguin Books, 1985.

Yergin, Daniel, and Joseph Stanislaw. *The Commanding Heights: The Battle for the World Economy.* New York: Simon and Schuster, 2002.

Made in the USA
Charleston, SC
03 April 2012